Business Studies GCSE

MACMILLAN

Acknowledgements

The author and publishers would like to thank the following organisations who have kindly given permission for the use of copyright material.

Examining Groups
LEAG – London & East Anglian Group
MEG – Midland Examining Group
NEAB – Northern Examinations and Assessment Board
NICCEA – Northern Ireland Council for the Curriculum, Examinations and Assessment
SEG – Southern Examining Group
WJEC – Welsh Joint Education Committee.

Other Organisations
Advertising Standards Authority, Amstrad, Austin Rover, Avon, Banking Information Service, BICC, Bradford City Council, British Standards Institute, British Telecom, Burton Group, CACI, Central Office of Information, Consumers' Association, Co-operative Wholesale Society, *Daily Express*, *Daily Mirror*, Department of Trade and Industry, *Economist*, *Guardian*, Grattan, International Stock Exchange, Kent County Council, *Kentish Gazette*, Lloyds Bank, Lonrho, National Westminster Bank, Nestlé, Transport & General Workers Union, *Telegraph & Argus*, Reuters, *Yorkshire Post*.

Every effort has been made to trace all copyright holders but if any have inadvertently been overlooked the publishers will be pleased to make the necessary arrangements at the first opportunity.

© Gerry Gorman 1989

All rights reserved. No reproduction, copy or transmission of this publication may be made without written permission.

No paragraph of this publication may be reproduced, copied or transmitted save with written permission or in accordance with the provisions of the Copyright, Designs and Patents Act 1988, or under the terms of any licence permitting limited copying issued by the Copyright Licensing Agency, 90 Tottenham Court Road, London W1P 9HE.

Any person who does any unauthorised act in relation to this publication may be liable to criminal prosecution and civil claims for damages.

First published 1989 by
MACMILLAN PRESS LTD
Houndmills, Basingstoke, Hampshire RG21 6XS
and London
Companies and representatives
throughout the world

ISBN 0–333 64355–0

A catalogue record for this book is available from the British Library.

Printed in Great Britain by Biddles Ltd,
Guildford and Kings Lynn

10 9 8 7 6 5 4
00 99 98 97 96 95

Good design
for effective revision

The Economic Framework 1

Syllabus analysis Ensures you only do the topics you need – no more, no less

Start and completion column Keeps tabs on your progress – see at a glance which areas still need to be worked through

Self assessment For you to note how well you've done or areas which need to be revised again

SEG	LEAG	NISEAC	WJEC	NEAB	MEG	Topic	Date attempted	Date completed	Self Assessment
✓	✓	✓	✓	✓	✓	1.1			
✓	✓	✓	✓	✓	✓	1.2			
✓	✓	✓	✓	✓	✓	1.3			
✓	✓	✓	✓	✓	✓	1.4			
✓	✓	✓	✓	✓	✓	1.5			
✓	✓	✓	✓	✓	✓	1.6			
✓	✓	✓	✓	✓	✓	1.7			

Contents

Introduction	vi
1 The Economic Framework	1
2 The Context of Business	10
3 International Trade	18
4 Private-Sector Firms	28
5 Public-Sector Firms	40
6 Finance for Business	48
7 Management of Business	56
8 Accounting for Business	67
9 Marketing	87
10 Production	108
11 Managing People	124
12 Recruitment and Training	133
13 Industrial Relations	146
14 Communication	155
15 The Government and Business	165
16 Aiding and Controlling Business	180
17 Coursework Assignments	193
Index	206

Exam Board Addresses

For syllabuses and past papers contact the Publications office at the following addresses:

Midland Examining Group (MEG)
c/o University of Cambridge Local
  Examinations Syndicate
1 Hills Road
Cambridge
CB1 2EU
Tel. 01223 553311

Southern Examining Group (SEG)
Publications Department
Stag Hill House
Guildford
Surrey
GU2 5XJ
Tel. 01483 302302 (Direct Line)

**Northern Examinations and Assessment
  Board (NEAB)**
12 Harter Street
Manchester
M1 6HL
Tel. 0161 953 1170
(Also shop at the above address)

**University of London Examinations and
  Assessment Council (ULEAC)**
Stewart House
32 Russell Square
London
WC1B 5DN
Tel. 0171 331 4000

**Northern Ireland Council for the
  Curriculum, Examinations and
  Assessment (NICCEA)**
Beechill House
42 Beechill Road
Belfast
BT8 4RS
Tel. 01232 704666

Welsh Joint Education Committee (WJEC)
245 Western Avenue
Llandaff
Cardiff
CF5 2YX

Scottish Examination Board (SEB)
for full syllabuses
Ironmills Road
Dalkeith
Midlothian EH22 1LE
0131–663 6601

or recent papers from the SEB's agent
Robert Gibson & Sons Ltd
17 Fitzroy Place
Glasgow G3 7SF
0141–248 5674

Remember to check your syllabus number with your teacher!

Introduction

How to Use this Book

This book has been designed to help you complete your coursework and prepare for the examination papers in GCSE Business Studies.

Each chapter gives a summary of the basic subject content of the various syllabuses. For more detail you should consult other books on the topics.

For each chapter there are suggested coursework assignments, which you should adapt as necessary for your interests and syllabus. Be careful to study the particular requirements of your syllabus. A summary and detailed guidance are given in Chapter 17.

At the end of every chapter are worked examples of examination questions, mostly from the specimen papers issued by the Examining Groups before the first GCSE examinations. These are followed by self-test questions, mainly from the first batch of papers set in 1988.

Although the book is divided into separate chapters for convenient reading, it is important to remember that GCSE Business Studies emphasises 'integration' of the subject content. In simple terms, this means that coursework assignments and examination questions should test knowledge from more than one subject area. You are likely to find that most questions ask for knowledge from at least two different chapters.

Types of Examination Question

There are three main types of examination question in GCSE Business Studies examination papers – *short-answer*, *data response* and *case studies*.

(a) **Short-answer Questions**

As their name implies, these ask for a very brief answer, from a single word to a couple of sentences. For example:

'Collective bargaining is a way of settling wage rates between employers and _____.' (*LEAG Specimen*)

'Give **two** functions of the Office of Fair Trading.' (*NISEC*)

(b) **Data Response or Structured Questions**

These give some information such as a short passage and/or a table of figures. You are then asked questions related to the data. An example from a MEG paper is given below.

Study the information below and answer the following questions.

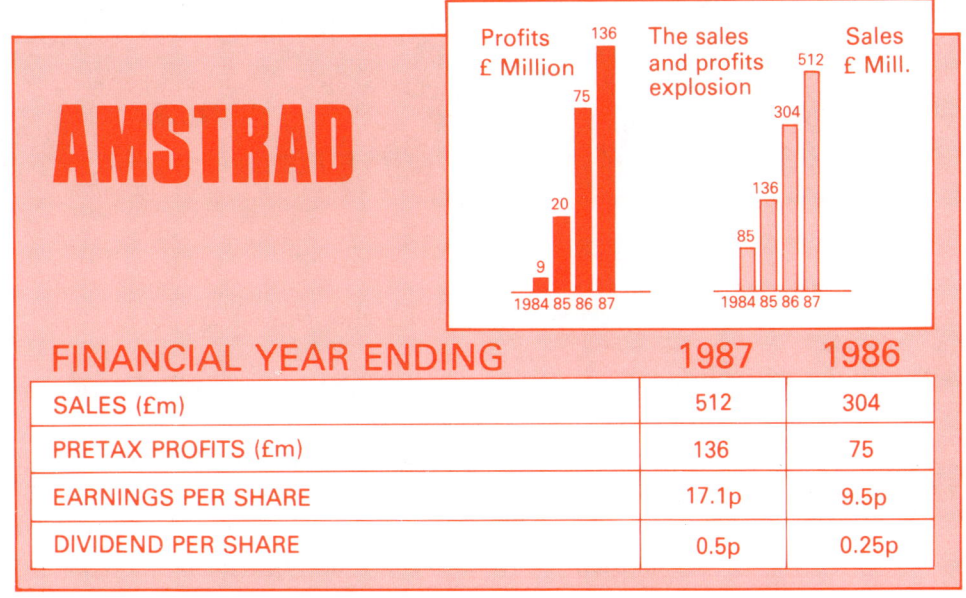

AMSTRAD

FINANCIAL YEAR ENDING	1987	1986
SALES (£m)	512	304
PRETAX PROFITS (£m)	136	75
EARNINGS PER SHARE	17.1p	9.5p
DIVIDEND PER SHARE	0.5p	0.25p

Extract from
The Guardian September 1987

(a) By how much did sales increase between 1984 and 1987? Show your working. (2)
(b) What was the percentage increase in profits between 1986 and 1987? Show your working. (4)
(c) Pretax profits are before tax is deducted. What is the name of the tax which AMSTRAD pays on its profits? (1)
(d) The table shows a number of ways in which the size of the business can be measured. Write down **two** other ways in which the size of AMSTRAD can be measured. (2)
(e) Types of business organisation include: sole trader, partnership, limited company, public limited company and nationalised industry. From the information given, what type of business organisation is AMSTRAD? Give a reason for your choice. (3)

> AMSTRAD is active in the video and audio markets. Since 1984 it has also moved into the low-price end of the computer market. It bought out Sinclair Electronics and is now moving into business computing.

    (f)   Why do you think AMSTRAD is involved in more than one market? (2)

    (g)   (i)   Why do you think AMSTRAD had concentrated upon the low-price end of the computer market? (4)

            (ii)   Suggest **one** difficulty there might be for AMSTRAD in selling business computers. (1)

(c) Case Studies

These are similar to data response questions but involve more detailed information and questions from a very wide range of the syllabus. In the MEG, NEA and SEG examinations, case studies make up a complete paper. A specimen case study from the NEA syllabus is given below.

Extended Case Study

Read the information given in the boxes and answer the questions which follow.

> Canteen supervisor redundant
>
> Sue Brown enjoyed her job as a canteen supervisor in Johnsons cotton mill where she had worked for twelve years. She lived close to the factory. In her job she was responsible for the other canteen staff.
>
> Her job was to plan the menus, buy in food and materials, supervise the cooking, make sure standards of hygiene were high, and to train the staff.
>
> Johnsons had not been doing well for the last few years. Profits were low and the work force had been gradually reduced. However, the news that the factory was to close still hit the town like a bombshell.

1   Explain what skills Sue may have gained in carrying out her present work as a supervisor in the kitchen. (16)

2   For what reasons might a business like Johnsons have been doing badly enough to decide to close down? (16)

3   Many people in the town apart from those working in Johnsons were afraid that their jobs and livelihoods might now be at risk. Why? (20)

> The Plan
>
> Sue: 'Well dad, if no-one else will employ me, I'll employ myself. I'll just have to start my own business. There are all kinds of things I can do with my experience, and I'll have £1,500 redundancy money to start me off.'
>
> Dad: 'I wish you luck lass, but I think you might be making a rod for your own back. The risks of failure in small businesses are very high, you know.'
>
> Sue: 'Oh come off it! I'm fed up with working for other people. I know what I'm doing, and anyway, if I start a Limited Company I can only lose the £1,500 redundancy money. Besides, I think I'd really enjoy being my own boss.'
>
> Dad: 'I hope you're right Sue, but remember, Johnson was self-employed himself at one time and look where it got him.'

4   Why do people in Sue's situation get redundancy money? (12)
5   Why might Sue want to be her own boss? (16)
6   What do you think Sue's father means by 'the risks of failure'? (16)

The Decision

Sue considered several possibilities for her own business and eventually followed up an idea for running a stall selling hot dogs and pizzas on the sea front at Blackpool, about 20 miles from home.

The stall cost £3000 to buy and equip; £1000 of this came from her redundancy money and she borrowed the rest from the bank. She agreed to repay the bank loan in two equal instalments, one at the end of the first year and the other at the end of the second year's trading. She prepared a forecast Profit and Loss Account.

Sue's forecast Profit and Loss Account for the first year

	£	£
Sales of hot dogs		6000
Sales of Pizzas		3000
Cost of Pizzas	1000	
Cost of hot dog sausages and rolls	2000	
Cost of hot dog sauces	100	
Wages	3000	
Electricity and Gas	140	
Rent for stall site	520	
Repairs/maintenance	100	
Loan interest	300	
Repayment of loan capital	1000	

---

7   Show your workings in each part of this question.
    (a) How much did Sue borrow from the bank? (4)
    (b) What rate of interest was charged by the bank? (4)
    (c) Using the information shown in the forecast Profit and Loss Account, say what the expected gross profit was on:
        (i) hot dogs;
        (ii) pizzas. (8)
    (d) How much net profit did Sue expect to make in the first year? (8)
8   (a) From the information given above, list the kinds of costs that Sue had to pay in:
        (i) setting up the business;
        (ii) running the business.
        (There is no need to include the amounts.)
    (b) Why is it difficult to make the distinction between setting up and running costs? (16)
9   When Sue applied for another loan to expand after the first year, the bank manager asked her to produce a forecast Profit and Loss Account. How useful would this information be to the bank manager? (20)
10 Describe ways in which Sue might increase her profits, pointing out the drawbacks or risks in the methods you describe. (20)

ix

The Structure of Examination Papers

For all syllabuses except that of the NEA, there are different papers for different abilities. This means that you will have to make a decision about whether to take the harder paper in order to have a chance of obtaining the A or B grades. The choice of papers is shown below.

Summary of examination papers

Examining Group	Paper	Time allowed (hours)	% of total marks	Type of questions	Designed for grades	Papers taken
London and East Anglian Group LEAG	1	2	75	Compulsory short answer multiple choice questions	G–D	Candidates take paper appropriate to their expected achievement plus coursework (25%)
	2A	2	75	Section A – short-answer questions 10% Section B – structured questions	F–B	
	3	2	75	Section A – structured questions Section B – open ended questions 30%	D–A*	
Midland Examining Group (MEG)	1	2$\frac{1}{2}$	70 (basic scheme)	Compulsory structured response questions	C–G D–A*	Basic scheme – Paper 1 only Candidates expected to gain grades C–G Extended scheme – Papers 1 and 2 Candidates expected to gain grades A–C If a candidate obtains grade C on the basic scheme and a higher grade on the extended scheme, the higher grade will be awarded
	2	1$\frac{1}{4}$	70 (extended scheme)	Written paper based on unseen case study	A*–C	
Northern Ireland Council for the Curriculum, Examinations and Assessment (NICCEA) incorporating NISEC	1	1$\frac{1}{2}$	40	Compulsory case study, compulsory short-answer, structured, and essay questions	C–G and A*–E	All candidates take Paper 1 plus Paper 2 and submit coursework
	2	2	40	4 compulsory multi-part questions	C–G and A*–E	
Northern Examinations and Assessment Board (NEAB) incorporating NEA	1	1$\frac{1}{2}$	35	3 structured questions based on case studies or stimulus material	A*–G	All candidates take both papers
	1	1$\frac{1}{2}$	35	Extended case study	A*–G	

x

Examining Group	Paper	Time allowed (hours)	% of total marks	Type of questions	Designed for grades	Papers taken
Southern Examining Group (SEG)	1	2	40	5 compulsory questions	A*–G	General level – Papers 1 and 2A Candidates expected to obtain grades C–G Extended level – Papers 1 and 2B Candidates expected to obtain grades A–D Candidates taking Paper 2B will be ungraded unless they obtain at least grade D
	2A	1½	30	Case study given to candidates 3–4 weeks before examination	C–G	
	2B	1½	30	Case study given to candidates 3–4 weeks before examination	A*–D	
Welsh Joint Education Committee (WJEC)	1	1¼	30	Compulsory structured questions	A*–G	Candidates take Paper 1 *plus* either Paper 2 (grades C–G) or Paper 3 (grades A–C)
	2	1½	40	Compulsory structured questions	C–G	
	3	1½	40	Compulsory structured questions	A*–C	

The Economic Framework

1

SEG	LEAG	NISEAC	WJEC	NEAB	MEG	Topic	Date attempted	Date completed	Self Assessment
✓	✓	✓	✓	✓	✓	1.1			
✓	✓	✓	✓	✓	✓	1.2			
✓	✓	✓	✓	✓	✓	1.3			
✓	✓	✓	✓	✓	✓	1.4			
✓	✓	✓	✓	✓	✓	1.5			
✓	✓	✓	✓	✓	✓	1.6			
✓	✓	✓	✓	✓	✓	1.7			

1.1 Scarcity and Choice

Any economic system has to solve the problem of *scarcity* of resources. This means that all resources such as land, raw materials, labour and machinery are limited in supply.

Resources are scarce because people have unlimited needs for goods and services. There are not enough resources to satisfy all of these needs.

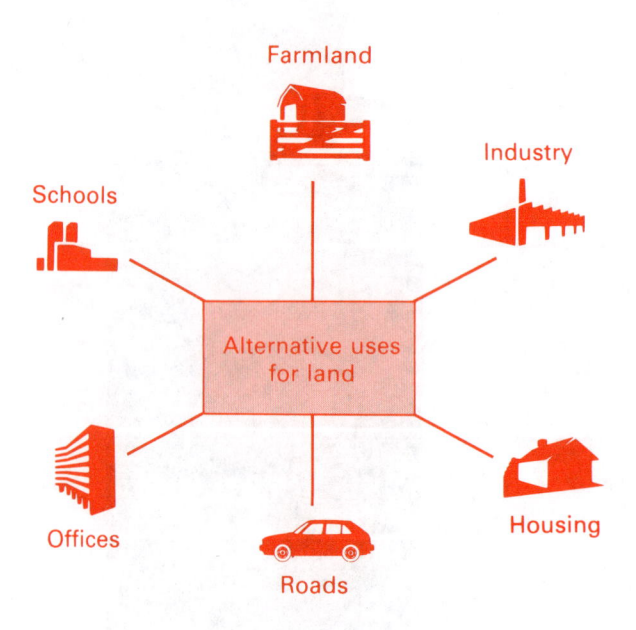

Figure 1.1 Alternative uses for land

For example, a plot of land might be used for any one of a number of purposes, as illustrated in Figure 1.1. However, using it for one of these purposes prevents its use for the others. A decision has to be made about which of the alternative choices is 'best'.

Any economy, however it is governed, has to make such decisions about how resources are to be used. There are three basic decisions to be made:

1. What is to be produced?
    e.g. should there be more soldiers and fewer firemen; should houses be built upon farmland in south-east England?

2. How is it to be produced?
   e.g. should electricity be produced by nuclear rather than coal-fired power stations; should machines be used instead of labour in a particular manufacturing process?
3. Who gets the goods and services produced?
   e.g. should people have to pay for medical care or should it be provided free by the Government?

Depending on the particular economy, decisions about production and distribution of goods and services may be made by private individuals, the Government, or a combination of the two.

Economies are often divided into three types, which vary according to who makes these decisions. Figure 1.2 illustrates the three types.

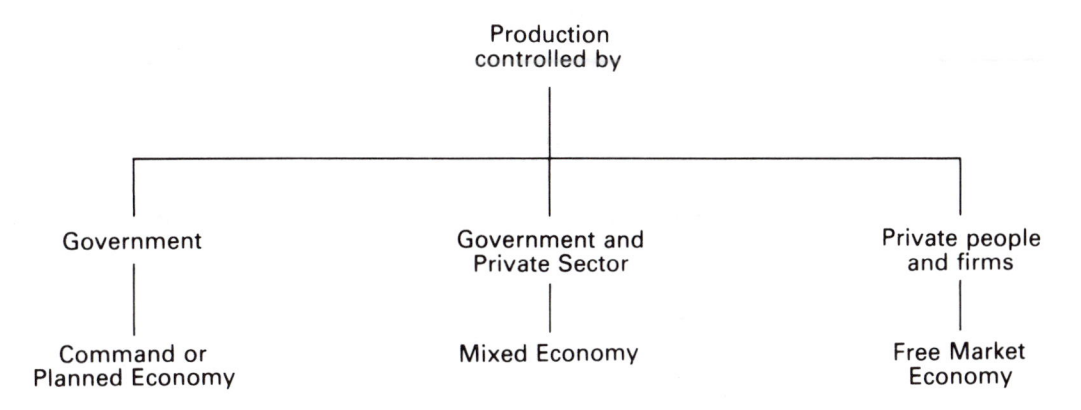

```
                    Production
                    controlled by
                         |
        ┌────────────────┼────────────────┐
    Government     Government and    Private people
                   Private Sector      and firms
        |                |                 |
    Command or      Mixed Economy    Free Market
  Planned Economy                     Economy
```

Figure 1.2 Three types of economy

1.2 The Free-Market Economy

(a) Free Enterprise

In a *free-market economy* decisions about production are made by private individuals and firms. The Government interferes as little as possible in business affairs. Its main purpose is to provide only those services which are necessary to protect the country's citizens, such as defence and the legal structure.

The basic principle of the free-market economy is that production is based upon *free enterprise*. Businesses are continually attempting to make as much profit as possible. They can only achieve this by producing goods and services that their customers want, and by producing them as cheaply and efficiently as possible.

(b) Role of Prices

Prices are the mechanism by which a free-market system works. The price of a good or service depends upon the *demand* (the amount that consumers wish to buy) and the *supply* (the amount that producers are willing to sell). Demand and supply are constantly changing, and this affects prices and the amounts produced.

For an example of this look at Figure 1.3 which shows the cost of renting offices in London in mid-1988. Many businesses want to be in the City of London

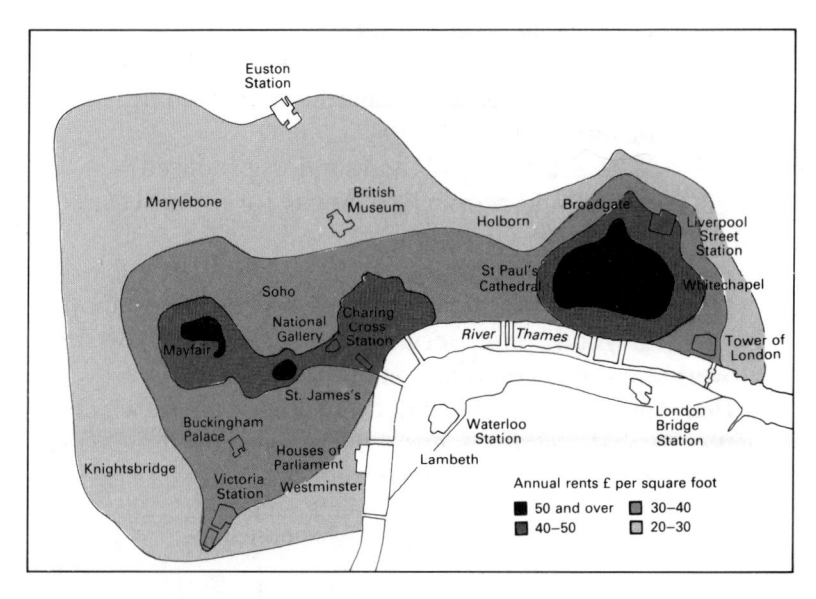

Figure 1.3 Office rents in London

area (the black-shaded area on the right-hand side of the map). Because of the competition for office space in the City, rents are far higher than elsewhere in London. Three miles away, offices can be rented for a third of the price.

This demand affects the way in which resources are used. Because it is so important to some firms to be in the City of London, owners of land will try to put as much office space as possible there. This is why skyscrapers are built in the centre of large cities, but not in areas where land is less scarce and therefore cheaper. Some firms will decide to locate elsewhere to save on the high rents payable.

In a free-market economy the consumer decides what is to be produced by buying goods and services. Businesses which provide goods and services that the consumer wants will be profitable. Those which don't will lose money and go out of business.

(c) Advantages of Free-Market Economies

- Producers have to satisfy the consumer in order to make a profit.
- Free enterprise encourages efficient production because firms must keep their costs low and produce high-quality goods and services. (This is sometimes referred to as the *profit incentive*.)
- There is as little Government intervention as possible in the economy, which leads to more freedom for people to make their own decisions.

(d) Disadvantages of Free-Market Economies

- The demand for products depends upon people's ability to pay for them. Poorer people may not be able to afford essential goods and services. Resources may be used to produce luxuries for the rich.
- Some public services such as education would not be provided for everybody.
- *Monopolies* may occur, which are often bad for consumers.
- Private producers will ignore the bad effects or *social costs* of their activities, such as pollution, if they are allowed complete freedom.

1.3 The Planned Economy

(a) Central Planning

A *planned* or *command* economy is one where decisions about production are taken by the Government. Planned economies are generally run by Communist Governments, which believe in state control of the economy in order to organise production for everybody's benefit rather than for private profit. The best-known example is the Soviet Union.

Planning a modern economy is a very complex process. The Government develops plans for the economy, usually for several years ahead. These plans set prices, wages and targets for production of different goods and services.

To take a simple example, let us suppose the Government wants to produce a particular number of machines over the next few years. In order to do this it will have to ensure that sufficient labour, steel, machinery and equipment are available to achieve this production. This involves issuing orders for production of steel, coal, machine components and so on.

Taking this a stage further, the coal industry will have to plan for extra production, which will require inputs of labour, machinery and other resources. Every decision about what to produce means that other adjustments have to be made in turn by the central planners. This is a massive task, too big for even the most sophisticated computer.

(b) Advantages of Planned Economies

- The Government can plan for the production of essential goods and services.
- Central planners can take into account social costs such as pollution which might be ignored by private producers.
- The Government can aim to make the distribution of income more equal.

(c) Disadvantages of Planned Economies

- Planning a large economy is very complicated, and impossible to do without making mistakes. Changes in demand or production problems often lead to shortages and surpluses of basic goods.
- A large and expensive bureaucracy is needed to make and carry through the Government's plans.
- Because there is no private profit there may be little incentive for people and firms to work hard or develop new products.
- If prices are fixed in advance, the advantages of the price system as a signal to producers are lost.

These problems have caused severe difficulties for planned economies such as the Soviet Union and China. During the 1980s these countries have gradually loosened the Government's control of the economy to allow more private enterprise. In the Soviet Union this change is called *perestroika* (which means 'reconstruction').

1.4 The Mixed Economy

A *mixed economy* is one in which production is controlled by both the Government and private producers. A good example is the United Kingdom.

To some extent, all economies are mixed economies, since none are completely dominated by private or Government production. However, the term is usually applied to countries where there is substantial production by both sectors.

In a mixed economy, production is largely undertaken by private producers, but the Government also intervenes in the economy in various ways. These are described in Chapter 15, and are summarised only briefly below:

1. The *public sector* (central and local Government and nationalised industries) produces many goods and services, such as education and medical care.
2. The Government influences spending on particular goods and services through its taxation and spending policies, e.g. heavy taxes on alcohol and cigarettes; tax relief on mortgages.
3. The sale of many goods and services is restricted, e.g. guns are licensed; some products such as drugs or legal advice can only be provided by qualified people.
4. Through social services such as social security, health care and education, the Government attempts to eliminate poverty and guarantee a minimum standard of living to all its citizens.
5. The Government regulates the economy in various ways, e.g. by influencing factors such as interest rates, investment and the location of industry.
6. Workers are protected by various laws which set maximum hours of work, minimum wages for some jobs, health and safety procedures and workers' rights such as maternity leave and redundancy pay.
7. Consumers are protected by laws such as the Weights and Measures Act and the Trades Descriptions Act.

1.5 Coursework Assignment

A local planning issue

Choose a local case of a firm seeking planning permission to extend its activities, such as a new building or extension or a 'change of use', e.g. from a shop to an office. Controversial issues will be easier to find information about.

Most proposed developments are likely to have both good and bad effects, e.g. creating trade and jobs, but causing more noise or traffic congestion. The assignment involves considering these effects and balancing them against each other.

Having chosen the issue you wish to investigate, phrase your title as a question, e.g.

> 'Should Tessbury's be allowed to build a new superstore in Oxford Road?'

The easiest way to start is to use local newspaper articles to build up a list of all the people and organisations with an interest in the issue. Figure 17.6 shows how this can be done. Addresses of local people, councillors and organisations should be in the telephone directory. For other addresses ask local newspapers and the Reference Library.

The best way to present your assignment is to use headings such as 'Environment' and 'Employment'. Using these headings, explain the case 'for' and 'against' the development.

Many of the arguments will be 'biased' one way or the other. They are also likely to be about what is likely to happen in the future. Try to work out whether suggested effects are likely to occur.

If you think that one case is obviously better, say so and explain your reasons. If you can't make up your mind, describe any information you would like to have before making a decision.

1.6 Worked Example

> **LOCAL AIRPORT TO BE DEVELOPED INTO A BUSINESS AREA**
>
> 1000 new jobs are to be created and it is hoped that it will attract an additional 200 flights per week for small business aircraft.
>
> Response to the news by local residents was mixed.
>
> "I don't want another Heathrow on my doorstep."
> "I've got young children who go to school in the area and the news means that there will be more traffic on the roads."
> "More work for the area."
> "Is it too late to stop it?"
>
> *Farncove Recorder* April 1986

(a) How would the following people feel about the news?
    (i) A young couple buying a house in the area. (4)
    (ii) A local hotelier. (4)
    (iii) A local bus company. (4)
(b) The local residents have decided to form themselves into a pressure group.
    (i) What is a pressure group? (4)
    (ii) From the passage explain the points that the pressure group might use to support their case. (8)
(c) Prepare a report for the local council to
    (i) show the problems that the new development might create and (8)
    (ii) explain how these problems might be overcome. (8)

(SEG Specimen)

Answers

(a) (i) Identify attitudes relating to nuisance problems e.g. noise, congestion. (1–2)

Explain other problems e.g. effect on house prices, quality of life. (3–4)

(ii) State that business will expand but without explanation. (1–2)

Identify cause and effect.
Note effect of increased business – more staff, expand business – how this might be achieved. (3–4)

(iii) Note that business will increase. (1–2)

Identify the effect upon the bus company. Give relevant solutions. Analyse problems that it will create. (3–4)

(b) (i) Answers may include 'people who try to change things'.
Some explanation as to how change can be carried out. (1–2)

Common interests.
Explain what a pressure group is and how 'pressure' may be applied. (3–4)

(ii) Identify one or two general points. (1–3)

Identify one or two relevant points from the passage e.g. additional flights, traffic. Attempt to explain how these could be used in pressure group campaign. (4–6)

Identify relevant points and show how the pressure group campaign might use them. (7–8)

(c) (i) Identify one or two problems with some explanation of their effects. (1–3)

Identify two or three problems and begin to show the effect upon the community. (4–6)

Have clear ideas as to what the problems are. Explain the effects upon the community: housing, burden on schools/hospitals, noise, road congestion, danger to old and young, increased use of public transport. (7–8)

(ii) Make an attempt to explain how the problems could be resolved. (1–3)

Identify the solution to some of the problems. (4–6)

Identify all relevant solutions to the problems. (7–8)

1.7 Self-Test Question

> *Economic Freedom*
>
> An essential part of economic freedom is freedom to choose how to use our income: how much to spend on ourselves and on what items; how much to save and in what form; how much to give away and to whom. Currently, more than 40 per cent of our income is disposed of on our behalf by government.
>
> Another essential part of economic freedom is freedom to use the resources we possess in accordance with our own values — freedom to enter any occupation, engage in any business enterprise, buy from and sell to anyone else, so long as we do so on a strictly voluntary basis and do not resort to force in order to coerce others.
>
> Today you are not free to offer your services as a lawyer, a physician, a dentist, a plumber, a barber, a mortician, or engage in a host of other occupations, without first getting a permit or licence from a government official. You are not free to work overtime at terms mutually agreeable to you and your employer, unless the terms conform to rules and regulations laid down by a government official.
>
> You are not free to set up a bank, go into the taxicab business, or the business of selling electricity or telephone service, or running a railroad, bus-line, or airline, without first receiving permission from a government official.
>
> M. R. Friedman *Free to Choose*

(a) What are the advantages of allowing people and firms to buy and produce goods and services without Government intervention?

(b) Choose three types of business which are restricted or licensed by the Government. Explain the case for such restrictions.

The Context of Business

SEG	LEAG	NISEAC	WJEC	NEAB	MEG	Topic	Date attempted	Date completed	Self Assessment
✓	✓	✓	✓	✓	✓	2.1			
✓	✓	✓	✓	✓	✓	2.2			
✓	✓	✓	✓	✓	✓	2.3			
✓	✓	✓	✓	✓	✓	2.4			
✓	✓	✓	✓	✓	✓	2.5			
✓	✓	✓	✓	✓	✓	2.6			
✓	✓	✓	✓	✓	✓	2.7			
✓	✓	✓	✓	✓	✓	2.8			

2.1 Specialisation and Exchange

Modern economies are based upon *specialisation*, with people producing one particular type of good or service, e.g. being a carpenter or typist.

Mass production, i.e. producing goods and services in large numbers, depends upon further specialisation, called *division of labour* (see Chapter 10).

Because people specialise, they do not produce all the things they need. For example, in Britain fewer than one in thirty workers is involved in producing food. Most people earn money by producing other goods and services and then buy their food.

The process by which people buy and sell products is called *exchange*. In primitive societies this was carried out through *barter*, the exchange of goods without using money.

Because individuals do not produce all the things they need, they rely upon other people and firms as consumers and suppliers. This is called *interdependence*.

2.2 Influences on the Business

Businesses have responsibilities to various groups of people, and to the community as a whole. Figure 2.1 shows how one large firm sees its duty to different groups.

2.3 Business and Change

Businesses have to cope with constant change in society and in the economy. These changes are illustrated throughout the book, but important recent changes include the following:

1. *Transport* has become faster with the growth in the motorway network. The Channel Tunnel will also speed transport between Britain and the Continent.
2. *Population changes* such as the growth in the number of over-65s have created new markets for products such as private nursing homes and sheltered accommodation. The fall in the number of teenagers during the 1990s will make it difficult for employers such as hospitals and building firms to recruit new workers, and will affect the sales of products aimed at teenagers.

BICC

Shareholders
BICC *seeks to:*

provide shareholders with a return on their investment which rewards their own financial risk.

maintain the involvement and commitment of shareholders by informing them promptly of any major actions or decisions affecting their investment.

develop the business, including new activities so as to provide long-term growth for investors.

Customers
BICC *aims to:*

develop and maintain good relationships with all its customers and deal at all times ethically and in good faith.

ensure rapid response to meet customers' needs.

achieve high standards in products, services and general approach so as to ensure customer satisfaction.

Employees
BICC *strives to:*

provide an open, challenging and involving environment for all who work in the company.

utilise, through selection, training and development policies and practices, the full talents, skills and abilities of all the people who work for the company at all levels.

promote the fullest possible understanding amongst employees of the goals, directions and performance of the company.

frame pay structures which reward individual abilities and personal performance.

provide a safe and healthy working environment for all employees.

The Wider Community
BICC *endeavours to:*

support and contribute to all communities in which it operates.

ensure that its employees have the opportunity to contribute in practical ways to local community interests.

respect the physical, economic and social environments of the communities in which it operates.

demonstrate the contribution of its activities and achievements to all groups in the community.

Figure 2.1 BICC PLC objectives

3. *New products* have created markets which were unknown only a few years ago. They also create opportunities for service industries such as video rental and computer programming.
4. *Changing tastes* mean that firms must always be prepared to adapt their goods and services. For example, food manufacturers now have to make 'additive-free' and 'low-sugar' products to keep their customers.
5. *Social changes* such as more women working affect a firm's attitude to its workers, e.g. firms may offer increasing opportunities for part-time work.

6. *Legislation* may force a business to make changes such as avoiding discrimination against women or changing products to meet new safety standards.
7. *Rising incomes* and *more leisure time* in recent years have led to increases in demand for many services such as sporting facilities and travel.
8. *International competition*, particularly for manufacturers, has made it increasingly difficult for firms to survive in the British and export markets.

2.4 Industrial Structure

Production can be classified into *primary*, *secondary*, and *tertiary* industries.

Main sectors of economic activity	Employees '000 (Dec. 1986)	Volume change in output % pa (1976–85)	% share of gdp (1985)
Agriculture, forestry, fishing	313	3.6	1.8
Energy and water supply	514	8.2	11.3
Manufacturing	5,153	−0.1	25.4
Construction	1,007	0.0	6.2
Distribution, hotels and catering	4,319	1.4	13.4
Transport and communications	1,399	0.8	6.9
Financial services	2,166	6.5	14.1
Ownership of dwellings	120	1.5	5.9
Education and health	2,942	1.6	8.7
Public administration	1,559	0.0	7.1
Other services	1,798	3.2	6.0
Adjustment and residual	–	–	−6.8
Gdp at factor cost	21,270	1.9	100.0

(*Source:* Lloyds Bank PLC)

Figure 2.2 The structure of industry in the United Kingdom.

(a) Primary Industries

Primary or *extractive* industries are those which produce food and raw materials. They include agriculture, mining, forestry and fishing. Their products are sometimes referred to as *commodities*.

(b) Secondary Industries

Secondary or *manufacturing* industries produce goods such as televisions and cars. The construction trades (building and civil engineering) are also included in this category.

Capital or *producer* goods such as machinery, buildings and lorries are used to help produce other goods and services.

Consumer goods are bought for their own sake to satisfy a need. They may be *single-use* goods such as food and washing powder or *durables* such as televisions and furniture, which are used repeatedly.

(c) Tertiary Industries

Tertiary industries produce services. These may be *commercial services*, such as banking and retailing, which are used to assist the manufacture and distribution of goods. These are sometimes called the *aids to trade*.

Other services such as education and entertainment are *direct services* which are enjoyed for their own sake. They are sometimes described as *quarternary* production.

(d) The Chain of Production

Primary, secondary and tertiary industries are the stages in the *chain of production* which is the process by which raw materials reach the consumer as finished goods or services. For example, the chain of production for a wooden table would be as follows:

Primary – a tree is cut down and sawn into planks

↓

Secondary – the wood is shaped into a table

↓

Tertiary – the table is transported and sold by a retailer.

(e) Changes in the Structure of Industry

As an economy becomes more developed, production and employment tend to shift away from primary and secondary production towards the tertiary sector. In the 17th century over 80 per cent of British workers were employed in agriculture. During the Industrial Revolution in the 17th and 18th centuries, workers moved away from agriculture to manufacturing industry such as textiles.

In the 20th century there has been a further shift from manufacturing to service industries such as tourism and banking. Agriculture now provides only 3 per cent of employment, and over 60 per cent of workers are involved in producing services. This type of change is normal for an industrial economy and has also occurred in the USA and Western Europe.

The decline in manufacturing industry is called *deindustrialisation*, and has been caused by three factors:

1. New technology has reduced the need for labour in many industries such as car manufacture and coal-mining.
2. Demand for products such as tobacco and cotton has fallen because of changing tastes and the development of substitutes.
3. Foreign competition has led to lower sales for British firms both in Britain and abroad. Britain now imports more manufactured goods than it exports. In 1950 exports of manufactures were three times as high as imports.

2.5 Social Costs and Benefits

All business activities create *benefits* and *costs*. Social benefits are advantages such as employment and income which occur because of business activity. Social costs are the problems caused by business such as pollution and traffic congestion.

For example, building a new factory on farmland might create the following costs and benefits.

(a) Benefits

- Jobs for workers in the factory.
- Higher income for the area because workers have more money to spend.
- Jobs in local shops and suppliers to the factory.
- Extra tax revenue for the Government.

(b) Costs

- Spoiling of local residents' views.
- Pollution and traffic congestion.
- Loss of output from farmland.
- Lost sales to competitors making the same product.

It is very difficult to estimate the social benefits and costs of business activity, especially when trying to forecast what will happen in the future.

For example, there have been many opposing arguments over the likely effects of building the Channel Tunnel. Jobs will be created for building workers, but may be lost by ferry companies and ports such as Dover and Ramsgate. Travel will be faster, but ships are also getting quicker and cheaper, and the tunnel may not save much time and money. It will be easier to transport goods abroad, but imports may also rise.

Detailed forecasts have been made about these effects, but no-one can predict exactly what will happen. It is also a matter of opinion whether faster travel is worth the sacrifice of ruining parts of the Kent countryside.

The case of the Channel Tunnel illustrates two important points about business activity:

1. It is often difficult to assess the results of any particular policy.
2. Sometimes there is no 'right answer' to business problems, and people will often have differing opinions about what should be done.

2.6 Coursework Assignment

What effect will a firm's closure have?

This assignment involves investigating the possible effects of a firm closing down or switching part of its business to another area.

Start by selecting a local example, preferably one which is featured in newspaper reports. Decide upon a specific title, e.g.

'What will happen to the local economy if _____ closes?'

You should then investigate the possible effects of the closure such as:

- Loss of jobs.
- Effect upon local businesses such as shops and suppliers.
- Cost of social security and redundancy payments.
- Loss of competition in the industry.

People and organisations which have an interest in the issue can be found in newspaper reports (see Figure 17.6). Addresses for local people, councillors and organisations should be in the telephone directory. For other addresses, ask local newspapers and the Reference Library.

Use headings such as 'jobs' and 'local businesses'. Explain the likely effects of the closure upon each of these. Point out any differing opinions about the possible effects of closure, using the figures you have obtained.

2.7 Worked Example

UK HOUSING STATISTICS		
	1976	**1986**
Stock of dwellings (*millions*)	20.6	22.6
% owner-occupied	54	63
% rented from local authorities and new towns	32	27
New dwellings completed (*thousands*)	325	205
Public	170	36
Private	155	169

Note: A *dwelling* is a house or flat

(a) What happened to the following between 1976 and 1986?
  (i) Owner occupation. (2)
  (ii) The number of private dwellings built. (2)
(b) How might the trends in council house building affect firms? (6)
(c) Explain how any three industries other than building might benefit from the changes shown in the data. (9)

Answer

(a) (i) Rose (1)
    From 54% to 63% of dwellings according to the percentages given (1)
  (ii) Rose (1)
    From 155,000 to 169,000 according to the figures given (1)

(b) Explain factors such as
- less business from council building
- more demand for private housing
- increased market for home improvements and repairs (2 each)

(c) State and explain examples, e.g.
- building supplies such as bricks and cement
- mortgage lenders such as banks and building societies
- DIY shops (3 each)

2.8 Self-Test Question

Study the following data and answer the questions printed below.

DISTRIBUTION OF EMPLOYMENT 1965–1985 in the county of Midshire			
% of Employment in:–	**1965**	**1975**	**1985**
Primary	20	?	10
Secondary	50	45	?
Tertiary	30	40	50
Unemployment %	4	6	10
Working Population *(thousands)*	300	320	350

(a) Give **two** different examples of **jobs** that might be classified as
    (i) tertiary activities. (2)
    (ii) primary activities. (2)
(b) What percentages of the workforce were employed in
    (i) primary activities in 1975?
    (ii) secondary activities in 1985? (2)
(c) How many people worked in tertiary activities in 1985? (Show your working.) (3)

International Trade

3

SEG	LEAG	NISEAC	WJEC	NEAB	MEG	Topic	Date attempted	Date completed	Self Assessment
✓	✓	✓	✓	✓	✓	3.1			
✓	✓	✓	✓	✓	✓	3.2			
✓	✓	✓	✓	✓	✓	3.3			
✓	✓	✓	✓	✓	✓	3.4			
✓	✓	✓	✓	✓	✓	3.5			
✓	✓	✓	✓	✓	✓	3.6			
✓	✓	✓	✓	✓	✓	3.7			
✓	✓	✓	✓	✓	✓	3.8			

3.1 Advantages of International Trade

There are several advantages to allowing *free trade* between countries without restrictions on imports and exports such as *tariffs* and *quotas*.

1. *Countries can obtain goods and services which they cannot produce themselves.*
   Without international trade, British consumers would be unable to obtain goods and services such as tea, bananas, holidays in Majorca and Australian soap operas.
2. *Countries can specialise.*
   Because of international trade countries can obtain goods and services which they could produce themselves, but which other countries produce more cheaply and efficiently. For example, Britain could produce more of its own food, but more land, labour and capital would have to be switched from other industries into agriculture. It is easier to import food and use British resources to produce other goods and services.
3. *International trade makes mass production possible.*
   International trade allows large-scale production, because firms can sell their products throughout the world. Many products such as aircraft, chemicals and oil are produced more cheaply because they are sold on a world-wide basis. All countries receive the benefits of higher world output and cheaper products because of *economies of scale*.
4. *Competition from abroad encourages efficiency.*
   If a British firm has foreign competition it will have to be efficient if it is to stay in business. One of the aims of the European Community is to increase competition throughout Europe to encourage firms to produce cheaper and better-quality products.
5. *Consumers benefit from international trade.*
   Because of the reasons given above, consumers get a wider choice of goods and services.
6. *Trade between countries leads to international peace and co-operation.*
   It is often argued that if countries trade with each other they are less likely to go to war. One of the reasons for establishing the European Community was to encourage international co-operation in order to avoid another World War.

3.2 Protectionism

Protectionism means placing restrictions upon free trade between countries.

(a) Methods of Protectionism

(i) Tariffs
Tariffs are taxes upon imports, making them more expensive than comparable domestic products.

(ii) Quotas
These are physical limits upon the amount of a good or service which can be imported e.g. 'x tons of tea' or 'x per cent of cotton shirt sales'.

(iii) Embargoes
This is a complete ban upon trade with a particular country (sometimes only in certain goods such as scientific or military equipment). It is usually used for political reasons.

(iv) Subsidies
Governments sometimes give money to domestic producers to help them compete against foreign firms in the home and export markets.

(v) Exchange controls
Importers need foreign currency to pay for imports. Governments sometimes limit the amount of currency which can be bought by people and firms. Exchange controls were abolished by the British Government in 1980.

(vi) Government procurement
A Government may tell its departments to buy domestically-produced goods and services whenever possible.

(vii) Special rules and regulations
Countries may deliberately design regulations about standards for products to make importing more difficult. For example, Japan banned imports of European skis on the grounds that Japanese snow is different.

(b) Reasons for Protectionism

The main reasons for protectionism are:

1. To cure a balance of payments deficit by increasing exports and/or reducing imports.
2. To protect domestic industry and employment.
3. To protect the exchange rate.

(c) Disadvantages of Protectionism

The disadvantages of protectionsim are:

1. It reduces the benefits of free trade.
2. If one country puts restrictions upon imports, others may retaliate, so that world trade falls.
3. The advantages of international specialisation and world-wide markets are lost.
4. Consumers get less choice and higher prices, e.g. cars and video-recorders would be cheaper if restrictions upon Japanese imports into Europe were removed.
5. It encourages inefficiency amongst domestic firms by limiting competition.

3.3 The Balance of Payments

EXPORTS

Visible
e.g. An American buys a British book;

A French firm buy A British machine

Invisible
e.g. A German holiday in London

A Greek shipping company insures a British broker

Foreign currency in

Foreign currency out

e.g. A Briton buys a Japanese stereo;

a British shop buys Italian

Visible

e.g. A British person holidays in Majorca;

a British firm hire, a Greek ship

Invisible

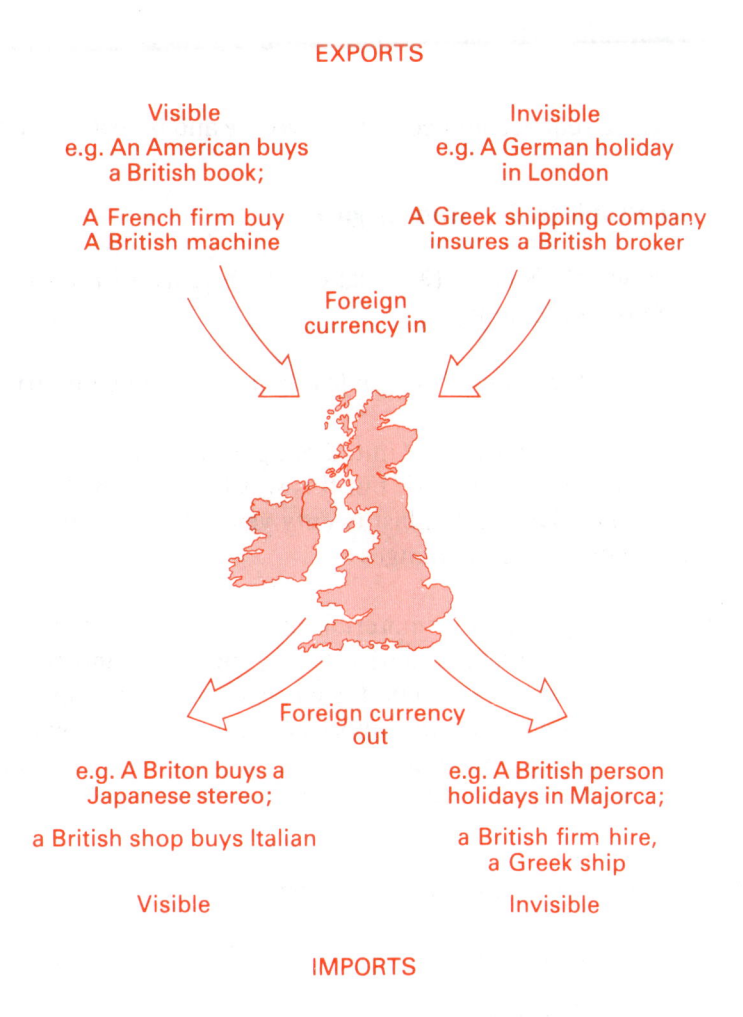

IMPORTS

Figure 3.1 Items in the balance of payments (current account)

The balance of payments is a record of all transactions between Britain and other countries. It is made up of:

- The *capital account*, which measures the flow of capital to and from other countries for purposes such as investment in foreign banks and industry.
- The *current account*, which records payments for goods and services to and by British residents. (The term residents is used to include people, firms and the Government.) This is discussed in more detail below.

(a) The Balance of Payments Current Account

Visible trade	£ million
Exports	79 422
Less Imports	89 584
Visible Balance	−10 162
Invisible trade	
Exports	80 010
Less Imports	72 352
Invisible Balance	7 658
Current Balance	−2 504

Figure 3.2 UK balance of payments, 1987 (current account)

The current account consists of *visible* and *invisible trade*.

(i) Visible trade – trade in goods

The *visible balance* (also called the *balance of trade*) is equal to visible exports minus visible imports.

Visible balance = visible exports − visible imports

Until the 1980s the United Kingdom generally exported more manufactured goods than it imported, but this was balanced by large imports of food and raw materials. During the last twenty years the pattern of visible trade has changed. Some of the major changes are:

- Food and raw materials have fallen as a proportion of imports, because of an increase in agricultural production and the development of synthetic substitutes for goods such as wool and cotton.
- Britain used to import all its oil, but is now a net exporter (exports are greater than imports) because of the exploitation of North Sea oil.
- Britain is no longer a net exporter of manufactured goods.

(ii) Invisible trade – trade in services

The *invisible balance* is equal to invisible exports minus invisible imports.

Invisible balance = invisible exports − invisible imports

Generally the United Kingdom has had a *surplus* (exports have been higher than imports) in invisible trade, particularly from insurance and financial services. British people and firms owned foreign assets of £90 billion pounds at the end of 1987, and received income from these.

(iii) The current balance

The *current balance* is equal to the visible balance plus the invisible balance.

Current balance = (visible exports − visible imports) + (invisible exports − invisible imports)

Since the Second World War the current balance has been positive (i.e. exports have been greater than imports) in about the same number of years as it has been negative.

In the early 1980s exports were consistently higher than imports, largely because of high earnings from North Sea oil exports. From 1986, as can be seen from Figure 3.3, imports started to exceed exports.

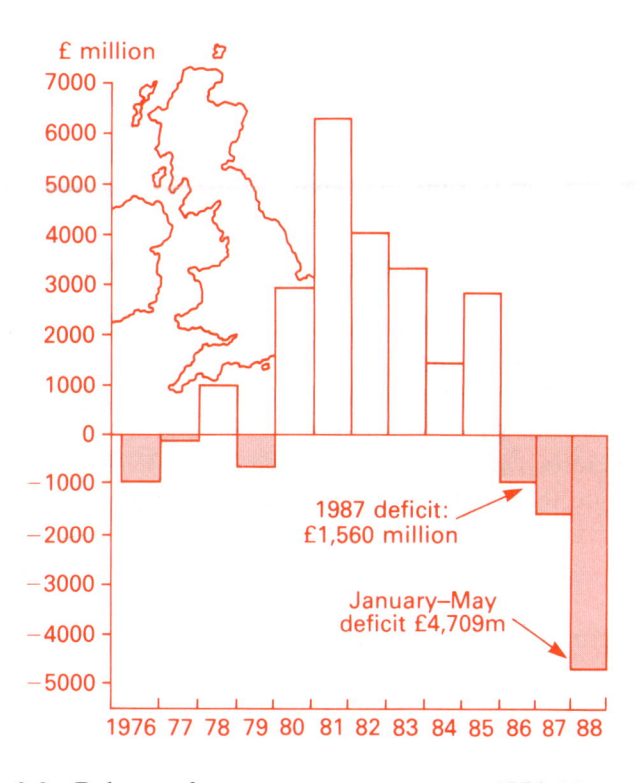

Figure 3.3 Balance of payments current account 1976–88

3.4 Difficulties of Exporting

Firms trying to sell abroad face special difficulties which do not occur when selling in Britain.

(a) Language

Documents, advertising and trade names may have to be translated into other languages.

(b) Information and Distribution

It may be difficult to obtain information about how to sell products abroad, or to arrange sales agencies and transport.

(c) Risk of Non-payment

The risk of bad debts is much higher in many other countries, especially those which are politically unstable.

(d) Laws and Regulations

Most exporters have to deal with different technical and legal rules in other countries, such as left-hand drive and safety regulations for car manufacturers. These are sometimes designed specifically to restrict imports.

(e) Currency Changes

The value of sterling may change, affecting both costs and income from exports. A rise in the value of the pound against the dollar, for example, would make British goods and services more expensive for foreign buyers.

(f) Tastes and habits

These can vary considerably between countries. For example, Rowntree Mackintosh had difficulty selling After Eights in France, because the French thought that combining mint and chocolate was very strange. (This problem was successfully overcome by advertising After Eights as 'so English'.)

Firms can obtain help from a variety of Government and private sources to overcome these difficulties (see Chapters 15 and 16).

3.5 The European Community (EC)

The European Community (EC) is an organisation of twelve countries with 320 million people. The twelve are responsible for 20 per cent of world trade. It is often known as the 'Common Market', because one of its main aims is to allow free trade and movement of workers and capital between its members.

In 1986 the twelve member countries signed the Single European Act, which is designed to remove all trade restrictions between member states. By 1992 it should be possible for an EC citizen to work anywhere in the Community, and for any good which can be sold legally in one country to be sold in any of the others.

This process will increase competition for firms throughout the EC. The twelve countries are trying to agree upon basic standards for products, so that goods can be sold freely in all member states.

THE EUROPEAN COMMUNITY

THE EUROPEAN COMMUNITY

Total population — 320 million
Total Gross Domestic Product — £1639bn
Total Exports from Community — £396390m
Total Imports to Community — £417413m

The European Community arose from a desire to establish a peaceful and prosperous Europe after the horrors of two World Wars. The twelve nations of the Community have agreed to merge their economic interests to form a 'common market' where trade may be conducted freely, people can work wherever they want, and money can be invested where it is most needed.

THIS . . .   . . . NOT THIS

What Britain puts into the Community

- A share of the running costs of the Community.
- Free access, for other Community countries, to Britain's market of 56 million people.
- Free access for Community citizens to jobs in Britain.
- Experience and traditions which result from being a stable, democratic nation.
- Experience of leading a multi-racial Commonwealth, and of helping many developing countries.

What Britain gets out of the Community

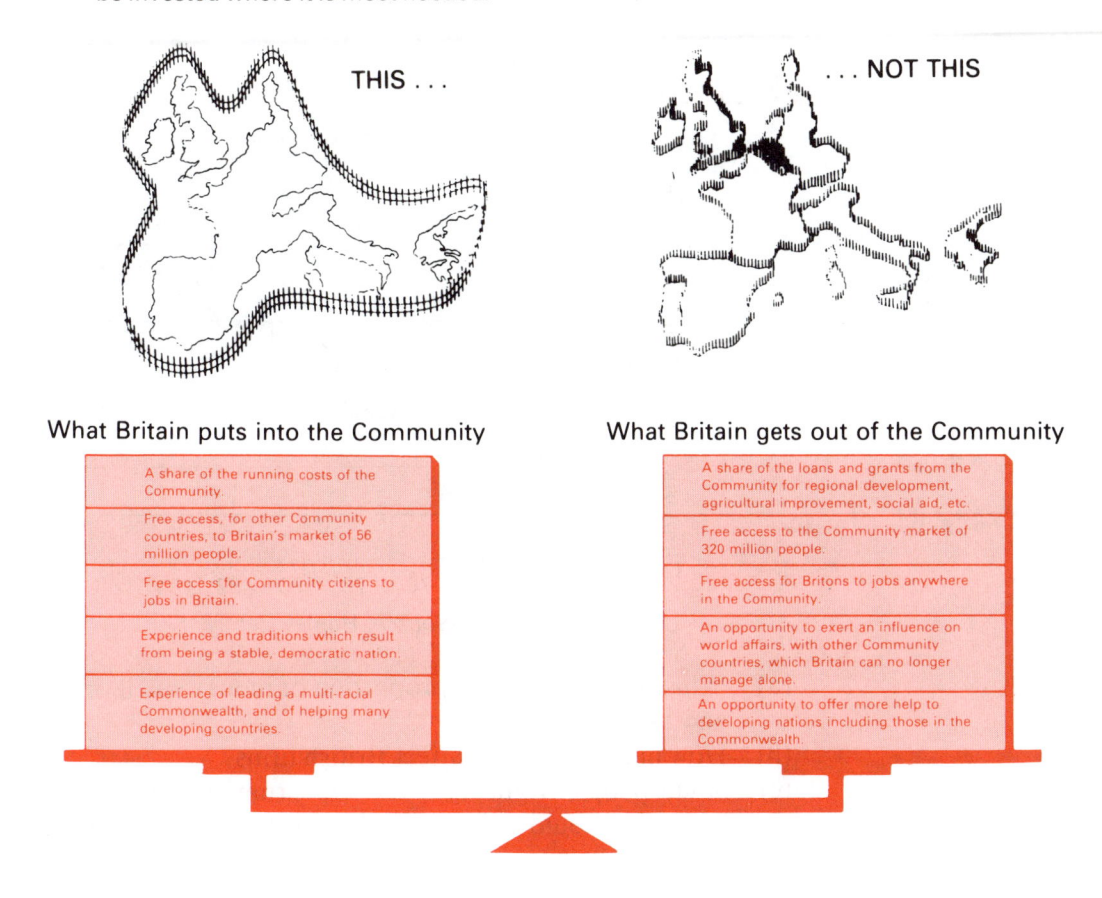

- A share of the loans and grants from the Community for regional development, agricultural improvement, social aid, etc.
- Free access to the Community market of 320 million people.
- Free access for Britons to jobs anywhere in the Community.
- An opportunity to exert an influence on world affairs, with other Community countries, which Britain can no longer manage alone.
- An opportunity to offer more help to developing nations including those in the Commonwealth.

Figure 3.4 Britain and the European Community in 1989

3.6 Coursework Assignment

What are the differences between domestic and foreign markets?

Choose a particular product or type of firm and investigate how selling abroad is different from selling in Britain. Issues which might be investigated include:

- Differences in tastes between countries.
- Special legal and Customs regulations, e.g. many food additives are legal in Britain but not in some other countries.
- Differences in advertising and packaging, e.g. green is associated with medicine in some countries.
- How goods are transported.
- Whether the same brand names can be used in all countries.
- Effects of changing exchange rates.
- Protectionist measures.
- Costs and profitability of exporting.

Try to find a local firm which is willing to help in providing particular information. It may be interesting to compare a small and a large firm selling the same product. Be careful to explain any differences between domestic and export markets, using facts and figures wherever possible.

3.7 Worked Example

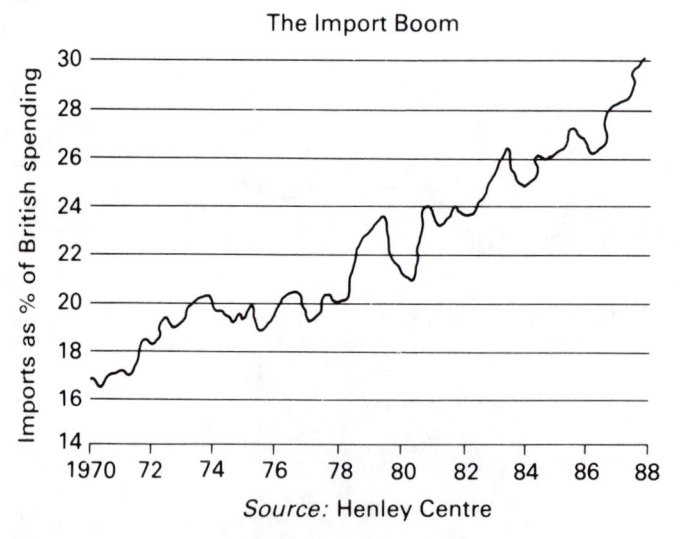

The Import Boom

Source: Henley Centre

(a) What happened to the proportion of money spent on imports between 1970 and 1988? (2)
(b) How might this trend affect British firms? (8)
(c) Some people argue that the Government should restrict imports. What arguments could be made against protecting British firms in this way? (12)

Answers

(a) Rose (1)
Percentage increased from 16% to 30% (1)
(b) Explain possible effects such as
- loss of trade
- lower profits
- may go bankrupt
- may have to sack workers. (2 each)
(c) Explain arguments such as
- retaliation by other countries
- encourages inefficiency in British firms by reducing competition
- consumers suffer from less choice and higher prices. (4 each)

3.8 Self-Test Question

Study the information below carefully, and answer the questions.

Oldport Docks			
Imports	'000 Tonnes	*Exports*	'000 Tonnes
Iron ore and other metals	1 900 000	Coal and coke	500 000
Timber	200 000	Iron and steel	150 000
Fruit	104 000	Chemicals	100 000
Others	55 000	Others	50 000

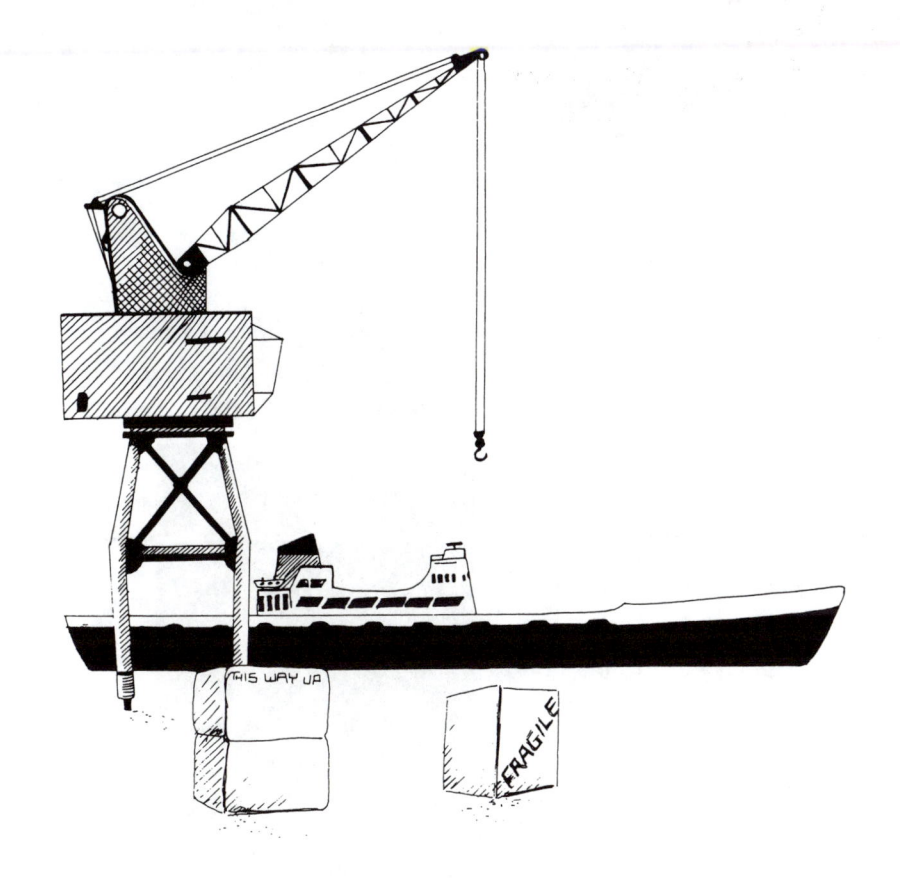

(a) Why does the United Kingdom import metals, timber and fruit? (5)
(b) Why do we buy cars from other countries when we can produce our own? (4)
(c) Draw a bar chart to show clearly the different amounts of exports from Oldport docks. (4)

(WJEC)

Private-Sector Firms 4

SEG	LEAG	NISEAC	WJEC	NEAB	MEG	Topic	Date attempted	Date completed	Self Assessment
✓	✓	✓	✓	✓	✓	4.1			
✓	✓	✓	✓	✓	✓	4.2			
✓	✓	✓	✓	✓	✓	4.3			
✓	✓	✓	✓	✓	✓	4.4			
✓	✓	✓	✓	✓	✓	4.5			
✓	✓	✓	✓	✓	✓	4.6			
✓	✓	✓	✓	✓	✓	4.7			
✓	✓	✓	✓	✓	✓	4.8			
✓	✓	✓	✓	✓	✓	4.9			
✓	✓	✓	✓	✓	✓	4.10			
✓	✓	✓	✓	✓	✓	4.11			

4.1 Types of Private-Sector Business

A *private-sector business* is one which is not owned by the Government. Apart from *co-operatives*, which are described in Section 4.8, there are four types of legal structure for privately-owned businesses:

1. Sole Trader.
2. Partnership.
3. Private Limited Company (Ltd).
4. Public Limited Company (PLC).

This order shows the usual size of the types of business in terms of *turnover* or total sales. Sole traders are usually small businesses and public limited companies are invariably large firms, such as Barclays Bank and Shell.

This is not always true. For example some partnerships in accountancy and law are bigger businesses than most private limited companies.

4.2 Important Principles of Business Organisation

(a) Limited Liability

Limited liability means that if a business is unable to pay its debts the owners of the company can only lose the money that they have paid for shares.

Sole traders and partnerships have *unlimited liability*. If the business cannot pay its debts, the owners have to pay them out of their own money. They may have to sell their house and other personal possessions to pay the business's creditors.

The importance of limited liability is that people can put money into a firm by buying shares, without risking the loss of all their money if the company fails. If limited liability did not exist, people would be less willing to risk investing in firms.

(b) Joint-stock Companies

Limited companies are sometimes called *joint-stock* companies because their shares or 'stock' are held jointly by a number of people.

The general rules for the running of joint-stock companies are set out by various Companies Acts dating from 1844 onwards. Rules are also made by Government Ministers and bodies such as the Stock Exchange. The purpose of these laws and regulations is to protect people who buy shares in or lend money to businesses.

(c) Incorporation

An *incorporated body* has a legal existence separate from its owners. Contracts can be signed in its name, and it has legal rights and duties of its own. Its owners also usually have limited liability.

(d) Business Names

Joint-stock companies have to register their name with Companies House, a Government organisation. Other types of business do not have to do this, but must display the name and address of the owners on their premises and stationery. Titles which include terms such as 'British' or 'Royal' are not allowed.

4.3 Sole Trader

(a) Features of the Sole Trader

The main features of the sole trader are as follows:

1. Owned and controlled by one person.
2. Usually small.
3. Common in industries such as farming, hairdressing, window cleaning and retailing.
4. Most common where personal service is important.
5. Can be set up with little capital.
6. Few legal formalities involved.
7. Unlimited liability.
8. Capital usually obtained from personal savings, borrowing and putting profit back into the business.
9. The sole trader is *unincorporated*, i.e. the owner is legally the same as the business.

(b) Advantages of the Sole Trader

The advantages of the sole trader include the following:

1. Easy to set up. Apart from any necessary licences or planning permission, there are very few legal formalities.
2. Although accounts are seen by the Inland Revenue they do not have to be made public.
3. The business is usually small, and the owner is in charge of the day-to-day management. Decisions can be made quickly.
4. The owner gets all the profit from the business, so he or she has an incentive to work hard.
5. Being small, the business can provide personal attention for its customers.

(c) Disadvantages of the Sole Trader

The main disadvantages of the sole trader are:

1. Prices may be higher. Sole traders are unlikely to be big enough to get the benefits of large-scale production. However, if *expenses* are kept down, e.g. by using the owner's home as premises, a sole trader may be able to keep prices low.
2. It may be difficult to raise finance to expand the business.
3. The sole trader has unlimited liability, and is personally responsible for the business's debts. He or she may have to risk home and savings to start the business.
4. The business depends very heavily upon the owner's abilities. He or she may be good at some tasks of running the business, but poor at others. For example, a person may have a technical skill as a car mechanic, but find it difficult to cope with accounts or staff when running a garage.
5. If the owner is ill the business may have difficulty in continuing.
6. Sole traders often have to work very long hours, particularly when setting up a business.

4.4 Partnership

(a) Features of the Partnership

The main features of a partnership are:

1. Two or more persons 'carrying on a business in common with a view to profit' (Partnership Act 1890). This definition excludes non-profit-making organisations such as charities and sports clubs.
2. Maximum of 20 partners (with some exceptions such as solicitors and accountants, which can exceed this limit). The exceptions are usually professions where members are not allowed to form limited companies.
3. Can be set up without legal documents, although this is inadvisable.
4. Capital is usually obtained from partners' personal savings, borrowing and retained profit.
5. Partners have *unlimited liability*. There are *limited partners* in a very small number of partnerships, but all must have at least one partner with limited liability.
6. Partnerships are *unincorporated*.

If there is no legal agreement the provisions of the Partnership Act 1890 apply. These are basically that:
- Profits and losses are shared equally.
- All partners have an equal say in the running of the business.
- All partners must agree before new partners can be admitted.

If a Partnership deed or agreement is drawn up it is likely to cover matters such as:
- The amount of capital to be contributed by each partner.
- The proportion in which profits and losses are to be shared.
- The management responsibilities of each partner.
- The maximum drawings of cash for personal use by each partner.
- Provisions for introducing new partners and the ending of the partnership.

Figure 4.1 Partnership deed

(b) Advantages of Partnerships

The advantages of partnerships are:

1. Compared to a sole trader, there are more people to put money into the business.
2. Can include people with different skills.
3. Fairly easy to set up.
4. As with sole traders, accounts do not have to be made public.
5. Partners are usually involved in the day-to-day running of the business, and have an incentive to see that it works efficiently.
6. Small partnerships can provide personal service.

(c) Disadvantages of Partnerships

The disadvantages of partnership are:

1. Usually too small for large-scale production, although there are exceptions to this.
2. The partners have unlimited liability (except for limited partners) and are responsible for any debts.
3. With more people in charge, decisions may take longer than for the sole trader.
4. Small partnerships may find it difficult to raise capital.
5. Each partner is legally and financially liable for the others. If one partner makes a mistake the others may lose money.
6. There may be problems if one of the partners leaves or dies. The partnership deed (see Figure 4.1) should allow for such changes.

4.5 Private Limited Company

(a) Features of Private Limited Companies

The main features of a private limited company are:

1. A private limited company is a joint-stock firm owned by two or more shareholders.
2. It has to be set up and registered according to certain legal procedures (see Section 4.7).
3. Shareholders have limited liability.
4. The company must use the word 'Limited' or the abbreviation 'Ltd' in its title.
5. Some shareholders may not take part in the daily management of the firm.
6. Capital is raised from retained profit, borrowing, share capital (but not public issues) and sometimes Government grants and loans.

(b) Advantages of Private Limited Companies

The advantages of private limited companies are:

1. Limited liability makes it easier to persuade people to put money into the business.
2. Many private limited companies are large enough to obtain the benefits of large-scale production.
3. Limited companies gain certain tax advantages compared to unincorporated businesses.

(c) Disadvantages of Private Limited Companies

The disadvantages of private limited companies are:

1. There are legal formalities to set up the business.
2. Accounts have to be filed with Companies House, and it is therefore difficult to retain privacy.
3. Shares cannot be sold to the public or on the Stock Exchange.
4. It may be difficult for shareholders to sell their shares and get their investment back.

4.6 Public Limited Company

(a) Features of Public Limited Companies (PLCs)

The main features of PLCs are:

1. A public limited company is a joint-stock firm owned by two or more shareholders, although most have hundreds or even thousands. They are all very large firms.
2. PLCs have to be set up and registered according to certain legal procedures (see Section 4.7). Most were originally private limited companies which later became PLCs.
3. Shareholders have limited liability.
4. The company must use the term 'public limited company' or the abbreviation 'PLC' in its title.
5. Most shareholders do not take part in the management of the firm. The firm is run by a Board of Directors elected by shareholders.
6. Capital is raised from retained profit, borrowing (often from international banks), share issues to the public and Government grants and loans.

(b) Advantages of Public Limited Companies

The advantages of public limited companies are:

1. Shareholders have limited liability.
2. They are large and can get the benefits of large-scale production.
3. PLCs can raise large amounts of capital through share issues and borrowing. They can usually borrow more cheaply than smaller firms.
4. Shares can be bought and sold easily through the Stock Exchange, so shareholders can get their money back (unless the value of the shares has fallen).
5. Being large firms, PLCs can afford to employ specialist workers such as lawyers, accountants and personnel staff.

(c) Disadvantages of Public Limited Companies

The disadvantages of public limited companies are:

1. PLCs are expensive to set up, because the regulations involved are very complicated.
2. Because of the size of the firm there may be *diseconomies of scale* such as decisions taking a long time to make.
3. As a large firm, the company may seem impersonal to customers and employees.
4. Shares in PLCs are often owned by people who buy them in order to make a quick profit (most large shareholdings are kept for less than two years). This means that they are always vulnerable to takeovers by other firms.

4.7 Registration of Joint-Stock Companies

When a joint-stock company is established certain documents must be submitted to the Registrar of Companies, a Government official. The two most important documents are the *Memorandum of Association* and the *Articles of Association*.

(a) Memorandum of Association

This governs the firm's external relationships with other people and organisations, and provides the world at large with certain basic information about the company. It contains several items:

1. Name of the company (which must not be the same as that of another firm). The title must include the term 'Ltd' or 'PLC'.
2. Address of registered office.
3. *Objects clause*. This states the type of business in which the company will be involved e.g. 'retailing' or 'building services'.
4. *Limitation clause*. This is a statement that shareholders have limited liability.
5. *Capital clause*. This gives details of the amount of share capital and the different categories of shares to be issued.
6. *Association clause*. This includes the names of the founder members and the number of shares for which each has subscribed.

(b) Articles of Association

These are the rules governing the internal affairs of a company, covering matters such as:

1. Voting rights of shareholders.
2. Election of directors.
3. Conduct of general meetings of shareholders.
4. The buying and selling of shares.

The Companies Acts contain a set of model rules which can be used. Alternatively, the founders may draw up their own rules.

(c) Statutory Declaration

This is a statement that the company has been set up within the regulations of the Companies Acts. It is sent to the Registrar of Companies along with the Memorandum and Articles of Association.

(d) Certificate of Incorporation

This is issued by the Registrar of Companies, and is necessary before the company can start trading.

(e) Certificate of Trading

This is also issued by the Registrar, and must be obtained by a public limited company before it can commence business. To obtain the certificate of trading the PLC must have raised a minimum amount of money. This is to ensure that the company will have sufficient capital to start trading. In addition, the company must also have satisfied the Council of the Stock Exchange (see Section 6.4) that it is a reasonable investment for the public.

4.8 Co-operatives

Co-operatives are a special type of private sector business. They are a fairly minor proportion of the total number of businesses. The Co-operative Development Agency (CDA) estimates that in 1986 there were 1,500 co-ops employing 14,000 workers, and that the number was growing every year.

There is no legal definition of a co-operative, but there are certain features which make most of them different from other types of firm:

1. Each member has one vote, no matter how much work or money they put into the co-op.
2. Shares keep the same value.
3. All profits made belong to the members. Some may be kept for future investment, but the remainder is distributed to members in a previously-agreed way.
4. The level of interest that can be paid for borrowing is limited.
5. Many are involved in political and social work, and the Co-operative movement sponsors several Members of Parliament.

Like shareholders of joint-stock companies, members of co-operatives have limited liability.

There are several types of co-operative.

(a) Producer Co-operatives

Producer co-operatives involve a central organisation such as the Milk Marketing Board buying and selling products upon behalf of its members. In Britain these are very common in agriculture.

(b) Worker Co-operatives

Worker co-operatives are businesses owned by their workers. The most famous examples are the Mondragon co-operatives in Spain. In Britain there are only about 2,000 worker co-operatives, a fairly small proportion of the total number of businesses. The main advantage of worker co-operatives is that the workers have an interest in the success of the business because they own it.

(b) Retail Co-operatives

UK CO-OPERATIVE MOVEMENT FACTS AND FIGURES

Co-Operative Retail Societies
Turnover	£5,350 million
Trading surplus	£99 million
Staff	82,000
Number of Societies	90
Members' Benefits/Dividend	£19 million
Number of shops	5,000 (65 Superstores)
Number of members	8,345,000

The Co-Operative Wholesale Society
Turnover	£2.4 billion
Staff	22,386
Factories	33
Farms	37,000 acres
Distribution centres	18
Co-op Brand Lines	2,000
Number of shops	320

The Co-Operative Bank Group
Assets	£1.64 billion
Staff	4,409
Branches	100
Handybanks	586
ChequePost (with cash-a-cheque support)	370
Cash-a-cheque points	2,370
Customer accounts	1.5 million
Financial Centres	49

The Co-Operative Insurance Society
Premium income	£768 million
Assets	Over £5 billion (market value)
Number of policies in force	12 million
Number of families insured	3.9 million
Staff	11,200
District Offices	220
Surplus on Life business for 1987	£234 million

Co-Operative Travel (all societies) — 160 branches

Shoefayre — 180 branches

Co-Operative Opticians — 93 practices

National Co-Operative Chemists — 150 branches

Worker Co-Operatives (UK) — 2,000   May 1988

Figure 4.2 The UK co-operative movement – facts and figures

Retail co-operatives are the largest group of co-operatives in Britain. The 'Co-op' is made up of 90 separate locally-based societies. These societies own the Co-operative Wholesale Society (CWS), which produces 60 per cent of the goods sold in Co-op stores.

The CWS is involved in many industries (see Figure 4.2), such as farming, insurance and undertaking. Its board is elected from the member societies.

The Co-op's customers receive a dividend on their purchases (some societies do not pay a dividend as such, but keep prices low). Dividends are often paid by giving customers stamps which can be exchanged for cash, goods or shares in the society.

4.9 Coursework Assignment

Investigation of local businesses

Draw a simple chart to show how any four local businesses are organised.

Select an example of a local sole proprietor's business and a local partnership, and describe four or five of the main features of each, e.g. size, ways in which customers are attracted, service provided. Make your own observations on the main features.

Suggest and comment upon the reasons for the existence of each of the businesses.

As a result of your own local investigation, prepare a report to show the differences between sole proprietors and partnerships in terms of ownership, simple legal requirements, the provision of capital, liability for losses and the way profits are used.

(LEAG Specimen)

4.10 Worked Example

John Cooke has just been made redundant from his job as a car worker. He has decided to set up a taxi and courier service to provide a service for the public and deliver letters and packages for businesses.

He still has to decide whether to work from home or to rent a small office in the town centre.

(a) Where would John obtain the capital to start up his business? (4)
(b) (i) What would be the disadvantages if John worked from home? (6)
    (ii) What would be the advantages if John decided to rent a small office in the town centre? (6)
(c) Which place of work would you advise John to choose? Give reasons for your choice. (10)
(d) John has received a number of applications for jobs as drivers with his business.
    (i) What qualities would be important for this type of work? (4)
    (ii) Draw up a contract of employment which could be used for one of John's employees. (10)

(SEG Specimen)

Answer

(a) Any form of borrowing. (1–2)

    Relate to redundancy payments. (3–4)

(b) (i) Problems referring to domestic only. (1–2)

    Additional problems mentioned e.g. nuisance value to neighbours, complaints from residents. (3–4)

    Highlight additional problems e.g. keeping business costs and private costs separate, obtaining planning permission to use premises for business. (5–6)

(ii) Mention one or two advantages. (1–2)

    Attempt to explain the advantages but do not necessarily relate to John Cooke's business. (3–4)

    Explain advantages relevant to John Cooke's business. (5–6)

(c) Attempt to give reasons for choice and make slight comparison between two sites. (1–3)

Make some comparison between the two sites. Supply final conclusion (relevant). (4–7)

Make logical judgement as to which of the two sites would be preferred. (8–10)

(d) (i) List one or two relevant qualities. (1–2)

    List three or four relevant qualities e.g. honesty, reliability, punctuality, driving licence. (3–4)

(ii) Only one or two relevant conditions included. (1–4)

    Three or four relevant conditions, but these begin to relate to type of occupation. (5–7)

    Four or five relevant conditions relating to type of work undertaken e.g. pay, hours, title, job description, pension, sickness, injury, termination of employment. (8–10)

4.11 Self-Test Questions

Question 1

Bill Jackson owned a small garden centre, and ran it as a one-man business selling plants and compost. He soon discovered that there was a large demand for a wide range of garden products from people in the surrounding area, so he decided to increase his product range. His brother Ken (a joiner by trade) came into the business as a partner to develop production of self-assembly sheds, greenhouses and garden furniture.

The business went from strength to strength and the brothers decided to form a Limited Company – Gardenparts Ltd – with Bill as Managing Director, and Ken as Production Manager. They took on more staff, and appointed Brian Willis as Sales Manager, who proved his worth by negotiating a contract to supply a National Chain Store Organisation, which will give the company a wider market.

The present workforce consists of three clerks (two working for the Sales Manager and one working for Bill). There are four joiners working in the joinery shop, and three men working in the nursery supervised by a foreman.

(a) Explain the **two** terms underlined. (4)
(b) Ken said 'If I become your partner, we must have a written agreement – it's illegal not to!' What are your views on this? (2)
(c) What may have been the reasons for the two brothers forming a Limited Company? (4)
(d) From the information available to you, draw up an organisation chart for Gardenparts Ltd as it is at the present time. (4)
(e) Suggest **three** ways in which Gardenparts Ltd could expand its operations. (6)

(NISEC)

Question 2

Study the following carefully, and answer the questions.

Tony works for a very large firm in mid-Wales but is unhappy in his job. He feels that his skills as a tradesman could be used to run his own business repairing farm machinery.

Tony does not know a great deal about the running of a business but believes that at first he will be able to work from home. He will need a telephone answering machine, a van, a range of spare parts and some more tools.

He has mananged to save £4,000 to start in business as a sole trader.

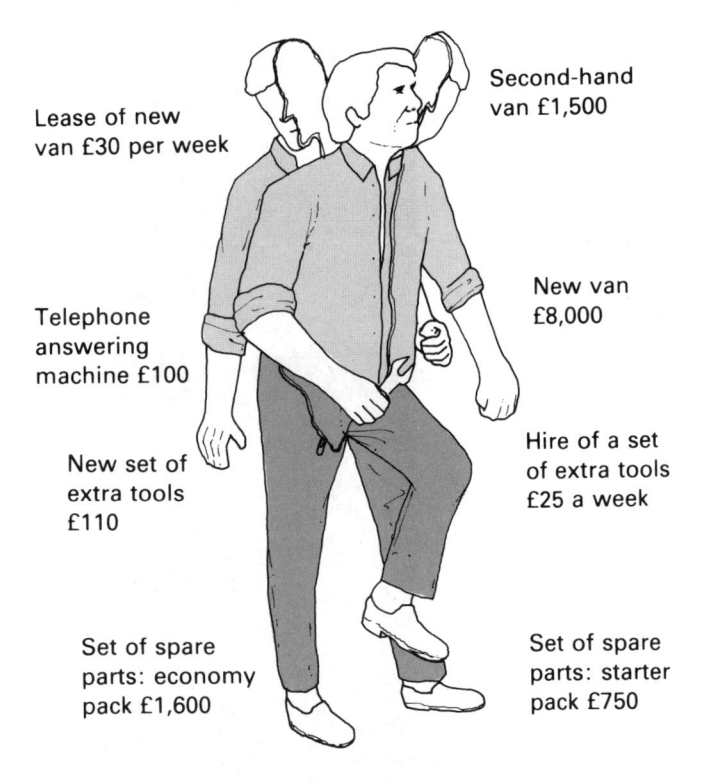

Lease of new van £30 per week
Second-hand van £1,500
Telephone answering machine £100
New van £8,000
New set of extra tools £110
Hire of a set of extra tools £25 a week
Set of spare parts: economy pack £1,600
Set of spare parts: starter pack £750

(a) (i) Why do you think Tony would prefer to work for himself? (4)
    (ii) What problems might arise if the new business is run as a sole trader? (5)
(b) (i) Where could Tony go to ask advice about setting up his business? (2)
    (ii) What advice might be most helpful to him? (4)
(c) How do you think he should spend his £4,000? (8)

(WJEC)

5 Public-Sector Firms

SEG	LEAG	NISEAC	WJEC	NEAB	MEG	Topic	Date attempted	Date completed	Self Assessment
✓	✓	✓	✓	✓	✓	5.1			
✓	✓	✓	✓	✓	✓	5.2			
✓	✓	✓	✓	✓	✓	5.3			
✓	✓	✓	✓	✓	✓	5.4			
✓	✓	✓	✓	✓	✓	5.5			
✓	✓	✓	✓	✓	✓	5.6			
✓	✓	✓	✓	✓	✓	5.7			
✓	✓	✓	✓	✓	✓	5.8			

5.1 Nationalisation

Nationalised industries (also called *public corporations*) are firms owned wholly or mainly by the Government. Most of the nationalised industries were created by the Labour Governments of 1945–51, 1964–70 and 1974–79. Usually this was done by the Government buying several firms from their private owners and merging them into one large public corporation.

A list of the nationalised industries at the end of 1987–88 and again in 1994, and those already *denationalised* (sold back to the private sector) is given in Figure 5.1. Further sell-offs to the private sector are planned for the mid-1990s.

The list of nationalised industries which remained in the public sector at the end of 1987–88 is as follows:
- British Coal
- Electricity (England and Wales)
- North of Scotland Hydro-Electric Board
- South of Scotland Electricity Board
- British Steel Corporation
- Post Office
- Girobank
- British Railways Board
- British Waterways Board
- Scottish Transport Group
- British Shipbuilders (Merchant)
- Civil Aviation Authority
- Water (England and Wales)
- London Regional Transport

The following industries have been privatised since 1979:
- British Telecom
- British Gas Corporation
- British National Oil Corporation
- British Airways
- British Airports Authority
- British Aerospace
- British Shipbuilders (Warships)
- British Transport Docks Board
- National Freight Company
- Enterprise Oil
- National Bus Company (assuming privatisation completed by early 1988).

The list of nationalised industries which remained in the public sector at the end of 1994 is as follows:
- British Coal
- Post Office
- Girobank
- British Waterways Board
- Scottish Transport Group
- British Shipbuilders (Merchant)
- Civil Aviation Authority
- London Regional Transport

The following industries have been privatised since 1979:
- British Telecom
- British Gas Corporation
- British National Oil Corporation
- British Airways
- British Airports Authority
- British Aerospace
- British Shipbuilders (Warships)
- British Transport Docks Board
- National Freight Company
- Enterprise Oil
- National Bus Company
- Electricity (England and Wales)
- North of Scotland Hydro-electric Board
- South of Scotland Electricity Board
- British Steel Corporation
- British Railways Board
- Water (England and Wales)

Figure 5.1

5.2 Features of the Public Corporation

The main features of the public corporation are that it:

1. Is owned wholly or partly by the Government.
2. Produces and sells goods and services.
3. Is controlled by a Board of Directors appointed by a Government minister.
4. Is answerable to the public for its activities (see Figure 5.2).
5. Works to financial and performance targets set by a minister.
6. Is usually a very large firm, whose products are vital to people and firms throughout the economy.

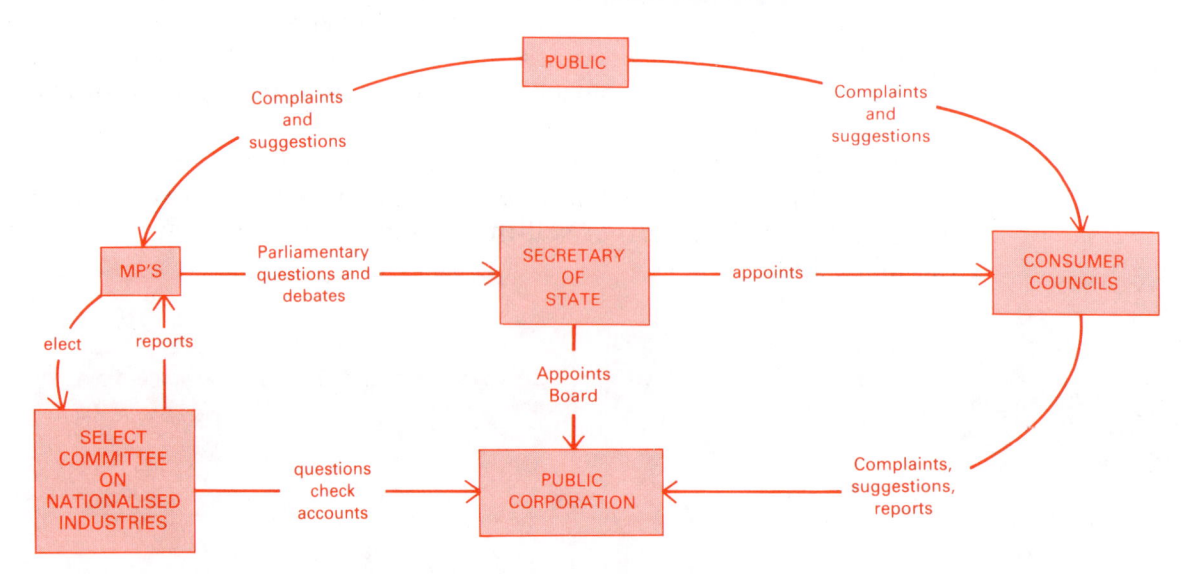

Figure 5.2 Control of nationalised industries

5.3 Arguments for Nationalisation

The arguments in favour of nationalisation are:

1. Nationalised industries may provide socially important services such as rural railway lines and postal services, which might not be supplied by a private firm because they are unprofitable.
2. Some industries are '*natural monopolies*'. It may not be financially worthwhile for more than one firm to provide a service such as gas or water. In these industries it is argued that it makes sense to have one producer, which should be owned by the Government to protect consumers.
3. Many industries require investment in expensive equipment and technology. For example an electricity power station costs several billion pounds. A private firm might be unwilling to risk such a large investment.
4. Industries such as fuel and steel are vital to the economy, and may be important in times of war. It can be argued that the Government should have control of these industries to ensure ample supply of important goods and services.
5. The Government should control the economy on behalf of its citizens. This is the major political argument for nationalisation.

6. Occasionally a private firm is nationalised to stop it going bankrupt and causing unemployment or other economic problems. British Leyland (now called Rover) was rescued in 1975 to prevent large job losses in the West Midlands. Rolls Royce Engines (not the car firm) was taken over in 1971 to ensure that Britain did not lose its capacity to make aircraft engines.

5.4 Arguments against Nationalisation

The arguments against nationalisation are:

1. Nationalised industries are inefficient because the Government will cover any losses that they make. The taxpayer is forced to support inefficient firms.
2. Lack of competition does not encourage efficiency or good service to customers. Most of the nationalised industries have had a *statutory monopoly*, which means that no other firm is allowed to compete with them.
3. Even vital industries can be trusted to private firms, as the Government can encourage or control production if necessary. For example, most defence equipment is provided by private-sector companies.
4. State control of industry is politically undesirable, giving the Government too much power over the way in which people make their living.
5. Nationalised industries are always subject to interference by the Government.

5.5 Privatisation

(a) The Three Methods of Privatisation

The Conservative Government which was elected in 1979 had *privatisation* as a major aim. Privatisation means switching production of goods and services from the public to the private sector. There are three basic methods of privatisation:

(i) Denationalisation

Denationalisation involves selling Government-owned enterprises to the private sector, e.g. British Steel, Girobank.

(ii) Deregulation

Deregulation involves removing statutory monopolies, e.g. abolishing restrictions on bus services.

(iii) Contracting-out

Contracting-out involves allowing private firms to bid for the supply of public services, e.g. hospital cleaning, refuse collection.

Gas cut-offs on increase

THE number of people cut off by British Gas North East rose by a sixth in the first full year after privatisation.

Right-wingers hit out at 'refusal to go private'

A RIGHT-WING pressure group has slammed Yorkshire's "appalling record" in refusing to save ratepayers' money by privatising council services.

Yorkshire local authorities had the worst record in the country in making efficiency savings from privatisation, said David Saunders, of PULSE, the Public and Local Service Efficiency Campaign.

Privatising can save rates, group claims

A POLITICAL pressure group claims rates could be cut by 30 per cent if Yorkshire councils privatised services.

Sell-offs help cut borrowing

THE proceeds of state sell-offs are helping to curb Government borrowing.

Privatisation threatens islands' ferry lifeline

Figure 5.3 Effects of privatisation

(b) Arguments for Privatisation

The arguments in favour of privatisation are:

1. It will lead to greater competition and efficiency. With more competition, producers will have to provide better and cheaper goods and services.
2. Consumers will benefit from greater choice and better services.
3. Taxpayers will benefit from cheaper Government services and lower payments to support nationalised industries. Denationalisation has provided several billion pounds of revenue to the Government.
4. Privatisation has increased the number of people owning shares in companies. By increasing share ownership among consumers and workers, the Government hopes that people will have a stake in the success and efficiency of British industry.

(c) Arguments against Privatisation

The arguments against privatisation are:

1. Privatisation does not necessarily increase competition or efficiency, e.g. the privatisation of British Telecom and British Gas has converted public sector monopolies into private sector monopolies. Contracting-out of public services has also led to complaints about the standard of work of private contractors in hospitals and Government offices.
2. Consumers have not always benefited, especially where competition has not been increased.
3. Privatisation costs the Government money. In some cases public corporations have been sold at less than their real value, and the profits from industries such as gas and telecommunications will be lost to future Governments. The Government has had to 'write off' debts to sell the corporations.
4. Increased share ownership has made little difference. Many people have sold their shares for a quick profit. They are still unwilling to buy shares with any real risk, such as those of Eurotunnel.

5.6 Coursework Assignment

Privatisation of _____ has been good for the economy

Choose a specific example of a firm or service which has been privatised. Local cases will usually be easier to find out about. Examples might include a public corporation being sold by the Government, or a local or central Government service which has been 'contracted out', e.g. hospital cleaners being replaced by a private company.

Concentrate upon issues such as:

- The purpose of privatisation, e.g. more competition, saving money.
- How customers are affected.
- Has competition increased?
- Effect upon workers, e.g. wages, conditions of service, number of jobs.

Information could be obtained from sources such as newspaper articles, trade unions, firms and councils. Local politicians are likely to have opinions about the issue. Try to obtain 'hard' information, e.g. about changes in costs or employment. Point out any interest a person or organisation may have.

Describe the benefits and costs of the privatisation you are investigating. If you have a definite opinion about whether the benefits of privatisation are greater than the costs in the case you have chosen, give reasons. If you are not sure, list any information you would like to obtain before deciding.

5.7 Worked Example

STEEL SHARES UP FOR GRABS

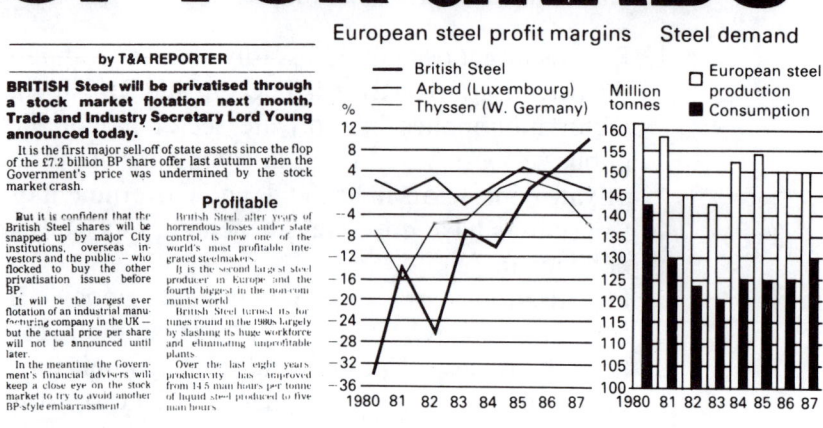

by T&A REPORTER

BRITISH Steel will be privatised through a stock market flotation next month, Trade and Industry Secretary Lord Young announced today.

It is the first major sell-off of state assets since the flop of the £7.2 billion BP share offer last autumn when the Government's price was undermined by the stock market crash.

But it is confident that the British Steel shares will be snapped up by major City institutions, overseas investors and the public — who flocked to buy the other privatisation issues before BP.

It will be the largest ever flotation of an industrial manufacturing company in the UK — but the actual price per share will not be announced until later.

In the meantime the Government's financial advisers will keep a close eye on the stock market to try to avoid another BP-style embarrassment.

Profitable

British Steel after years of horrendous losses under state control, is now one of the world's most profitable integrated steelmakers.

It is the second largest steel producer in Europe and the fourth biggest in the non-communist world.

British Steel turned its fortunes round in the 1980s largely by slashing its huge workforce and eliminating unprofitable plants.

Over the last eight years productivity has improved from 14.5 man hours per tonne of liquid steel produced to five man hours.

T&A, Thursday October 6, 1988

Source: Phillips & Drew

(a) Look at the graph 'steel demand'. Describe the trends in production and consumption between 1984 and 1987. (6)
(b) How might these figures affect the profits of steel manufacturers? (6)
(c) What was happened to British Steel's profit margins between 1980 and 1987? (4)
(d) Explain how British Steel has managed to become profitable. (9)
(e) What risks would a buyer of British Steel shares take? (3)

Answer

(a) Production down (1)
    Figures show a fall of approx 153 to 150 million tonnes (1)
    Consumption up (1)
    Figures show a rise of approx 125 to 130 million tonnes (1)
    The gap between production and consumption is narrowing (1)
    Figures show the gap has decreased from approx 28 to 20 million tonnes (1)
(b) Production greater than consumption; may be difficult to sell steel. (2)
    Explain possible effects, e.g. more competition, falling prices, some firms go out of business. (4)

(c) Increased (1)
Figures show an increase from – 34% to 10% (1)
Explain that BS making losses until 1985 (2)
(d) Price may fall (1)
Explain possible reasons, e.g. overproduction in industry, general fall in stock market (2)

5.8 Self-Test Question

Read the information below and answer the following questions.

Royal Mail

'The Post Office Users' National Council criticised the Post Office about their service. They claimed that only 75% of First Class mail arrives on the next day of posting.'

'The Post Office hopes to have automated all sorting offices by 1989.'

'Postal workers today claimed that they worked longer hours than the average worker but received less than the average wage.'

'The Chairman of the Post Office said today that a pay claim by the postal workers would put up the price of letters by 2p.'

'The Communication Workers' Union has agreed to continue pay negotiations in the hope of reaching a settlement in the near future.'

(a) What type of organisation is the Post Office? (1)
(b) (i) What type of organisation is the Post Office Users' National Council? (1)
(ii) Why is it thought necessary to have such a group? Give **two** reasons. (2)
(c) From the information give **two** arguments that the Communication Workers' Union could present to support the pay claim for Post Office workers. (2)
(d) From the information give **one** argument the Post Office would make against the pay claim. (1)
(e) List **three** examples of industrial action the Communication Workers' Union might take if pay negotiations break down. (3)
(f) State **two** economic costs and **two** economic benefits to the Post Office of further automation in postal sorting. (4)
(g) (i) What is meant by a social cost? (1)
(ii) Give **one** example of a social cost that might result from automation. (1)
(h) The Post Office could be a candidate for privatisation in the future. State the business reasons why the Post Office should or should not be privatised. (7)

6. Finance for Business

SEG	LEAG	NISEAC	WJEC	NEAB	MEG	Topic	Date attempted	Date completed	Self Assessment
✓	✓	✓	✓	✓	✓	6.1			
✓	✓	✓	✓	✓	✓	6.2			
✓	✓	✓	✓	✓	✓	6.3			
✓	✓	✓	✓	✓	✓	6.4			
✓	✓	✓	✓	✓	✓	6.5			
✓	✓	✓	✓	✓	✓	6.6			
✓	✓	✓	✓	✓	✓	6.7			

6.1 The Need for Finance

All firms need finance to stay in business. This may be for purposes such as:

- Running costs such as wages, materials and rent.
- New premises and equipment.
- Developing new products.
- Ensuring adequate *cash-flow* through the business.

Finance may be obtained from either *internal* or *external* sources.

6.2 Internal Finance

Internal finance is obtained from within the business itself. It is by far the most important source of capital for firms, accounting for over two-thirds of the total. For smaller businesses it may be the only means of raising finance. It can be obtained from:

1. *Retained profit*. This is also referred to as *ploughed-back profit*, or undistributed profit. At the end of the financial period (usually every six or twelve months), the firm will divide its profits in three ways, as shown in Figure 6.1.

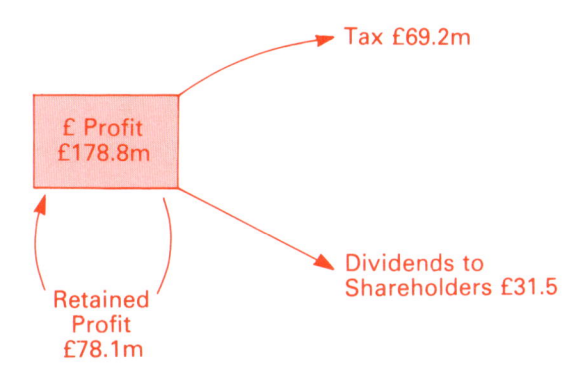

Figure 6.1 Allocation of profit by Reuters PLC (1987)

2. Past reserves of cash.
3. Reducing the credit period allowed to customers, or persuading suppliers to give longer credit.
4. Reducing the level of stocks of materials and goods kept.
5. Selling off unprofitable assets such as buildings or subsidiary companies.

6.3 External Finance

External finance is money obtained from outside the business, through means such as the following.

(a) Borrowing

This accounts for 20–30 per cent of firms' capital. Businesses borrow money from several different types of lender.

(i) Commercial banks

These are the major High Street banks such as Barclays and Midland. They offer two major types of loans to business, the overdraft and the fixed-term loan.

Overdraft
This allows the firm to spend more than it has in its account, up to an agreed limit. The period of the overdraft is fixed, but is often renewed indefinitely. This is the cheapest form of borrowing, as the borrower pays interest only upon the actual sum owed at any particular time.
  Overdrafts are suitable in cases such as a shop stocking up for Christmas or a manufacturer supplying goods on credit.

Fixed-term loan
This is suitable for a business wishing to invest in fixed assets such as premises or machinery. A fixed amount is borrowed and paid back in instalments over a definite period.

Apart from these basic loans, banks often have schemes specially designed for particular types of business such as farms or franchises.

(ii) Specialist banks and finance houses

These specialise in lending to commercial borrowers. A well-known example is Investors in Industry (known as '3i'), which lends to firms in return for a proportion of the shares.

(iii) International banks and consortia

Large public limited companies may need to borrow millions of pounds. A single bank might be unwilling to risk lending all this money, so an international bank such as Chase Manhattan or Barclays International will arrange for a number of lenders to share the loan and risks. This is called a *consortium loan*.

(iv) Leasing

If a firm needs expensive equipment or vehicles it may lease them through a bank or finance house. The leasing house buys the equipment and hires it out to the user over an agreed period. The firm does not have to commit large amounts of capital.

(v) Factoring

A *factor* will pay a proportion of all the debts owed to a firm, which gets immediate payment instead of having to provide credit. The factor then collects the full amount owing from the firm's creditors.

(vi) Debentures

Public limited companies can issue debentures on the Stock Exchange. A debenture is an IOU from the firm, which promises to repay it in a few years' time. The holder of the debenture receives interest every year. Debentures are *negotiable*, i.e. they can be bought and sold. They are not shares, and their holders have no say in the running of the firm.

(b) Issuing Shares

Limited companies can obtain capital by issuing shares. Private limited companies cannot advertise shares for sale, but are allowed to admit new shareholders – often banks and finance companies. A private company can also 'go public' by becoming a public limited company.

Public limited companies can issue two main types of shares, preference shares and ordinary shares.

(i) Preference shares

Preference shares earn a dividend before other types of shares. They carry a fixed dividend rate; for example the holder of £100 worth of 9 per cent preference stock would receive £9 per year.

Preference shares may be *cumulative* – if profits are too low to pay a dividend in one year, they get double dividends the next year.

Preference shares provide a steady and safe income. They are often non-voting shares, but some companies issue *participating preference shares* which do carry a vote.

(ii) Ordinary shares

The majority of company shares are ordinary shares. The rate of dividend varies from year to year, depending upon the level of profits. Ordinary shareholders only receive their dividend after preference shareholders have been paid. Most ordinary shares carry a vote for each share held. In a good year they will usually receive a higher return than preference shares.

(c) Government Assistance

The Government has various schemes which assist firms for certain purposes, such as investing in particular regions or types of production. Some of these are listed in Chapter 15.

6.4 The Stock Exchange

(a) Functions of the Stock Exchange

The Stock Exchange is a market for both new and second-hand shares, debentures and Government securities. It is also responsible for supervising *new issues* of shares when firms become public limited companies.

By providing a market for new and second-hand shares, the Stock Exchange makes it possible for firms to raise capital, and for investors to convert their shares into cash. Without a market of this type it would be more difficult for companies to persuade people to invest their money in new shares.

In December 1987 there were 3,062 companies listed on the Stock Exchange. Of these, 400 were quoted only on the *Unlisted Securities Market* (USM) or the *Third Market*. These markets allow shares in smaller companies to be traded on the Exchange.

(b) The Big Bang

Until October 1986 there were two types of members of the Stock Exchange:

- *Brokers* worked as agents for buyers and sellers, who could only trade in shares through a broker. The broker received a commission (which had a fixed minimum rate) for buying and selling shares.
- *Jobbers* bought and sold shares for themselves. They made their living from the profit (called *jobber's turn*) on their dealings.

The main feature of the system was *'single capacity'*. A person could only be a broker or a jobber. Brokers were not allowed to buy or sell shares for themselves. Jobbers were not allowed to deal directly with the public. This was to prevent members of the Stock Exchange from advising their clients to buy shares in which they had a personal interest.

In October 1986 this system was completely changed by the 'Big Bang'. The aim of Big Bang was to make dealing in shares more competitive and efficient. The key changes were:

1. All members can now operate in *'dual capacity'*, trading shares for themselves and clients.
2. Scales of minimum commission were abolished.
3. 'Corporate membership' by banks and financial institutions was allowed. Members can now have limited liability.
4. Protection for investors was increased, particularly through the electronic recording of all transactions.
5. A computerised dealing system called the *Stock Exchange Automated Quotation* (SEAQ) system was established (see Figure 6.2).

There is now only one type of Stock Exchange member – the broker/dealer. Some members will act as *market-makers* in particular types of shares, such as oil or chemicals, buying and selling these shares on a regular basis.

All members can deal with the public, but they must always tell the client whether they are buying or selling the shares themselves, or for a client. The SEAQ system ensures that the client gets the best price available at the time.

Figure 6.2 The SEAQ system

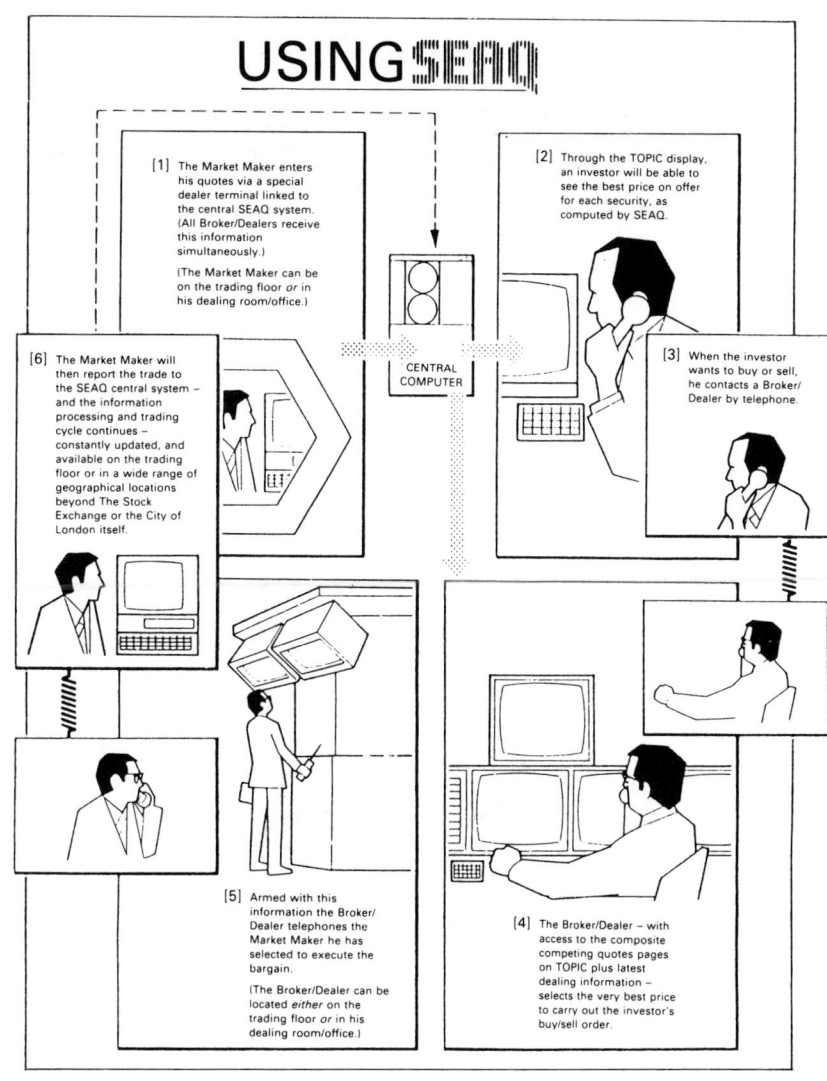

Figure 6.3
How share-buying works

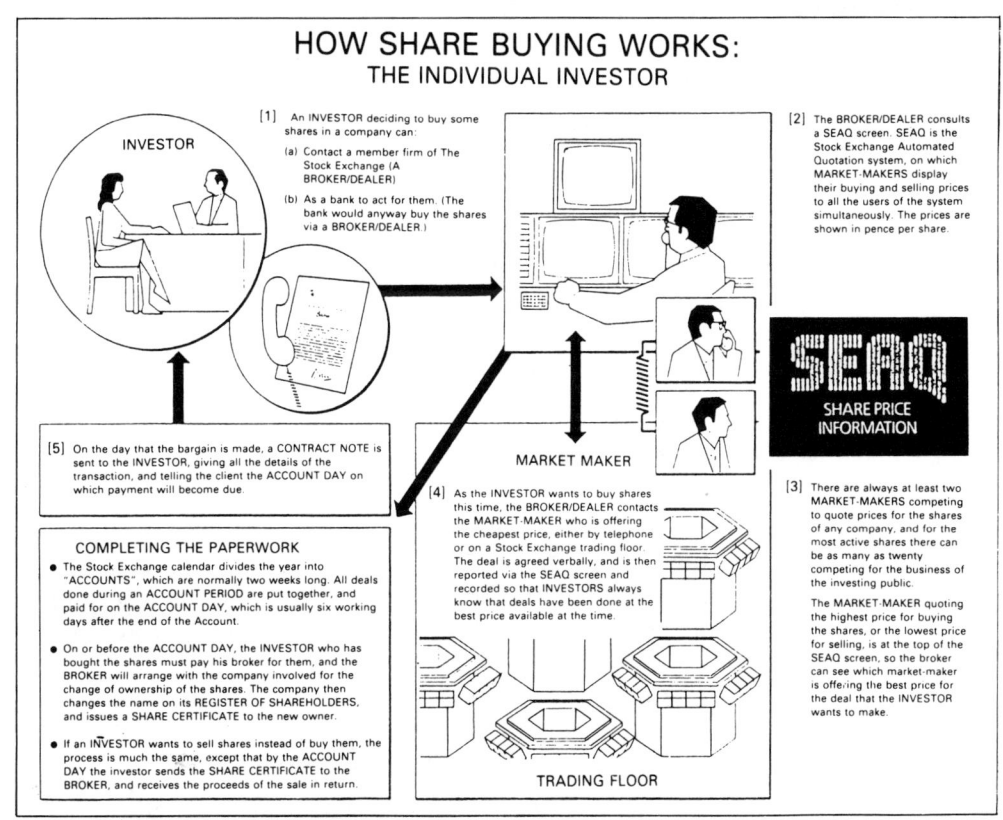

(c) New Share Issues

A firm wishing to issue shares through the Stock Exchange must follow the rules made by the Stock Exchange Council. These are intended to ensure that a firm advertising shares to the public is reputable and safe for investors to trust with their money.

The firm will employ an *issuing house*, which is usually a department of a merchant or commercial bank. A prospectus must be issued, containing information such as:

- The company's financial record e.g. past profits, turnover and assets.
- The number and type of shares to be sold.
- Future plans.
- Date of share issue.
- An application form to buy shares, with details of how shares will be allocated if the issue is *oversubscribed*.

Applications for shares are unlikely to exactly equal the number offered for sale. The issue will usually be *undersubscribed* (too few applications) or *oversubscribed* (too many).

If the issue is undersubscribed the shares will be paid for by the *underwriters*, usually one or more financial institutions which have agreed in advance to buy any unsold shares at a particular price.

If the issue is oversubscribed, shares will be allocated according to the formula described in the prospectus.

6.5 Coursework Assignment

Is it better to buy or lease equipment?

Choose an example of a piece of equipment or property which a firm could lease or buy outright, e.g. vehicles, shops, photocopiers, computers or tools.

A decision about whether to buy or lease could involve issues such as:

- The cost of buying, including interest if money has to be borrowed.
- Rental charges.
- Depreciation.
- Tax relief.
- Cost of updating equipment.
- Maintenance costs.

You will need to investigate the effect of these factors on the costs of buying or leasing.

Information could be obtained from sources such as price lists and brochures, letters and personal interviews. A local firm or organisation may be prepared to help.

Present your assignment by describing the factors which would have to be considered in making the choice about buying or leasing. Use tables or graphs to show the financial costs of the two options.

If you think that one of the options is better, explain why you think so.

6.6 Worked Example

Patrick McNab, who owns a manufacturing business, decides to acquire his own fleet of delivery vehicles instead of using independent road haulage contractors. He also decides to lease, rather than buy, the vehicles.

(a) Why do you think he chose to acquire his own fleet? (6)
(b) How does leasing help to reduce the initial cost of the vehicles? (3)
(c) What other advantages are there for Patrick in leasing rather than purchasing outright for cash? (6)

(LEAG Specimen)

Answers

(a) Greater control: more security; vehicle advertising; reduced damage by handling. (6)
(b) Payments spread over period of years; monthly/annual lease rent paid. (3)
(c) Obsolescent vehicles can be replaced with new models; lease rent is tax deductible; no permanent commitment to equipment as circumstances change; precise outgoings known in advance; any cash released through not purchasing outright can be used elsewhere. (6)

6.7 Self-Test Question

The following information is included in the Chairman's Annual Report and Accounts presented to the shareholders of Glaxo PLC for the year to 31 March 1988.

Authorised Capital 600,000 £1 Ordinary Shares	
Issued Capital 400,000 £1 Ordinary Shares (fully paid)	
Profits <u>retained or ploughed back</u> in the business up until 31 March 1987	£74,000
Gross Profit for the year to 31 March 1988	£162,000
<u>Net Profit</u> before taxation for the year	£110,000
Estimated taxation to be paid	£34,000
<u>Turnover</u> in year	£1,265,000
Proposed Dividend 12%	
Cash at Bank	£27,500

(a) Explain briefly the words underlined. (6)
(b) (i) What is the meaning of the term 'Authorised Capital'? (2)
    (ii) What is the meaning of the term 'Issued Capital'? (2)
(c) How much will a shareholder receive in dividends if he holds 20,000 £1 shares? (2)
(d) (i) State whether you consider (from the information above) that the company has had a reasonably good year's trading. Give reasons. (2)
    (ii) What other information would have helped you? (3)
(e) Calculate the profits retained or ploughed back which the Chairman will quote in his next Annual Report. (Show your calculations.) (3)

(NISEC)

7 Management of Business

SEG	LEAG	NISEAC	WJEC	NEAB	MEG	Topic	Date attempted	Date completed	Self Assessment
✓	✓	✓	✓	✓	✓	7.1			
✓	✓	✓	✓	✓	✓	7.2			
✓	✓	✓	✓	✓	✓	7.3			
✓	✓	✓	✓	✓	✓	7.4			
✓	✓	✓	✓	✓	✓	7.5			
✓	✓	✓	✓	✓	✓	7.6			

7.1 Functions of Management

The functions of management can be divided into planning, organising, command, co-ordination and control.

(a) Planning

Management must decide upon the *objectives* of the business and how these will be carried out. Decisions must be made about matters such as which goods and services will be produced, where the firm will locate and how it will market its products.

(b) Organising

Organising involves ensuring that plans are carried out. People must be given responsibility for different functions of the business. Everybody must know who is responsible for making decisions and ensuring adequate supplies of materials, labour and equipment. In larger businesses these functions are usually split between departments, such as those shown in Figure 7.2.

(c) Command

Managers must ensure that employees work towards the company's objectives. The word 'motivation' is more commonly used nowadays, because it is generally believed that workers are more efficient if they are involved in their work rather than simply being told what to do. Motivation of workers is discussed in Chapter 11.

(d) Co-ordination

Within businesses, particularly larger firms, workers may have different objectives and priorities. If they are not co-ordinated to work together, problems may occur.

For example, a machine may be the cause of complaints from customers. This may be because of production problems such as bad design or defective parts, or because sales staff are exaggerating what it can do. Whatever the cause,

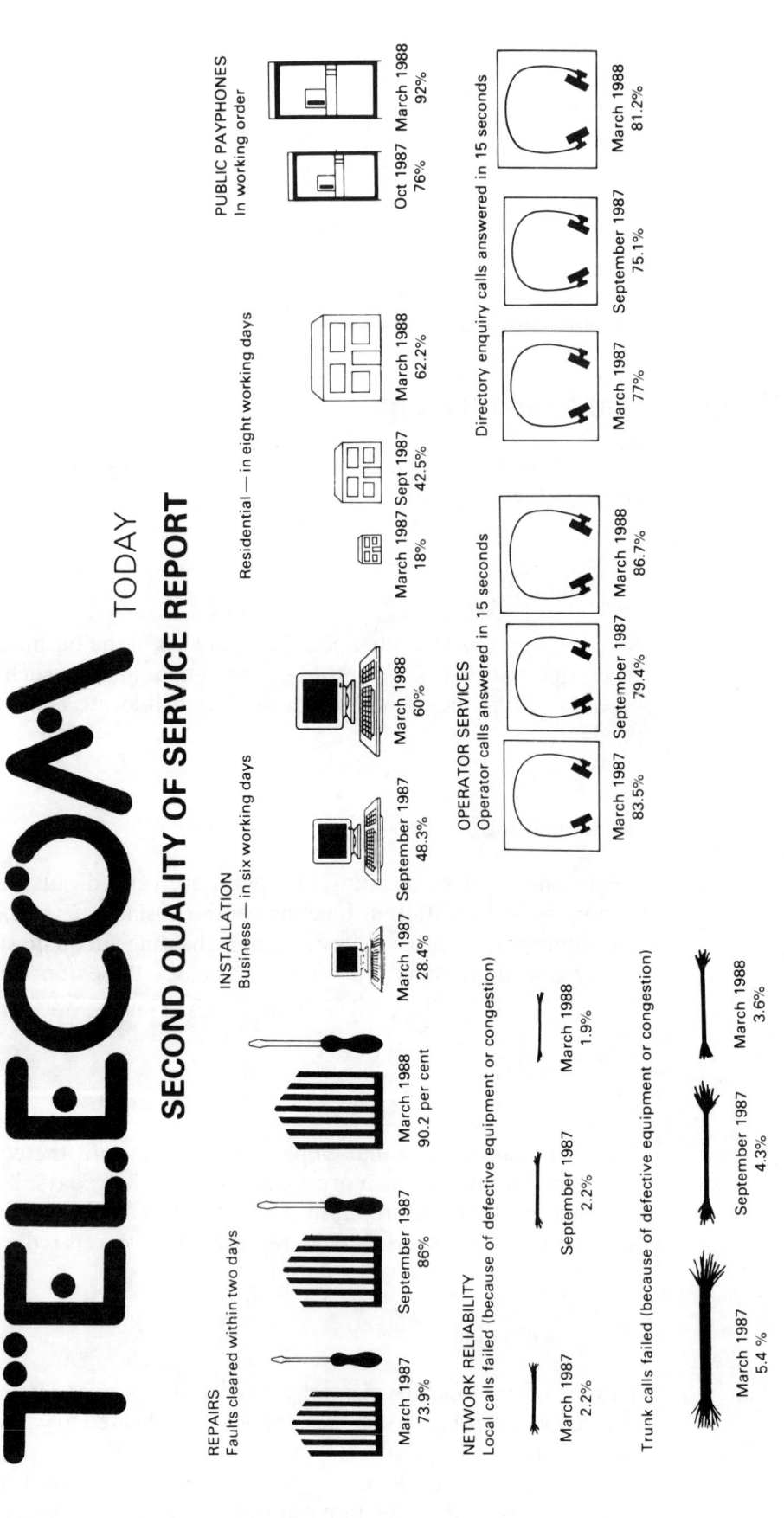

Figure 7.1 British Telecom quality of service report

management must ensure that the problem is solved by getting production and sales staff to work with each other.

(e) Control

Control means setting up systems to check that plans are being carried out. The business will usually have targets for items such as sales, costs and profits. There may also be performance targets for certain parts of the business (see Figure 7.1).

For example, in 1988–89 British Rail set the following targets for its InterCity trains:

- At least 90 per cent should arrive within 10 minutes of the set time.
- Only 1 in 200 at most should be cancelled.
- Customers should not have to queue for more than five minutes to obtain tickets.
- 95 per cent of telephone calls should be dealt with within 30 seconds.

If a business's targets are not being achieved the management must either set more realistic targets or improve performance to meet the plans.

7.2 Business Objectives

(a) Maximise Profits

Maximising profit means making the highest possible profit. It is the main aim of a privately-owned business, although some may follow other objectives such as those described below.

Profit is important for the following reasons:

1. To provide a financial reward to the owners of the business for putting their money into it.
2. As a source of finance for future investment.
3. To allow the business to survive.

(b) Maximise Sales

The firm may attempt to obtain the highest possible sales, even if unprofitable business is taken on. This policy will often be based upon increasing the firm's *market share*, which is its proportion of the sales of the industry as a whole.

(c) Maximise Share Price

This applies to public limited companies, whose directors may wish to maintain a high share price. This pleases shareholders and puts off potential takeover bids.

(d) Provide a Service

All firms have to provide an efficient service to stay in business. For private firms this is essential in order to keep customers and be profitable. Organisations such as public corporations may have other objectives which are not profitable, such as maintaining a nationwide postal service or providing transport to remote country areas. These services may be provided at less than their cost.

7.3 Internal Organisation of Business

(a) Organisation Charts

In small businesses a single owner may be responsible for all the functions of management. In larger organisations, however, the business is likely to be split into departments. Figure 7.2 is an *organisation chart* showing the departments of a typical medium-sized manufacturing firm.

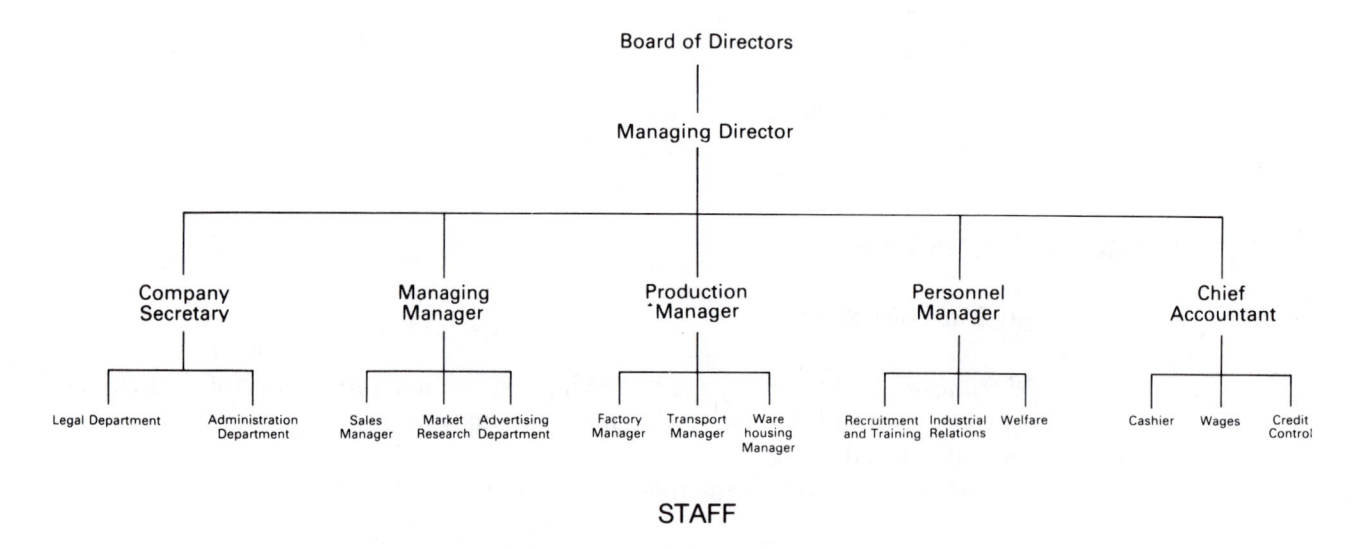

```
                        Board of Directors
                              |
                       Managing Director
    ┌─────────────┬───────────┼───────────┬─────────────┐
  Company      Managing   Production   Personnel      Chief
  Secretary    Manager     Manager      Manager    Accountant
   ┌─┴─┐        ┌─┴─┐      ┌─┴─┐        ┌─┴─┐        ┌─┴─┐
 Legal  Admin  Sales Market Advert  Factory Transport Ware  Recruit Industrial Welfare  Cashier Wages Credit
 Dept   Dept   Mgr   Res.   Dept    Mgr     Mgr      housing and     Relations                      Control
                                                     Manager Training
```

STAFF

Figure 7.2 An organisation chart

This chart is only one example, and the exact division into departments will vary between firms. The titles used for particular people are also different.

(b) Departments

The *Board of Directors* is elected by the shareholders to manage the company. They appoint a *Managing Director* to control its daily management. Some of the Department Managers such as the Company Secretary or Chief Accountant may also be members of the Board.

In Figure 7.2, the Managing Director has direct control over the five Department Managers, whose responsibilities are given below.

(i) Company Secretary

The Company Secretary is responsible for all the business's legal affairs and administration. He or she will often sign contracts and carry out duties such as informing shareholders about the financial state of the company. The Secretary may also be in charge of organising the company's offices and paperwork such as mail and internal communication (see Chapter 14).

(ii) Marketing Manager

The Marketing Manager will control the activities involved in selling the firm's products, such as advertising and sales. In many large firms there may be separate Marketing and Sales Departments. Marketing is discussed in Chapter 9.

(iii) Production Manager

The Production Manager has to ensure that the firm's products are made as efficiently as possible. Labour, materials and equipment must be arranged and used without wastage or delays. Production is discussed in Chapter 10.

(iv) Personnel Manager

The Personnel Department is responsible for all matters involved in employing staff. Its duties include recruitment and training (see Chapter 12) and industrial relations (Chapter 13).

(v) Chief Accountant

The Chief Accountant is in charge of the financial affairs of the company. His or her duties would include arranging for wages and suppliers to be paid, and advising the Board of Directors on matters such as how capital should be raised and used (see Chapter 6). The Chief Accountant will also be responsible for organising company accounts and explaining their relevance to people inside and outside the company (see Chapter 8).

(b) Other Methods of Organisation

Larger businesses, particularly those selling many different products, may be organised in different ways. Many are organised with a *holding company* owning several *subsidiaries*. Each subsidiary firm will sell different products or operate in different markets. Grattan PLC, itself owned by the Next group, is a good example of this (see Figure 7.3).

Multinationals, which produce in many different countries, often have a separate company for each part of the world, or for particular countries.

(c) Principles of Internal Organisation

(i) Delegation

All organisations depend upon the *delegation* of responsibility. For example, in a large public company the shareholders have ultimate control. However, they do not usually have the time or willingness to run the day-to-day business. They

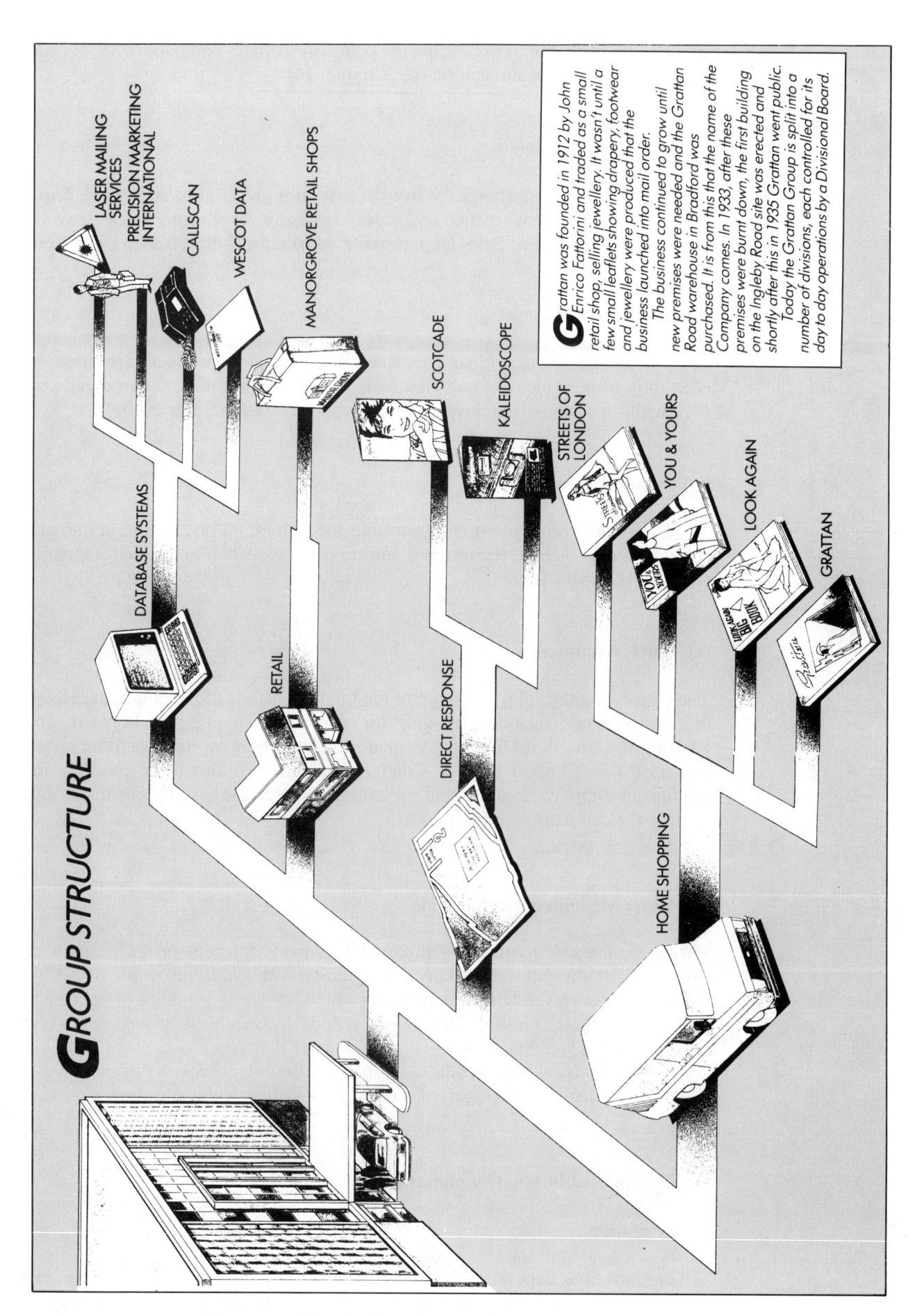

Figure 7.3 Organisation of Grattan PLC

62

elect a Board of Directors, which in turn delegates this responsibility to the Managing Director.

Although the Managing Director is responsible for management of all the business's activities, he or she cannot directly control hundreds or thousands of workers. Department Managers are appointed to control different activities, such as finance or production. Each Manager then appoints other workers to take on smaller responsibilities, such as managing an individual factory or recruiting junior staff.

Delegation does not mean giving up responsibility. For example, a product may sell badly because of poor work in the factory. The Managing Director does not directly control production, but may still be held responsible because he or she should have set up systems to ensure that such problems did not occur.

(ii) Chain of command

The *chain of command* refers to the way in which power is passed down through the organisation. In a small firm workers may be directly supervised by the owner or manager. In larger firms, however, the chain of command will be more complicated.

Suppose, for example, that the Managing Director of a car manufacturer decides that more cars should be painted red. This decision will be passed down through the chain of command as shown in Figure 7.4.

```
          Managing Director
                  │
                  ▼
         Production Manager
                  │
                  ▼
          Factory Manager
                  │
                  ▼
    Paint Department Supervisor
                  │
                  ▼
           Paint Sprayers
```

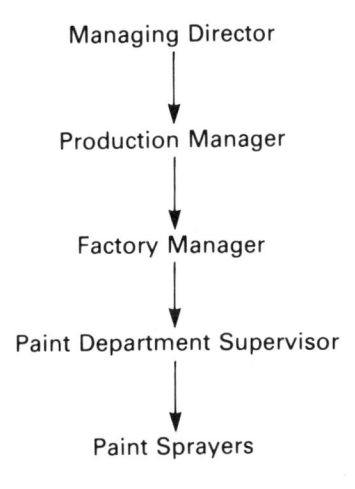

Figure 7.4 A chain of command

At each stage the employee has both *responsibility* and *authority*. The Paint Department Supervisor has a responsibility to tell the paintsprayers to use red paint, but cannot be blamed if red cars sell badly. He or she has no authority to refuse the order, but does have the authority to order more red paint.

(iii) Span of control

The *span of control* is the number of people directly controlled by one person. In Figure 7.2 the Managing Director has a span of control of five managers.

The number of people which can be directly controlled varies according to the type of work involved. The five people in the Managing Director's span of control all have complicated responsibilities. It would be difficult to control a large number of people with similar jobs.

For simple work which can be checked easily, the span of control can be larger. The Paint Department Supervisor could easily control ten or more paintsprayers.

(iv) Centralisation and decentralisation

Authority within an organisation may be *centralised* or *decentralised*. If it is centralised, decisions are taken by the top managers and passed down through the chain of command. Multiple chains of shops often work upon this basis. Individual shop managers have little or no control over which goods to stock and what prices to charge. In a *decentralised* company local shop managers would have more power to make decisions.

Centralised and decentralised management both have advantages. Centralised management makes it easier to co-ordinate the ordering and marketing of products. National advertising campaigns can feature special offers, knowing that local branches will stock the products.

The main advantages of decentralised management are that it allows individual managers to react quickly to changes, and makes people feel more involved in their work.

7.4 Coursework Assignment

Why are firms organised in different ways?

Draw up organisation charts for at least two firms or other organisations such as Council Departments. Figure 7.2 gives a simple example of an organisation chart.

You will need to obtain the co-operation of local firms. Some may be able to give you a ready-prepared chart, but otherwise you will have to interview a manager to obtain this information.

Once you have obtained your charts try to find information about factors such as:

- The chain of command. Is there a long chain of command between senior management and shop-floor workers?
- The span of control. Why do some managers or supervisors control more people than others?
- How 'centralised' is authority within the firm, e.g. do people feel that they have much control over decisions?

If the two firms are in similar businesses, check to see if their organisation is similar. If they are in different businesses, can any differences in organisations be explained by the goods they produce?

7.5 Worked Example

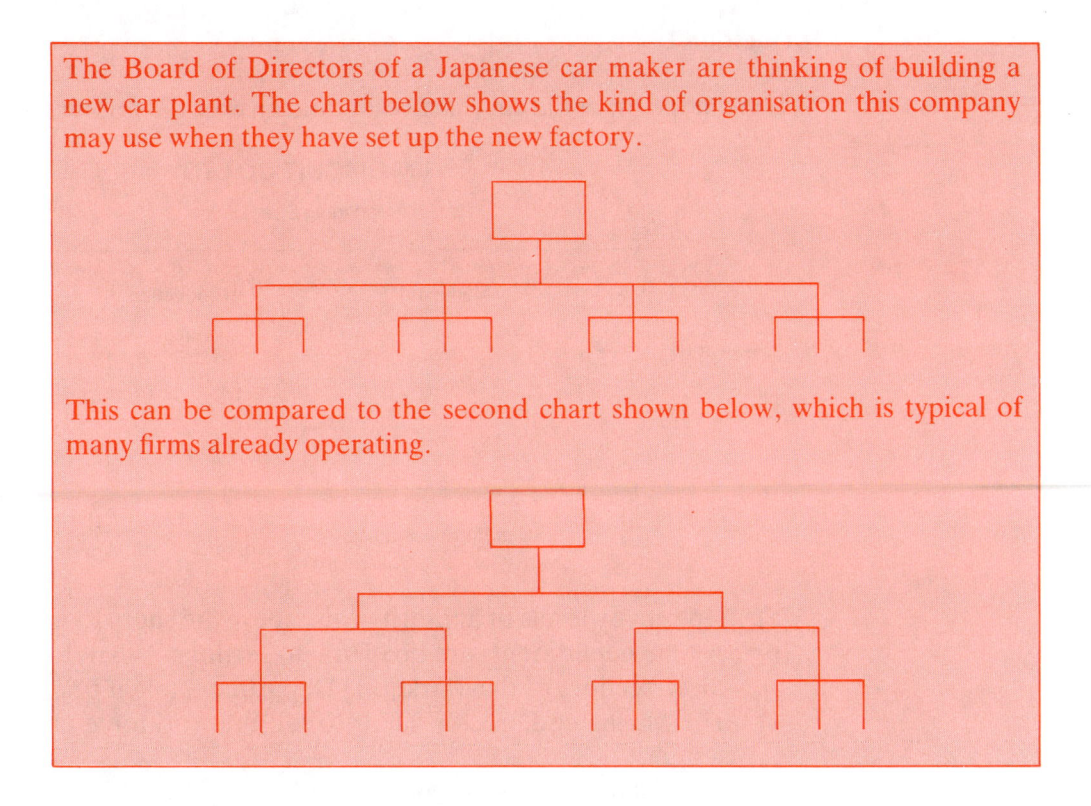

> The Board of Directors of a Japanese car maker are thinking of building a new car plant. The chart below shows the kind of organisation this company may use when they have set up the new factory.
>
> [organisation chart — flatter structure]
>
> This can be compared to the second chart shown below, which is typical of many firms already operating.
>
> [organisation chart — taller structure]

What are the main differences between these two organisations and what might this mean for the people who work in them?

(NEA Specimen)

Answers

State one difference relating purely to the appearance e.g. the first is flatter. (0–2)

Explain a difference relating to the meaning of the charts e.g. the people in the second have fewer people below them. (3–4)

Describe more than one factor e.g. the supervisors in the second have fewer people responsible to them, there is a shorter chain of command. (5–6)

Explain one factor in detail to show the implications for the people, e.g. shorter chain of command means the top is more accessible. (7–8)

Explain more than one factor developed as in 4. (9–12)

Show an awareness of most of the differences and their implications i.e. chain of command, span of control, access to senior people, individual responsibility, team decision making, control of large groups. (13–16)

65

7.6 Self-Test Questions

Question 1

Look at the organisation chart below and answer the following questions.

LM BISCUIT CO LTD

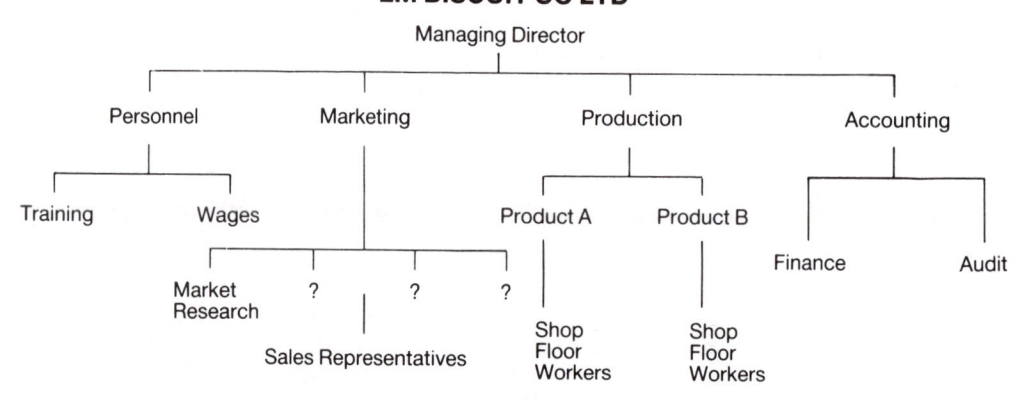

```
                        Managing Director
       ┌──────────┬──────────┬──────────┐
   Personnel   Marketing  Production  Accounting
   ┌────┬──┐      │      ┌────┬────┐   ┌────┬────┐
Training Wages    │   Product A Product B Finance Audit
              ┌──┬──┬──┐    │       │
           Market ? ? ?  Shop    Shop
           Research      Floor   Floor
                │        Workers Workers
          Sales Representatives
```

(a) How many levels of authority exist **above** the shop floor? (1)

(b) All the departments are divided into sections. What do you think the other **three** sections of the Marketing Department might be? (3)

(c) The Managing Director needs to tell the workforce about a new payment system.
   (i) List **three** ways in which he could do this. (3)
   (ii) Choose **one** way from your list and explain why it would be an appropriate method in this situation. (2)

(MEG)

Question 2

Read the following paragraph carefully and answer the questions printed below.

J. Hamilton Ltd is a medium sized textile manufacturer with two plants five miles apart. The firm has five departments concerned with market, production, finance, personnel and distribution. There has been a serious accident and the **Board of Directors** have told all **Departmental Managers** to remind employees of their **duties and obligations** under the Health and Safety at Work Act.

(a) Show what you understand by the following terms used above.
   (i) **Board of Directors** (2)
   (ii) **Departmental Managers** (2)
(b) State **three** suitable methods of communicating these '**duties and obligations**' to all employees. (3)
(c) To which Departmental Manager would you expect the following employees to report?
   (i) salesman
   (ii) lorry driver
   (iii) accounts clerk
   (iv) machinist (4)

(MEG Specimen)

Accounting for Business

SEG	LEAG	NISEAC	WJEC	NEAB	MEG	Topic	Date attempted	Date completed	Self Assessment
✓	✓	✓	✓	✓	✓	8.1			
✓	✓	✓	✓	✓	✓	8.2			
✓	✓	✓	✓	✓	✓	8.3			
✓	✓	✓	✓	✓	✓	8.4			
✓	✓	✓	✓	✓	✓	8.5			
✓	✓	✓	✓	✓	✓	8.6			
✓	✓	✓	✓	✓	✓	8.7			
✓	✓	✓	✓	✓	✓	8.8			
✓	✓	✓	✓	✓	✓	8.9			
✓	✓	✓	✓	✓	✓	8.10			
✓	✓	✓	✓	✓	✓	8.11			
✓	✓	✓	✓	✓	✓	8.12			
✓	✓	✓	✓	✓	✓	8.13			

8.1 The Need for Financial Records

All firms have to keep financial records, which serve various purposes, as illustrated in Figure 8.1.

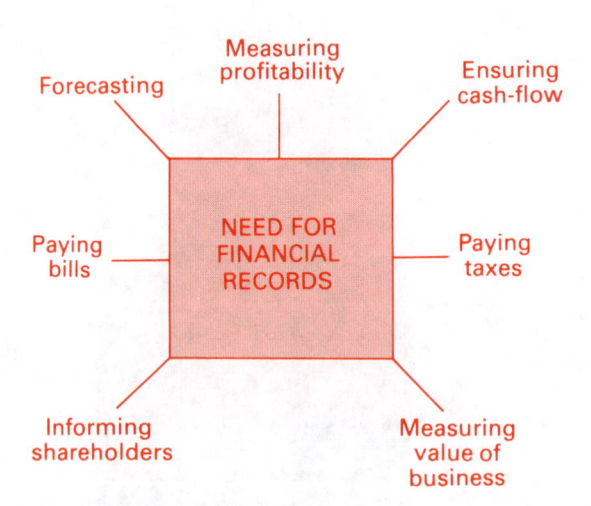

Figure 8.1 Need for financial records

As well as the firm's accounts, records are kept by using documents such as those described in Section 8.9.

8.2 Costs, Revenues and Profit

(a) Costs

Costs are the money paid by a firm to workers and suppliers.

(i) Fixed costs

Fixed costs (also called *overheads* or *indirect* costs) stay the same whatever the business's sales or production. Fixed costs include items such as rent and rates, hire of machinery and vehicles and management salaries. If the firm is to continue these have to be paid even if sales are zero.

(ii) Variable costs

Variable costs (also called *direct* costs) increase as output increases. They include items such as materials, fuel and wages.

(iii) Total costs

Total costs = Fixed costs + variable costs

(iv) Average or unit costs

$$\text{Average or unit costs} = \frac{\text{Total costs}}{\text{Output}}$$

This is the cost of producing one unit of a product, e.g. a single car or a ton of sand.

(b) Revenues

Revenues are the money received by a business for selling its goods or services.

(c) Break-even Analysis

Break-even analysis is a means of forecasting the minimum sales necessary before a good or service becomes profitable. It is best illustrated by means of an example.

Siobhan Quinn plans to earn money by making and selling badges on a market stall. Her costs are as follows:

1. Fixed costs (hire of badge-stamping machine and market stall, transport etc) are £20 per day.
2. Variable costs (purchase of badges and other materials) are 10 pence per badge.

She decides that a competitive price is 30 pence per badge. Her costs and revenue at different levels of sales are plotted in Figure 8.2.

The *break-even point* is the levels of sales where

Total costs = Total revenue

In this case Siobhan will have to sell 100 badges before she starts to make any profit. If she sells less than this she will make a loss, because she has to pay £20 in fixed costs no matter what her sales are.

If Siobhan could not sell this many badges she would have to do one or more of three things:

- Cut her fixed costs, e.g. by looking for a cheaper machine hirer or market stall.
- Reduce her variable cost by buying cheaper materials.
- Increase her prices (if she doubled her price to 60 pence she would only have to sell 50 badges to break even).

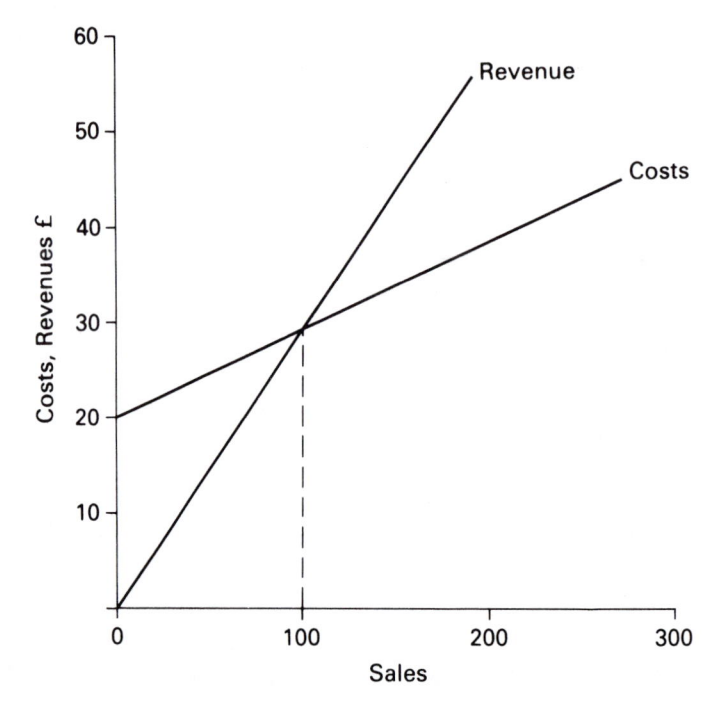

Figure 8.2 A break-even graph

8.3 Cash-Flow

All businesses have to make or receive payments at different times. It is often necessary to pay for purchases or expenses before payment is received from customers. This is particularly likely in businesses where customers normally buy on credit. Small firms may also have to pay cash for supplies because they are regarded as a bad risk.

This means that a business may be operating profitably, but will need to have cash or borrowed money available at certain times. A *cash-flow* forecast such as that in Figure 8.3 sets out the likely cash position of a company over the near future.

The forecast is prepared by John Cartwright, who runs a small business making toys and novelty gifts. Some are sold direct to the public through his own shop and at craft fairs. He also sells to large retailers, who insist upon being allowed three months to pay.

As can be seen from Figure 8.3, the peak sales periods are in the summer and just before Christmas. However, the goods have to be made throughout the year, and materials and other expenses must be paid for. Although the business makes a profit during the six months, it is not until December that the firm actually has cash in its account.

This situation will not be serious if it is anticipated, and loans can be arranged to keep the business going. However, many small firms fail because of cash-flow problems, even though they are actually making a profit.

Month	Jul	Aug	Sept	Oct	Nov	Dec	Total (July–Dec)
Balance at start of month	(4000)	(4000)	(5000)	(6000)	(4000)	(1000)	–
Sales	4000	5000	3000	6000	7000	8000	33 000
Purchases	2000	2000	2000	2000	1000	1000	10 000
Expenses	2000	4000	2000	2000	3000	3000	16 000
Net profit for month	0	(1000)	(1000)	2000	3000	4000	7 000
Balance at end of month	(4000)	(5000)	(6000)	(4000)	(1000)	3000	–

Notes
1. Figures in brackets are negative
2. Balance at start of month is the amount of cash the firm has in the bank e.g. at the start of July the firm has an overdraft of £4000
3. Net profit = sales − (purchases + expenses)
4. Balance at end of month = net profit + balance at start
   This figure becomes the balance at start for the next month.

Figure 8.3 Cash-flow forecast

8.4 The Balance Sheet

A *balance sheet* is a picture of the business at any particular time. It records *assets* (items owned by the firm) and *liabilities* (items owed by the firm).

A simple balance sheet is illustrated in Figure 8.4. There are different ways of presenting a balance sheet. This is one particular style.

Balance sheet of Jack & Jill's Hardware Store at 31 August, 1989

LIABILITIES £			ASSETS £		
Capital at 1.9.88	130 000		*Fixed assets*		
Net profit for year	20 000		Freehold premises	125 000	
			Shop fittings	10 000	
Less			*Less*		
Drawings	10 000		Depreciation	3 000	
		140 000			132 000
Current liabilities			*Current assets*		
Creditors	800		Stock for sale	1 600	
			Debtors	400	
		800	Bank account	6 800	
					6 800
		140 800			140 800

Figure 8.4 Balance sheet

This balance sheet is a very simple one, but illustrates some important accounting terms.

(a) Capital

This is the money that the owners have put into the business plus the net profit which has been retained in previous years.

(b) Net Profit

Net profit is explained later in this chapter. It is added to the capital of the business.

(c) Current Liabilities

These are debts which have to be paid within the year. The *creditors* are people or firms who have supplied goods on credit.

(d) Fixed Assets

These are assets which will stay in the business for more than a year. They may increase in value (*appreciate*) or fall in value (*depreciate*). For example the premises would probably appreciate, but the shop-fittings would depreciate as they become worn or out-of-date. This is shown in the balance sheet by deducting £3,000 from the business's fixed assets.

(e) Current Assets

These change constantly during the year as the business buys and sells goods and services.

- *Debtors* are people and firms who owe the business money.
- *Stock for sale* is measured at its *cost price* (what the business paid for it).

The two sides of the balance sheet are always equal.

8.5 The Trading, Profit and Loss Account

A business's profits are calculated from its trading, profit and loss account. A simple example is illustrated in Figure 8.5.

Smallco Ltd Trading, Profit & Loss Account for year ending 31 August, 1989

	£		£
Stock at 1.9.88	90 000	Sales	330 000
Purchases	120 000		
	210 000		
Less			
Stock at 31.8.88	80 000		
Cost of sales	130 000		
Gross profit	200 000		
	330 000		330 000
		Gross profit	200 000
Less			
Wages	60 000		
Rent	5 000		
Advertising	10 000		
Transport	25 000		
Other costs	20 000		
Expenses	120 000		
Net profit	80 000		

Figure 8.5 Trading, profit and loss account

Important items in the trading, profit and loss account are as follows:

1. *Sales*. The income received from selling goods.
2. *Purchases*. The amount spent on buying goods for resale.
3. *Stock*. The unsold goods held by Smallco. The stock at the end of year (*closing stock*) is £80,000, £10,000 less than the stock at the beginning of the year (*opening stock*).
4. *Cost of sales*. This is equal to
    Value of stock used + purchases
    =   £10,000   + £120,000
    =   £130,000

5. *Gross profit*. The profit made from buying and selling goods or services before expenses involved in the sale are subtracted.

73

$$\text{Gross profit} = \text{Sales} - \text{Cost of sales}$$
$$= £330,000 - £130,000$$
$$= £200,000$$

6. *Expenses*. The costs involved in selling goods and services, such as wages, transport, advertising and rent.
7. *Net profit*. The profit made by a business after all expenses are paid.

$$\text{Net profit} = \text{Gross profit} - \text{expenses}$$
$$= £200,000 - £120,000$$
$$= £80,000$$

8.6 Stock Turnover

Stock turnover or *rate of stock-turn* measures the speed with which stock moves in or out of the business, i.e. the time taken from buying goods until they are sold.

To calculate the rate of stock-turn it is necessary to work out the *average stock* held during the year.

$$\text{Average Stock} = \frac{\text{Stock at start of year} + \text{Stock at end of year}}{2}$$

For example, if a business has £20,000 in stock at the beginning of the year, £40,000 at the end, and its cost of sales is £120,000:

$$\text{Average Stock} = \frac{£20,000 + £40,000}{2} = £30,000$$

The rate of stock-turn is measured by the equation:

$$\text{Rate of stock turn} = \frac{\text{Cost of sales}}{\text{Average stock}} = \frac{£120,000}{£30,000} = 4$$

In this case goods are replaced on average four times a year, that is, goods are held in the business an average of three months. If stock was being turned over every day, e.g. fresh milk or newspapers, the rate of stock-turn would be 365.

The firm will try to achieve the highest possible rate of stock-turn, since keeping stock ties up capital and storage space. If goods are kept too long they may deteriorate or go out of fashion.

The ideal rate of stock-turn will depend upon the type of goods stocked. A rate of four might be acceptable for jewellery or furniture, which could be stored for several months. It would be far too low for fresh fruit or fashionable clothes.

8.7 Accounting Measures and Ratios

There are several measures and ratios which are important in showing a business's value, efficiency and profitability.

(a) Net Worth of the Business

This is also called the *owner's capital*. The net worth of Jack & Jill's Hardware (Figure 8.4) is measured by the equation:

$$\text{Net worth} = \text{Assets} - \text{current liabilities}$$
$$= £140,800 - £800$$
$$= £140,000$$

The net worth will increase if the business makes a net profit, and will fall if it makes a loss.

(b) Return on Capital

This is measured by the formula:

$$\text{Return on capital} = \frac{\text{Net profit}}{\text{Capital}} \times 100$$

In the case of Jack & Jill's Hardware (Figure 8.4) this is:

$$\frac{£20,000}{£130,000} \times 100$$

$$= 15\% \text{ (approx)}$$

Whether this percentage is satisfactory depends upon the return which could be achieved elsewhere, for example by putting the money into a bank or another type of business. If a bank account pays 10 per cent interest an investment of £130,000 would earn £13,000 a year. Jack & Jill might be pleased to have made £20,000 profit from the same amount of capital.

(c) Working Capital

This is the money that is needed to pay expenses such as wages, stock and other day-to-day purchases. In Jack & Jill's case:

$$\text{Working capital} = \text{current assets} - \text{current liabilities}$$
$$= £8,800 - £800$$
$$= £8,000$$

(d) Liquid Capital

Liquid capital measures the assets of the business which can be quickly converted into cash. Stocks of goods are not included because they take time to sell, and could only be sold quickly at less than their true value.

$$\text{Liquid capital} = \text{Working capital} - \text{stock}$$
$$= £8,000 - £1,600$$
$$= £6,400$$

(e) Mark-up

Mark-up is the percentage which is added on to the cost of goods to fix the price at which they are sold. It is calculated from the trading, profit and loss account.

The mark-up of Smallco Ltd (see Figure 8.5) is equal to:

$$\frac{\text{Sales}}{\text{Cost of sales}} \times 100 = \frac{£330{,}000}{£130{,}000} \times 100 = 254\% \text{ (approx)}$$

(f) Gross Profit Margin

Gross profit margin for Smallco is measured by the formula:

$$\text{Gross profit margin} = \frac{\text{Gross profit}}{\text{Sales}} \times 100 = \frac{£200{,}000}{£330{,}000} \times 100 = 61\% \text{ (approx)}$$

The mark-up and gross profit margin will vary between businesses. For example, if goods have to be kept for a long time, or expenses are high, the mark-up and profit margin will tend to be high. Storing goods ties up capital, and expenses have to be paid from the gross profit. If goods are sold quickly and expenses are low, the mark-up and margin are likely to be lower.

(g) Net Profit Margin

Smallco's *net profit margin* can be calculated using the equation:

$$\text{Net profit margin} = \frac{\text{Net profit}}{\text{Sales}} \times 100 = \frac{£80{,}000}{£330{,}000} \times 100 = 24\% \text{ (approx)}$$

The net profit margin will also tend to vary between businesses. For example, it will tend to be lower when there is strong competition or falling sales in an industry.

8.8 Improving Profitability

In considering whether its profits are high enough a firm would have to consider questions such as:

- Is it as good as or better than that earned by similar firms in the same business?
- Is it rising or falling compared to past years?
- Is it high enough to provide a reasonable return on the owners' capital?
- Does it allow enough capital for future investment?

If the net profit is too low, there are a number of measures that the firm may take. If

Net profit = Gross profit − Expenses

the business must increase gross profit and/or reduce expenses. It could do this by:

- Cutting prices, hoping to increase sales by enough to make up for the lower profit on each item.
- Increasing prices, hoping to keep enough custom to increase revenue from sales.
- Spending more on advertising.
- Offering better credit or delivery terms to customers.
- Diversifying by offering a wider range of goods and services.
- Cutting the cost of purchases and other expenses by changing suppliers or buying in bulk.
- Reducing expenses by employing fewer workers, cutting advertising, holding less stock and reducing the quality of service offered.
- Examining the profitability of different products or departments to discover whether any should be dropped.

As can be seen, some of the measures suggested contradict each other, e.g. profits might be increased by cutting or increasing prices. This shows that the effects of any policy are unpredictable and there can often be disagreement about the right choice.

8.9 Business Documents

Buying goods or services is a contract under law, even if no documents are signed. Every day millions of such oral contracts are made in shops when people buy their daily paper or a packet of washing powder.

For many transactions, however, details are recorded in writing. Firms keep records for their own use, and to show to accountants, shareholders and tax officials.

Various standard documents are used in business transactions:

1. An *enquiry* asks a supplier about its products and terms of sale such as prices, delivery, discounts and credit.
2. A *quotation* is sent by the supplier, giving the information asked for in the enquiry.
    In some cases a catalogue and price list will give all the necessary information, but in others a quotation will be specially prepared.
3. An *order* is sent to the supplier stating the amount to be purchased and the terms of sale. Figure 8.6 gives an example.
4. An *acknowledgement* may be sent by the supplier when the order is received. It confirms the quantities, prices and other conditions of sale, as previously agreed.
5. An *advice note* tells the buyer that the goods are being sent, and that he should contact the supplier if they are not delivered within a certain time.
6. The *delivery note* is sent with the goods, and usually has a space for the customer to sign for receipt of the goods.
7. An *invoice* (see Figure 8.7) is a bill for goods.

ORDER

K. Wharton Printers Ltd
206 Edinburgh Road
Glasgow
G41 0BG
Tel: 041-658 8838

Order No. KW88 64358
VAT Reg No 21 0432 817
Delivery Address
As above
June 21, 1988

To

NAB Supplies Ltd
11 Cardiff Street
Bradford
BD41 5GN

Account No. 36001

Quantity	Description	Unit Price	Total
100	11.2/3 × 9.1/4 PART PLAIN PAPER	19.20	192.00

Terms: Nett 30 days from invoice date
Delivery: Carriage paid

Total 192.00
VAT 28.80
Invoice Total 220.80

Figure 8.6 An order

INVOICE

NAB Supplies
11 Cardiff Street
Bradford
BD41 5GN

INVOICE No. 8928
Tel. No. 0274 699842

VAT Reg. No. 33 6158 942

Invoice Address:-	Delivery Address:-	Tax Point
K. Wharton Printers Ltd 206 Edinburgh Road Glasgow G41 0BG	As Invoice Address	24/06/88 Delivery Note 013576 01/07/88
Customer Account No:- 3G001	Customer Order No:- KW88 64358	

To supply of goods in accordance with your instructions

Quantity	Product Description	Unit Price	Total
100	LP11 × 9–7 11.2/3 × 9.25 1 PART PLAIN LISTING TO 70 GSM	19.20	192.00

Terms: Nett 30 days from invoice date.
Special Instructions

TOTAL GOODS	192.00
VAT at 15%	28.80
INVOICE TOTAL	220.80

Figure 8.7 An invoice

8. A *pro forma invoice* contains the same details as a normal invoice, but is sent to the buyer when payment is expected before the goods are delivered. When payment is made the goods will be sent.
9. A *credit note* is sent to the buyer if goods are damaged or some are found to be missing.
10. A *statement of account* is sent to regular customers who are paying for and receiving goods continually. It is usually sent monthly and shows the customer's *debits* (charges for goods received) and *credits* (payments and allowances for damaged or incomplete deliveries). The *outstanding balance* shows the amount owed by the customer.
11. *Receipts* may be sent to the buyer as proof of payment. However, except for cash payments, these are often omitted unless requested by the customer.
12. A *remittance advice note* may be sent by the buyer to inform the supplier that a payment has been made through the banking system.

8.10 Coursework Assignment

How could a club improve its finances?

This assignment involves applying business principles to the workings of a club or other non-profit-making organisation.

Choose a local organisation such as a youth club or professional sports club. Consider the ways in which the club could improve its service or raise more money. Use one of your ideas as the title for your assignment, e.g:

- How could £500 be raised to buy equipment for a playgroup?
- How could Glamorgan County Cricket Club increase its attendances?
- Is a school magazine financially viable?

Once you have decided on the problem to investigate, consider ways of solving it. If you are thinking about organising an event you will need to consider requirements such as premises, equipment, supervision etc.

Whatever you decide to investigate, try to think of at least two different ways of approaching the problem. Obtain as much detailed information as possible, especially about the possible costs of staging an event.

Information can be found from different sources such as interviewing people and using questionnaires to find out why people use or don't use a service. Prices of equipment, services etc can be obtained from local firms, Yellow Pages, trade directories and magazines.

Your presentation should include tables, graphs, profit and loss accounts etc. Describe some of the possible solutions to your problem, and the information you have obtained about each of these.

8.11 Worked Examples

Question 1

Carol Roach owns and runs a small manufacturing business making children's toys. She always plans ahead and often makes monthly estimates. From past experience Carol makes the following estimates for one month: raw materials £1500, rent and rates £360, wages and salaries £3500, other running costs £540. The average price of the toys is £14 and she hopes to sell 530 each month.

(a) Show the firm's financial position for the month. (8)
(b) During the month of December Carol estimates that sales will increase by 20 per cent.
    (i) How would this change Carol's revenue? (2)
    (ii) How would Carol meet the increase in sales? (6)
    (iii) Explain what the possible effects might be on profit. (10)
(c) After the rush during December, Carol decides that she should try to sell her toys to Japan.
    (i) What problems could Carol's firm face when selling toys to Japan? (5)
    (ii) Explain how these problems might be overcome. (9)

(SEG Specimen)

Answers

(a) (i) Attempt to group costs and calculate total sales. (1–3)
    (ii) Separate costs and revenue – giving final total figures. Attempt to calculate profit. (4–6)

    Provide an organised trading and profit loss account. Show profit made. (7–8)

(b) (i) Effect is increase of 20%. (1)

    Relate increase to monetary value. (2)

    (ii) Give solution (but no attempt to explain effect e.g. increase production). (1–2)

    More relevant solutions to problem. Begin to explain how increased sales could be met e.g. overtime, shift work. (3–4)

    Analyse problem and able to give relevant solutions e.g. productivity, stockpiling. (5–6)

    (iii) Explain that profits will increase. Attempt to explain why. (1–4)

    Begin to relate answer to effect on costs and revenue.
    Explain how these will effect profit, although not automatically assuming that profits will increase. (5–7)

(c) (i) Reiterate production problems. Attempt to link to problems of exporting. (1–3)

    Explain that problems are exporting ones. Identify the problem and expand upon it e.g. language, customs, control, transport, product suitability. (4–5)

    (ii) Attempt to explain how simple problems can be overcome e.g. language, transport. (1–3)

    Provide solutions to problems given, although solutions may not be in depth for some problems. (4–6)

    Ability to analyse problems in depth and produce relevant solution to the problems. (7–9)

Question 2

Ahmed Akhtar buys T-shirts in different colours and sizes. He then prints designs on the T-shirts, (e.g. pop groups, school names, etc.) and re-sells them.

The graph below was prepared by Ahmed.

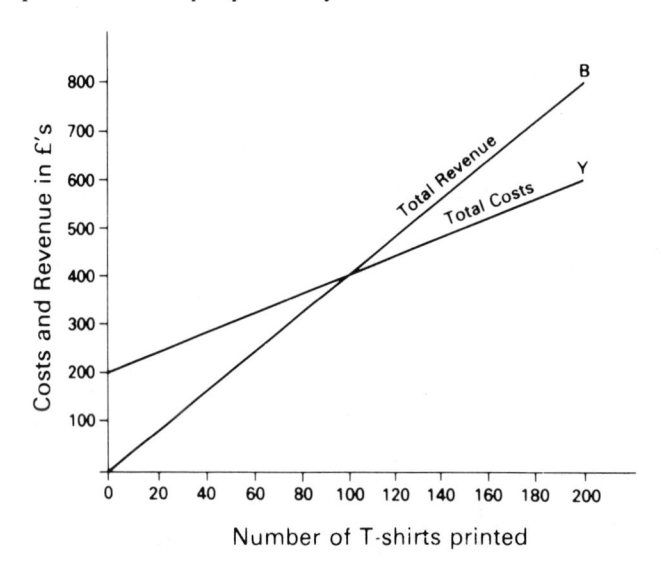

(a) Use the graph to find the following:
 (i) the total revenue of 120 T-shirts (1)
 (ii) the number of T-shirts printed if total costs are £300 (1)
 (iii) the value of fixed costs (1)
 (iv) the value of the variable costs when 80 T-shirts are sold (1)
 (v) the profit made when 160 T-shirts are sold (2)
(b) Why might such a graph be useful to Ahmed Akhtar? (6)
(c) Ahmed finds that he can only sell 70 T-shirts each week.
 (i) What problems would this create for the business? (6)
 (ii) Explain how these problems could be overcome. (8)
(d) Ahmed wishes to expand his business and decides to try and sell sweat shirts with a wider variety of designs. Ahmed employs a friend to carry out market research.
 (i) What is the purpose of market research for Ahmed's business? (4)
 (ii) Design a questionnaire which would be suitable to use for market research for Ahmed's business. (10)

(SEG Specimen)

Answers

(a) (i) £480 (1)
 (ii) 50 (1)
 (iii) £200 (1)
 (iv) £160 (1)
 (v) £120 (2)
(b) Show costs and revenue. (1–2)

 Show costs and revenue, and explain significance of break-even point. (3–4)

 Explain significance of break-even point. Project costs and revenue. (5–6)

(c) (i) Make a loss (little or no further expansion). (1–2)

 Identify loss amount. Explain inability to meet costs – indicate shortfall. (3–4)

 See the problem in short and long term. Explain fixed costs covered. (5–6)

(ii) Provide one solution to the problem. Attempt to explain e.g. advertising. (1–2)

Mention additional alternatives e.g. alter prices, reduce prices but with little cause and effect. (3–4)

Analyse solution to problem e.g. effect of reduced costs, increasing or decreasing prices. (5–6)

(d) (i) Method of asking public questions. (1–2)

Significance of research – suitability, marketability. (3–4)

(ii) Supply a few relevant questions – in no particular sequence. (1–4)

More questions, related to business and with a logical sequence. Begin to introduce different styles of questions. (5–7)

Supply questions relevant to product.
Show sequence to questions.
Use different types of questions effectively, bringing out all aspects of the product. (8–10)

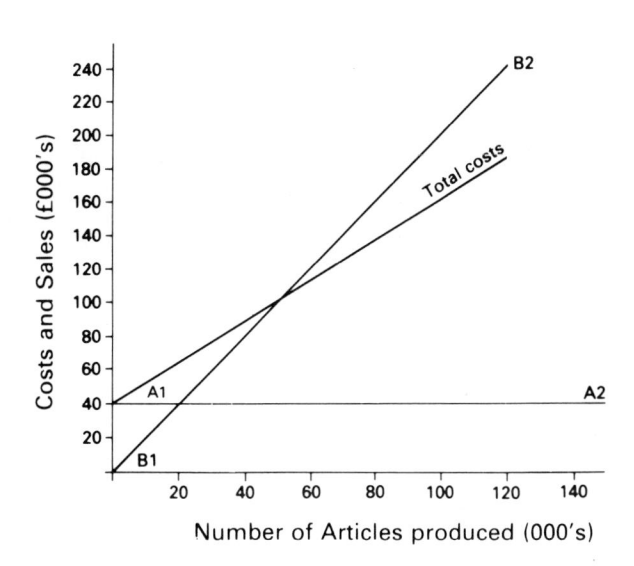

Question 3

The graph below was prepared for the marketing manager of Mammoth Enterprises Ltd. It is used as part of a test given to applicants for a job vacancy in the marketing department. Complete the test as best you can.

(a) What do the following lines on the graph represent?
  (i) A1 to A2 (1)
  (ii) B1 to B2 (1)
(b) What is the level of output at the break-even point? (1)
(c) What is the income from sales at the break-even point? (1)
(d) Use the graph to find
  (i) the profit and loss if 100,000 articles are sold (1)
  (ii) the total revenue if 80,000 articles are sold (1)
  (iii) the output if total costs are £88,000. (1)
(e) What is the selling price of an article produced by Mammoth Enterprises? (1)
(f) Explain why total costs increase as production increases. (2)

(LEAG Specimen)

Answers

(a)	(i)	Fixed costs	(1)
	(ii)	Sales	(1)
(b)		50,000	(1)
(c)		£100,000	(1)
(d)	(i)	£4,000 profit	(1)
	(ii)	£160,000	(1)
	(iii)	40,000	(1)

(e) £2 i.e., $\dfrac{\text{Total Revenue}}{\text{Total Production}}$ (1)

(f) Total costs include variable costs (as well as fixed costs) and these change as production changes. (2)

Question 4

Study the balance sheet of XYZ Ltd and answer the questions printed below.

Balance Sheet as at 31 December 1985

Authorised Capital	£		£
30,000 £1 Ordinary Shares	30,000	Premises	22,000
		Machinery	12,000
Issued Capital		Stock	8,000
25,000 £1 Ordinary Shares	25,000	Debtors	5,000
10% debentures	4,000	Cash	1,000
Reserves	8,000		
Creditors	4,000		
Overdraft	7,000		
	48,000		48,000

(a) Give **one** example of a fixed asset owned by XYZ. (1)
(b) Give **one** example of a current liability owed by the company. (1)
(c) How much does the company pay each half year to debenture holders? (1)
(d) Calculate the working capital of XYZ (2)
(e) What indications are there that XYZ is a private company? (2)
(f) Why do you think that XYZ Ltd may wish to remain a private company? (3)

(LEAG Specimen)

Answers

(a) Premises, machinery (1)
(b) Creditors, overdraft (1)
(c) £200 (1)
(d) £14,000 – £11,000 = £3,000 (2)
(e) 'Limited' in title/less than £50,000 authorised capital (2)
(f) The particular benefits of this form of organisation, e.g. control of a family business. (3)

8.12 Self-Test Questions

Question 1

Jane Murphy left school with no qualifications but with one special skill – she was great at carving things from wood. It had been her hobby for a long time. She decided to go into business by herself, selling high quality carved ornaments connected with local stories and legends. The local interest helped to make them different from the competition and created interest amongst buyers. She hired a small shop in a side street, and decided to employ an assistant on Saturdays in the shop.

Jane Murphy's Trading Account year ending 31 March 1988

	£	£
Sales		5,000
Cost of Sales	1,000	
Gross profit	4,000	
	5,000	5,000

Jane Murphy's Profit & Loss Account year ending 31 March 1988

	£	£
Gross profit		4,000
Less costs:		
Rent & Rates	2,610	
Wages	450	
Light & Heat	150	
Repairs	100	
Insurance	190	
Net profit	500	
	4,000	4,000

'This is hopeless – my work seems to be selling well but I'm not making enough to live on. I'm seventeen now and I still have to depend on my mum and dad for everything'

(a) How much did Jane have to live on from her business in her first year's trading? How much per week is this? (6)
(b) Which of the costs in the account above are variable costs and which are fixed costs? Explain your answer. (15)
(c) What proportion of Jane's total costs are her overheads? (10)

(NEA)

Question 2

A. Green owns and runs 'The Bright Owl' bookshop. On 1 June the firm's draft balance sheet was as follows.

Assets				(1)
(i) *Assets*				
Premises	25,000			
Equipment	9,000	(ii)		(1)
(iii) *Assets*				(1)
Stock	6,000			
Debtors	800			
Cash	125			
		(iv)		(1)
Current Liabilities				
Creditors	1,600			
Working capital		(v)		(2)
Net Assets			(vi)	(2)
Represented by				
Capital		35,000		
Add				
Net Profit	(vii)			(2)
Less Drawings	3,000			
		(viii)		(2)
		39,325		

(a) Write down the numerals i–viii and by each one write down the missing figure or word from the balance sheet. (12)
(b) The rate of stock turnover is five. Why is this figure important to Green? (4)
(c) The bookshop has a mark-up of 200%.
   (i) What does this statement mean? (2)
   (ii) Explain two reasons why this business should have high mark-up. (6)
(d) The firm wishes to increase its sales revenue without raising its prices. Explain how this could be done. (10)

(SEG)

9 Marketing

SEG	LEAG	NISEAC	WJEC	NEAB	MEG	Topic	Date attempted	Date completed	Self Assessment
✓	✓	✓	✓	✓	✓	9.1			
✓	✓	✓	✓	✓	✓	9.2			
✓	✓	✓	✓	✓	✓	9.3			
✓	✓	✓	✓	✓	✓	9.4			
✓	✓	✓	✓	✓	✓	9.5			
✓	✓	✓	✓	✓	✓	9.6			
✓	✓	✓	✓	✓	✓	9.7			
✓	✓	✓	✓	✓	✓	9.8			
✓	✓	✓	✓	✓	✓	9.9			
✓	✓	✓	✓	✓	✓	9.10			

9.1 What is Marketing?

The Institute of Marketing defines marketing as

> 'the management process responsible for identifying, anticipating and satisfying consumer requirements profitably'.

Successful marketing involves:

1. Recognising the goods and services that customers want at present and in the future.
2. Ensuring that these products are available to the customer in acceptable quantities and prices.
3. Selling at a profit.

9.2 The Marketing Mix

Marketing requires decisions to be made about the 'four Ps':

1. *Product* – the type of good or service produced, e.g. size, quality, design and packaging.
2. *Price* – this includes discounts, credit terms and special offers.
3. *Promotion* – products have to be advertised and brought to customers' attention.
4. *Place* – how and where products are sold, e.g. through shops or direct to customers.

The combination of these four Ps is called the *marketing mix*.

9.3 Product

(a) What is a Product?

Products come in many different forms. A business producing goods or services must consider factors such as:

- Size and shape.
- Colour.
- Quality of materials.
- Services offered, e.g. delivery, after-sales service.
- Image.
- Brand name.
- Credit terms.
- Packaging.
- Price.
- Fashion.
- Type of customer.

Marketing

To launch a new product can take between two and four years and cost millions of pounds. Much depends on whether massive investment in new production technology is required and if development is to be via a trial plant.

So before embarking on a costly exercise we thoroughly research the market.

One of the first steps is to examine existing products to see if there is a need for change. The COMA* report's recommendations for less fat, sugar and salt in the diet led to the company taking a close look at the standard variety of beans, spaghetti, soups, etc.

The result was the development of the Healthy Balance range of products.

We are always researching new products to fill gaps in the market – for example, Crosse & Blackwell Oil-Free French Dressing.

Ideas are put to consumers in their homes and public halls. The questions asked of the testers and tasters are: Are you interested in the product? What do you expect from it? Would you buy it at this price?

If the product meets with approval it must then be decided how to brand it. Should a low calorie product be sold under the Findus Lean Cuisine brand, Carnation Slender range or Crosse & Blackwell Waistline?

Packaging can be in carton, jar, sachet or plastic pot but it must carry a label which informs, meets legal requirements and has impact. Packaging is the first line of advertising! However, while the product must stand out against the competition it must fit within the chosen Nestlé range.

Next, we must get the price right – the product must always be competitive. Advertising on television, in the quality newspapers, the popular press, women's glossy magazines, posters or bus sides depends on which group of consumers the product is aimed for and what fits its image best.

Sales are forecast and factory production programmes geared to meet demand. Results are carefully monitored on a daily basis.

*Committee on Medical Aspects of Food Policy

Figure 9.1 Nestlé marketing strategy

The importance of these factors will vary for different products and customers. Colour, image and fashion are fairly unimportant for matches, but crucial for the sale of clothing. Customers also have different priorities. When buying a car some may be most interested in speed and acceleration, others in comfort and fuel consumption.

A product may not even be a specific good or service, and need not necessarily be marketed by a commercial business. For example, Bradford City Council successfully markets the city as:

- A cultural attraction, e.g. theatres and museums.
- A specialist shopping centre for woollen and Asian goods.
- A tourist resort, e.g. the Brontë Country.
- A convenient location for firms.

(b) Market Segments

Market segments are the different parts of a market for the same product. For example, a hotel may cater for:

- Business travellers.
- Weekend tourists.
- Wedding parties.
- Lunches.
- Evening meals.
- Casual drinkers.
- Conferences.

Each of these activities will require the hotel to provide different facilities and services, such as entertainment or photocopying facilities. Customers will have different needs – lunchtime eaters may expect faster service but accept a smaller choice of meals than evening diners.

A successful business will try to satisfy as many of the 'segments' as possible, or concentrate upon the most profitable. Each segment requires a different marketing mix.

(c) The Product Mix

Almost all businesses sell different types of product. The range of products sold is called the *product mix*. In choosing its mix a business may follow different policies such as:

1. Concentrating upon a single market segment, e.g. sports cars; Far East holidays; health foods.
2. Covering all or most segments of a particular market, e.g. Honda sell cars ranging from small hatchbacks to large luxury models; the Burton Group has clothes shops for different types of customer (see Figure 9.2).
3. Selling many different products, e.g. by becoming a *conglomerate* (see Figure 10.5 for an example).

The Young Market: Dorothy Perkins The Style Market: Principles The Teenage Market: Top Shop/Top Man The Larger Market: Evans

The secret of successful retailing is giving the market what it wants.

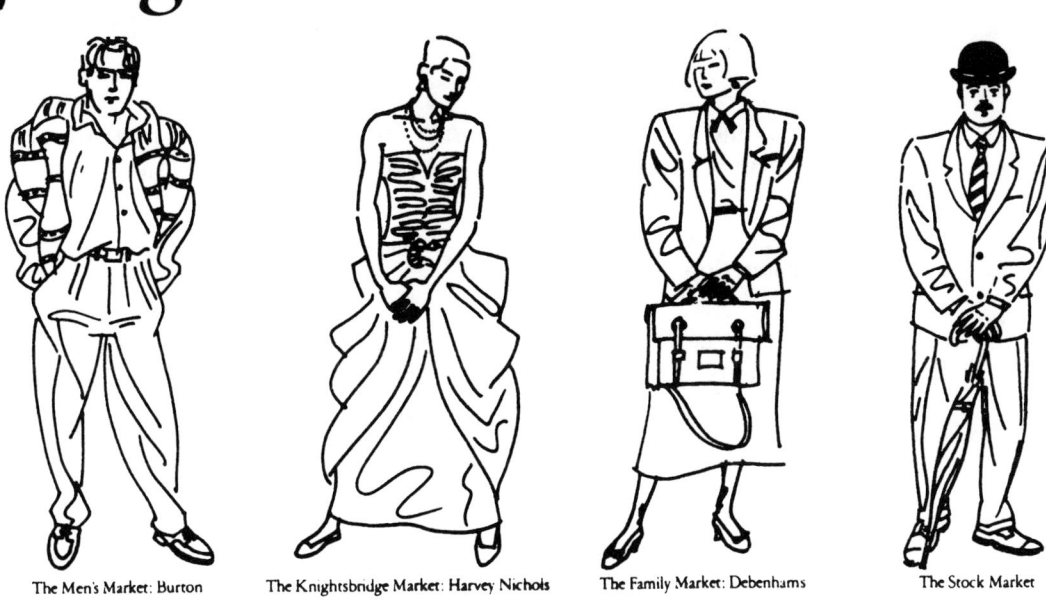

The Men's Market: Burton The Knightsbridge Market: Harvey Nichols The Family Market: Debenhams The Stock Market

Figure 9.2 The Burton Group

If a firm wishes to increase its profits it may change its product mix by:

1. Expanding the mix by selling a wider range of services, e.g. a restaurant may offer take-away meals; a newsagent may rent out videotapes. Larger firms may expand their mix by taking over other firms, e.g. Nestlé bought Rowntree Mackintosh to obtain important brands such as KitKat and Lion Bars.
2. Contracting the mix by cutting out unprofitable or poorly-earning products, e.g. Woolworths has reduced food sales and closed smaller stores; ASDA has sold MFI.
3. Changing products, e.g. car manufacturers change models approximately every ten years.

(d) The Product Life-cycle

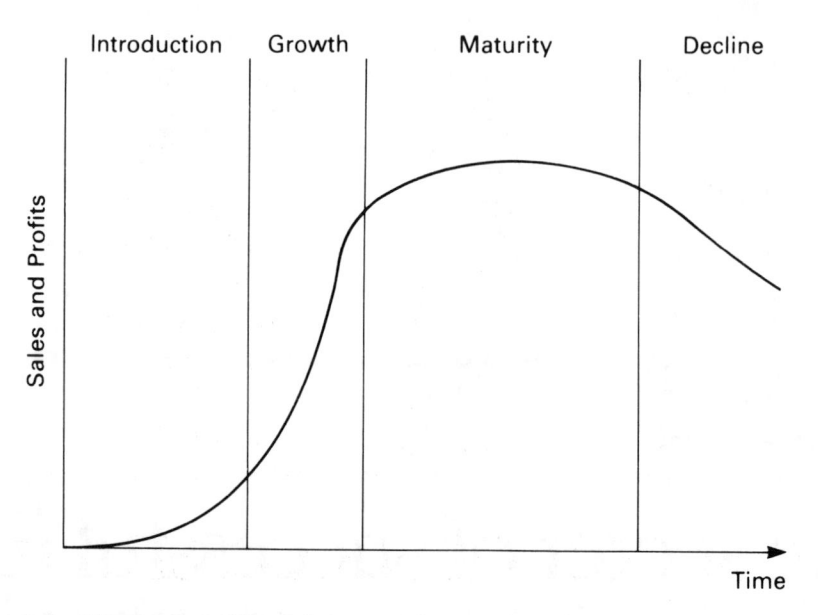

Figure 9.3 The product life-cycle

All goods and services have a *product life-cycle* which describes the way in which sales rise and eventually fall. The life-cycle is divided into four stages.

(i) Introduction

The product is developed and launched on the market. Sales will be low and large amounts will be spent on advertising and promotion. Profits may be low, or the product may make no profit at all. Many products fail at this stage.

(ii) Growth

Sales and profits increase steadily.

(iii) Maturity

This is usually the longest stage. Sales and profits may still be rising, but at a slower rate. Eventually the product will reach its *saturation point*, when sales are at their highest level. A high proportion of sales may represent 'replacement' by existing customers, e.g. colour televisions or fridges in Britain.

The business may try to maintain sales by price-cutting, heavy advertising or launching 'improved versions'. Inefficient producers will be forced out of the market.

This is the stage in which new products or markets should be developed, before the 'decline' stage is reached. For example, some stereo manufacturers have bought record companies because the market for recorded music is growing faster than sales of hi-fi equipment.

(iv) Decline

Eventually sales and profits will start to fall. The business may accept this, or abandon the product altogether. Even if profits are still being made, the product may be taking up capital or management time which could be used more profitably on other products.

The length of the product life-cycle and its different stages varies considerably between products. Citizen's Band radio and skateboards had very rapid growth for a couple of years, followed by almost instant decline. The maturity stage was very short. At the other extreme, basic goods such as salt and coal have had life-cycles lasting hundreds of years.

(d) Branding

Many products have *brand names* such as Heinz or Crosse & Blackwell. Branded products are usually advertised heavily to persuade people to buy them rather than another product of the same type. Sometimes, as in the case of petrol and washing powder, there is little or no difference between the products of different firms, apart from the brand name. By advertising, a business hopes to encourage loyalty to its product.

Figure 9.4 Brands used by Nestlé

9.4 Price

Businesses have different methods for setting prices. Generally they will try to ensure that the price is higher than the cost of producing a product. Policies for pricing include:

1. *Cost-plus*. The cost of producing a product is calculated, and a percentage added on for profit.
2. *Penetration*. The price is set lower than that of competitors. A firm often uses this policy to increase its share of the market. Amstrad personal computers have been successfully sold in this way.
3. *Skimming* or *creaming*. This is very common with new products such as compact disc players. The product is sold at a high price, because some customers are keen to be the first to have it. The price will eventually fall, especially when competitors enter the market.
4. *Price discrimination*. Prices vary between different customers and markets. For example, rail and air travel both sell 'off-peak' tickets at lower prices.
5. *Loss-leading*. A product may be sold at a low profit, or even below cost, in order to attract new customers. This is often done by means of special offers or discounts.
6. *Dumping*. Products may be sold at a loss simply to obtain some revenue from them. Hotel accommodation is often sold very cheaply during the winter months to help pay for the fixed costs of running the hotel all the year round.

9.5 Promotion

Promotion is the process of telling customers about the firm's products. The two main methods of promotion are personal selling and advertising.

(a) Personal Selling

Sales staff or agents may be used to approach customers directly. Personal selling can be expensive because of the cost of wages, so it is most suitable where the orders obtained are large.

Because of this expense, personal selling is most common for industrial products sold to firms, and for more expensive consumer products such as life insurance and home improvements. However, companies such as Avon (Figure 9.5) do successfully sell cheaper goods through agents.

(b) Advertising

For many products advertising is very important, especially for branded goods and services such as Heinz baked beans and Avis car hire. Over £5 billion a year is spent on advertising in Britain, from people selling second-hand goods in local papers to million-pound national advertising campaigns.

AVON
The Beauty Business

THE WORLD'S NO. 1 NAME IN DIRECT SELLING

Knowing what you're good at

Avon sells direct because that's what we know about and that's what we do best.

Avon is one of the acknowledged leaders in the field of direct selling – after all, we've been doing it for more than 100 years. We know the joys and sorrows, advantages and disadvantages of selling direct and we're a leader in the cosmetics world.

Advantages

The advantages of selling direct are numerous:

All of our products are factory fresh. Customers know our products have not been stored in a warehouse for months or displayed on a shop counter.

Customers can choose products in the comfort and convenience of their own home at times to suit them.

Every Representative provides her customers with a friendly and reliable service.

There is no competition for our products at the point of sale unlike a store where there can be several brands on the same counter.

Representatives seek out customers and their earnings opportunity – we don't have to wait for customers to come to us. We have a territory system that provides for every home within that territory to be serviced every campaign.

Since Avon sells in three-week cycles, it gives our customers time to plan their purchases and set money aside for those special occasions.

We have little need of advertising. Representatives talk to customers and place brochures in the homes in their territory. It's a tremendously personal way of advertising and it happens every three weeks.

Direct selling means we can quickly change or introduce new products to meet customers' demands and changes in fashion. We constantly strive to improve our customer service, because at the end of the day, direct selling represents service in a time of diminishing service and that's why a direct selling business such as Avon is good, and will remain good, for those who work at it.

Figure 9.5 Avon – an example of direct selling

(i) Informative advertising

Informative advertising is concerned with giving information, e.g. about timetables, changes in prices and new Government legislation.

(ii) Persuasive advertising

Persuasive advertising aims to get people to buy a product in order to increase sales. Advertising of goods such as petrol is often included in this category because the competing products are virtually identical. Persuasive advertising is often used to establish and maintain *brand names*.

In practice the distinction between informative and persuasive advertising is rather artificial, as most advertisements are a combination of both methods.

(c) Advertising Media

CAMPAIGN TO BOOST ALL CO-OP PRODUCTS

A 30-second television commercial will spearhead the new Co-op Brand Fusspots campaign, with the first showing scheduled for the middle of April.

Press advertising and posters will launch around the end of April.

Copy and artwork have been prepared for the first press advertisements, with each one promoting a specific range of Co-op Brand products.

The advertisements, which are all in full-colour, will appear in magazines including *TV Times*, Sunday supplements and many women's magazines, including *Woman* and *Woman's Own*.

The aim of the campaign is to convey the message to customers that Co-op Brand products really are excellent quality and offer good value for money. Ultimately, its purpose is to increase sales of Co-op Brand products through Co-op foodstores.

Additionally, it must:
- make sure everyone knows how good Co-op Brand really is;
- reinforce the value-for-money attractions of Co-op Brand;
- increase awareness of the breadth of the Co-op Brand range;
- create an association between the Co-op Brand range and healthy eating;
- link the positive and modern image of Co-op Superstores to Co-op Brand.

Five products will feature in the first TV commercial — orange juice, cheese, tea bags, cereals and soups — while eight products will feature in the first series of press advertisments. These are: tea, fruit squash, muesli, biscuits, wholemeal plain flour, soups, cheeses and frozen gateaux.

An artist's impression of the kind of advertisement which will appear in magazines.

Figure 9.6 An advertising campaign

(i) Television

Commercial television is the most effective medium for reaching large numbers of people, and has been proven by research to be the most noticed and remembered. It is also the most expensive, with peak-time adverts costing £30,000 or more per minute.

Television advertising can be very effective, but has several drawbacks. Because of the cost, TV adverts have to be very brief, most being for less than 30 seconds. They cannot be very informative, and they display images rather than information. Television advertising is not very selective – it is hard to reach a particular group of people.

(ii) Radio

Local radio advertising is fairly cheap and can be effective in reaching certain types of people such as housewives.

(iii) National press

National press advertising is expensive, but much cheaper than television. It allows detailed information to be given. It is also fairly easy to reach a particular audience as the readership of newspapers is well-researched – for example, *Daily Express* readers are mostly over 30, and *The Times* readers are mostly well-educated.

(iv) Magazine and trade press

These are a cheap and effective way of reaching a specialised group of customers, e.g. doctors or coin collectors. Magazines have a much longer life than TV or newspapers and people often study the advertisements at length.

(v) Local press

The local press is the main market for classified or 'small ads'. It is very cheap, and people who want a new house, a second-hand car or somewhere to go for the night out will buy a local paper mainly for the adverts.

(vi) Posters and hoardings

These are cheap and effective if good locations can be found. They have to be easy to read quickly, and are usually used together with other forms of advertising.

(vii) Sales promotions

These include free gifts, competitions, giveaway samples and special offers. They are very common for products such as petrol, where there is little price competition.

(viii) Direct mail

This is often used by advertisers such as the AA and Readers' Digest. Using databases such as ACORN (see Figure 9.10) it is easy to 'target' particular groups of people.

(ix) Sponsorship

Sponsorship is very common for sporting and cultural events. Sponsorship connects the sponsor's name with a popular cause. If a sponsored event is televised the sponsor can obtain good publicity very cheaply.

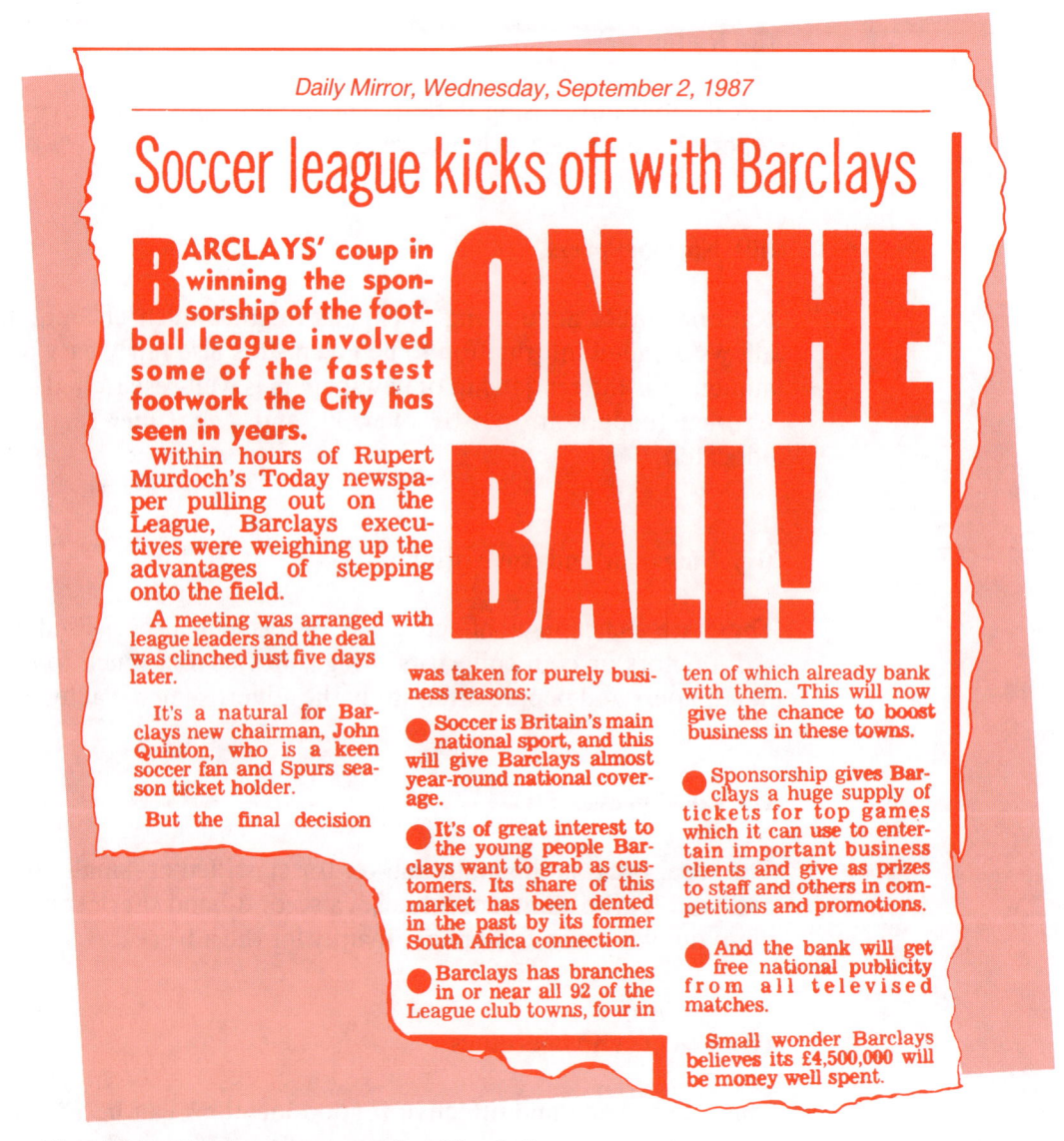

Daily Mirror, Wednesday, September 2, 1987

Soccer league kicks off with Barclays

ON THE BALL!

BARCLAYS' coup in winning the sponsorship of the football league involved some of the fastest footwork the City has seen in years.

Within hours of Rupert Murdoch's Today newspaper pulling out on the League, Barclays executives were weighing up the advantages of stepping onto the field.

A meeting was arranged with league leaders and the deal was clinched just five days later.

It's a natural for Barclays new chairman, John Quinton, who is a keen soccer fan and Spurs season ticket holder.

But the final decision was taken for purely business reasons:

● Soccer is Britain's main national sport, and this will give Barclays almost year-round national coverage.

● It's of great interest to the young people Barclays want to grab as customers. Its share of this market has been dented in the past by its former South Africa connection.

● Barclays has branches in or near all 92 of the League club towns, four in ten of which already bank with them. This will now give the chance to boost business in these towns.

● Sponsorship gives Barclays a huge supply of tickets for top games which it can use to entertain important business clients and give as prizes to staff and others in competitions and promotions.

● And the bank will get free national publicity from all televised matches.

Small wonder Barclays believes its £4,500,000 will be money well spent.

Figure 9.7 Barclays' sponsorship of football

(x) Advertising agencies

These are professional companies whose purpose is to design advertising campaigns and book advertising slots for products. They will also carry out *market research*. One of the best-known agencies in Britain is Saatchi and Saatchi.

9.6 Place

'Place' refers to the way in which a product is *distributed*. Distribution is the process by which products are sold to the customer. In the case of goods it includes *transport* (see Section 16.3).

Traditionally, goods are sold through a *channel of distribution* such as that shown in Figure 9.8.

```
Producer
   ↓
Wholesaler
   ↓
Retailer
   ↓
Consumer
```

Figure 9.8 The traditional channel of distribution

Nowadays, however, many products are sold by different channels. The wholesaling and/or retailing stages may be missed out, as shown in Figure 9.9.

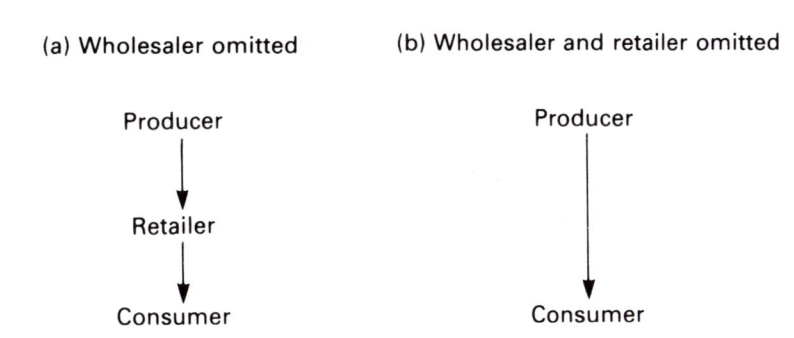

```
(a) Wholesaler omitted          (b) Wholesaler and retailer omitted

     Producer                            Producer
        ↓                                   ↓
     Retailer                            Consumer
        ↓
     Consumer
```

Figure 9.9 Alternative channels of distribution

The wholesaler may be omitted in circumstances such as large supermarket chains buying in bulk, or retailers buying specialist goods and services such as machinery or insurance.

Many services such as banking are sold direct to the customer. In these cases the producer usually has its own retail outlets – a good example is 'tied' pubs owned by breweries, which buy only one brewery's products. A business may also sell by direct mail, with people ordering by post from advertisements or catalogues.

Many producers use more than one channel of distribution. For example, building societies operate through their own branches, but also have 'agencies' at the offices of solicitors and estate agents. Food manufacturers may produce 'own-brand' goods for supermarket chains, and also sell through wholesalers.

9.7 Market Research

(a) What is Market Research?

Market research is the process of obtaining information about the market for new and existing products. A business may look for information about matters such as:

- Potential sales of a new product.
- Consumers' attitudes to a product, e.g. do they like the colour/taste/packaging/name?
- Future trends in a market.
- Potential new markets e.g. in different areas or countries.
- Possible effects of changes in products or prices.
- Effectiveness of advertising.

Market research includes many different activities. At its simplest it might involve checking the suitability of a site for a shop by counting the number of people going past it at different times of the day. A sophisticated campaign may involve spending thousands of pounds on questionnaires, consumer interviews and test marketing.

(b) Desk Research

Desk research involves using published information or secondary data. There are many potential sources of secondary data:

1. *Firms' own data*, e.g. records of how much certain types of customer spend and which areas have the best sales for particular products.
2. *Official statistics*. The Government publishes statistics and reports on many topics such as population changes, foreign trade and consumer spending. An example is given in Figure 15.3.
3. *Trade associations* and *trade magazines* supply information for almost all types of business.
4. *Commercial directories* of different types of company and buyers of particular products.
5. *Market reports* on different products are published by firms such as Mintel.
6. *Commercial databases* such as ACORN contain valuable information for finding customers.

(c) Field Research

If the information the business wants is not already available, it will be necessary to use field research to find it. Methods of field research include the following.

(i) Surveys

These involve questioning large numbers of people by personal interview. A *sample* of people will be chosen, as it is impossible to interview every potential customer.

Characteristics of ACORN Types

	13	36	UK average		KEY
	43.0%	89.7%	55.7%		% households owner-occupied (1981 census).
	24.6%	84.1%	48.8%		% economically active population employed in white collar jobs (1981 census).
	21.8%	16.4%	19.3%		% population under 15 (CACI updates, 1985).
	14.6%	13.9%	15.0%		% population over 64 (CACI updates, 1985).
	20.1%	4.4%	11.3%		% workforce unemployed (Dept of Employment/CACI July 1987).
	38.1%	6.6%	20.7%		% adult population watching 20+ hours IBA Channels weekly (National Readership Survey, 1986).
	6.2%	44.2%	18.5%		% households with 2+ cars (BMRB Target Group Index, Apr 86-Mar 87).
	4.0%	38.0%	14.0%		% adults owning any stocks & shares (NOP Financial Research Survey, Oct 86-Mar 87).
	13.0%	61.0%	34.0%		% adults owning any bank credit card (NOP Financial Research Survey, Oct-Mar 87).

The ACORN system divides addresses into 38 different types. 2 of these are illustrated here.

TYPE 13
Older Terraces, Lower Income Families

Type 13 includes those areas where local authorities have been active in purchasing and improving poor quality pre-1914 terraced housing.

This type is often seriously disadvantaged by low levels of industrial skill and high unemployment amongst its population. It is particularly common in cities such as Liverpool, Hull, Teesside and Sunderland where docks, steelworks and chemical plants have often provided well paid but physically strenuous work for an unskilled labour force.

In contrast to type 12, married women are less likely to work and families are much larger so that the proportion of children in the community is therefore much greater.

TYPE 36
Detached Houses, Exclusive Suburbs

Of all 38 types, this is the one with the highest status, whether measured by car ownership or by the proportion of professional or managerial workers.

These therefore are areas of large detached houses, in mature grounds, in locations of choice landscape value, such as Esher and Solihull.

Most of these areas were developed in the 1930's so that this type attracts mostly the older professional with school age or grown-up children. Younger families are seldom able to afford the house prices, and those who can do are more likely to prefer more modern executive estates.

Low unemployment and very affluent lifestyles predominate.

Figure 9.10 The ACORN system

The sample may be *random*, with no attempt to choose the type of person interviewed. This is likely to be used for a product such as biscuits which is bought or used by many different types of people.

Random sampling is not suitable for products aimed at particular groups, e.g. a 40-year-old man's opinion about a teenage girls' magazine or brand of perfume is unlikely to be useful for market research.

Because of this disadvantage, *quota* sampling is more common. This involves choosing people of a particular type, such as professional men over 40 or mothers of small children, who are likely to use the product.

(ii) In-depth interviews and group discussions

These allow more detailed questions to be asked. They are often used to discover people's attitudes to new products or advertisements before they are tried out on the public.

(iii) Observation

This involves watching people in different situations. It is sometimes used in shops to see how people react to displays of products, One ice-cream manufacturer discovered that its products were selling badly because children could not see over the top of the freezer. The problem was solved by altering the design.

(iv) Test marketing

A product may be tried out on a small scale before launching it to all customers. For example, the Wispa chocolate bar was sold in north-east England as an experiment.

9.8 Coursework Assignment

Where should a retail outlet be sited?

This assignment involves choosing a site which may be suitable for a retail outlet such as a small shop, superstore, market stall, tool hire business or estate agent. Choose a business in which you are interested. It will be helpful if you know somebody with some expertise in the particular business.

Having chosen your example, think about the essential requirements for a site. Consider issues such as:

- The good or service to be sold.
- The space needed for display, storage, parking etc.
- Whether the site should be in a particular type of area, e.g. in the town centre or on a main road.
- Will customers be prepared to travel to the outlet, e.g. specialist hobby shop, or is local and passing trade important, e.g. newsagents?
- The type of customer, e.g. people with children; OAPs; teenagers.
- How much competition is there in the area?

Draw up a list of the requirements for the ideal site. Choose three or four local sites which look suitable and investigate them in more detail. Information can be obtained from sources such as estate agents, newspaper advertisements, Council Planning Departments, census statistics, local retailers and personal observation (see Figure 17.5 for an example).

When writing your assignment use maps and tables to show the important features of the alternative sites such as costs (rent/rates/capital), people and traffic flows and the position of competitors. Describe the advantages and disadvantages of each potential site, using the criteria that you have set for the ideal site.

9.9 Worked Examples

Question 1

Read the information given in the boxes and answer the questions which follow.

> Franco's is a small firm making ice cream in a variety of flavours. The ice cream is sold from vans in nearby seaside resorts. Their sales vary a lot throughout the year. This means that they have a number of production and financial problems which they would like to reduce. The most they have sold in any one month is 20,000 litres.

(a) (i) Draw a graph to show how their sales might vary from January to December. (16)
    (ii) Explain your reasons for drawing the graph in the way that you have. (12)
(b) Explain what 'production and financial problems' the firm might suffer from because 'their sales vary a lot throughout the year'. (18)

> At the moment Franco's only sells ice cream. The sales have not been increasing as much as they would like. They want to expand the business but are not sure of the best way to do it. These are the choices they are considering:
> 1. Sell ice cream in containers to shops and supermarkets.
> 2. Make and sell iced lollies as well as ice cream.
> 3. Buy in and sell soft drinks as well as ice cream.

(c) Consider these three options and advise the firm on the choice they should make. Give reasons why this choice of action would be best. (16)
(d) How useful do you think market research would be in helping this firm? (20)
(e) What factors must the firm take into account before launching an advertising campaign to sell their new line? (16)

(NEA Specimen)

Answers

(a) (i) Line showing some relationship but with unspecified axes. (0–2)

Graph showing line relationship between two variables. (3–6)

Graph showing seasonal rise in summer months, but crude, e.g. no scales or labels, unrealistic winter sales levels. (7–8)

Attempt to model the data given realistically, e.g. showing peak of 20,000 litres in high summer. (9–12)

Show an approximation to accurate modelling of data, e.g. positive low sales October to March, rise through April and May, relationship with holidays, peaking in July/August, with slowdown to winter low. (13–16)

(ii) Statement about changing sales patterns. (0–2)

Show awareness of some cyclical pattern. (3–6)

Explain the reasons lying behind a cyclical pattern e.g. visitors, weather, vans dependent on weather. (7–10)

Explain all aspects of the graph as well as the summer high, e.g. positive sales levels in winter, Christmas increase, rates of change. (11–12)

(b) Make an unexplained statement about either a financial or production problem e.g. changing levels difficult to deal with. (0–4)

Make a specific statement about a production or financial problem e.g. not much money being earned at one time of year. (5–6)

Specific statement about a problem in each of the two areas e.g. storage, cost of storage, staff layoffs, underutilised capital, cash flow. (7–10)

Attempt to explain the problems. (11–14)

Attempt to identify the likely central problems from a range e.g. the central production problem is storage and the central financial problem is cash flow in the slack period. (15–18)

(c) Simple choice, no reason. (0–2)

Choice with reason but no development e.g. 'I would recommend . . . because . . .' (3–6)

Choice with valid reasons explained with no reference to the other two possibilities. (7–8)

Show awareness of reasons requiring balancing shown by reference to other possibilities but essentially one-sided argument. (9–12)

Make a balanced argument considering the relative merits of each possibility. (13–16)

(d) Make a single statement of what it may do e.g. predict sales. (0–4)

Show more than one of the things market research may achieve without explaining how e.g. predicting sales, consumer attitudes and spending power, location and type of target. (5–6)

Show some of the possibilities above, explaining how market research may do these e.g. predicting sales either by analysing past trends and/or directly questioning consumers. (7–10)

Show a clear grasp of what market research is and its potential contribution e.g. giving a business the knowledge to accurately target the most likely group, how best to do this and to predict the likely results. (11–14)

Show an awareness of its limitations of market research. (15–20)

(e) Single factor suggestion with no explanation e.g. choice of an advertising medium. (0–2)

More than one suggestion with no explanation e.g. choice of an advertising medium and the extent of the campaign. (3–4)

Recognise that two choices are needed, a choice of medium, and a decision on the amount and type of advertising within the chosen medium. (5–8)

More than one suggestion with an attempt to explain or suggest possible courses of action e.g. advertising in the trade press would be appropriate, and the decision on the type and extent of the campaign would depend on research or previous experience. (9–12)

Show an awareness that any advertising must be judged by the balance between cost and effectiveness. (13–16)

Question 2

Jane Wright and Alak Patel have decided to rent a small shop in a local shopping centre to sell fashion jewellery. They have a budget of £500 to spend on advertising.

(a) Suggest **four** ways they could use this money to advertise their new shop. Give reasons for your suggestions. (4)
(b) Give **two** motives to which that advertising could appeal. (3)
(c) Explain **two** ways, other than advertising, which Jane and Alak could use to promote sales. (4)
(d) State, with reasons, which one of the forms of sales promotion you have described in (c) is likely to be the most effective for the business of Jane and Alak. (4)

(LEAG Specimen)

Answers

(a) Local press, radio, window advertising, posters, leaflets, etc. plus reasons. (4)
(b) Romance; keeping up with the Jones etc. (3)
(c) Seasonal sales, price reductions on selected lines, free gifts, competitions. (4)
(d) Explain, giving reasons for choice e.g. price reduction may attract people into shop. (4)

9.10 Self-Test Questions

Question 1

The Sales Manager of Aroma Perfumes has produced the following diagram showing the life cycle of their (products)

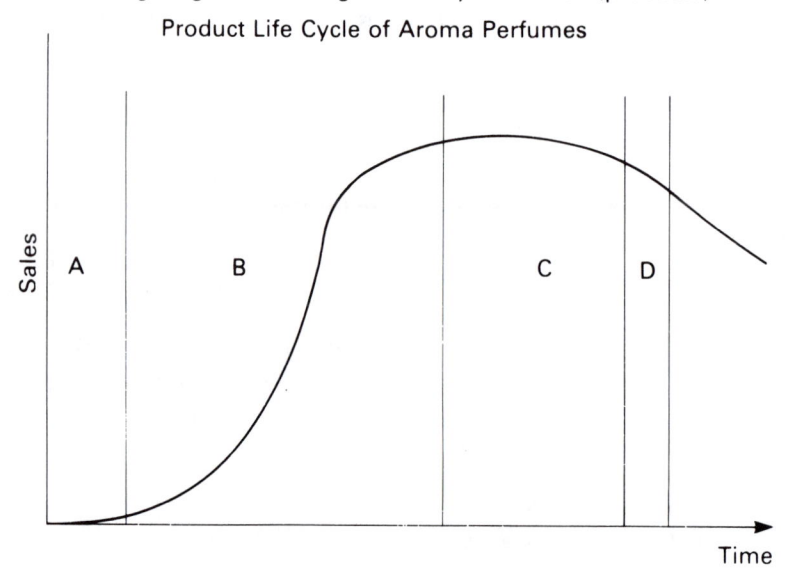

Product Life Cycle of Aroma Perfumes

Explain what has happened to the sales of Aroma Perfumes throughout their life cycle. (10)

At a recent meeting in Aroma Perfumes, the Sales Manager explained part of their sales policy in recent years.

'With our line of perfumes we had got to the stage where we had a saturated market. We could only increase sales by changing fragrances and advertising heavily every so often. Men had very strong sales resistance because wearing perfume was seen as a totally feminine habit. So we launched a perfume for men by linking it with shaving and calling it aftershave lotion.'

(i) What did the Sales Manager mean by a 'saturated market'? What does this mean for a firm? (15)
(ii) What did the Sales Manager mean by 'sales resistance'? (6)
(iii) How did the firm go about dealing with the sales resistance in the market? (12)

(NEA)

Question 2

F. Brown is the sole owner of a small market garden business. It is on the edge of a medium sized town. The firm has a small shop on the site, selling its produce. Brown has decided to expanded the shop and buy in flowers, vegetables and garden equipment from wholesalers. Brown is a good gardener but has few business skills.

(a) What extra costs might be involved in expanding the business? (8)

(b) Brown needs advice on how to finance this expansion. Where could he get this advice? (4)

(c) Brown considers two alternatives:
  (i) Borrowing the money from a bank
  (ii) Taking on a partner
What are the advantages and disadvantages of each? (12)

(d) To increase his sales Brown decides he will need to advertise.
  (i) How could he find out the type of consumer he should be trying to reach? (8)
  (ii) What methods of advertising is Brown likely to use? Give reasons to support your ideas. (8)

> **BROWN'S GARDEN SHOP**
> Now Open
> The Cheapest Garden Produce in Town
> Our Carrots improve your Eyesight
> **ALL HOME GROWN PRODUCE**
> On the A599 2m south of the Town Centre
> "You know what you are getting at Brown's"

(e) He produces the above advertisement. In what ways would you change it to make sure that it did not break the Advertising Standards Authority's Code of Practice? (6)

(SEG)

10 Production

SEG	LEAG	NISEAC	WJEC	NEAB	MEG	Topic	Date attempted	Date completed	Self Assessment
✓	✓	✓	✓	✓	✓	10.1			
✓	✓	✓	✓	✓	✓	10.2			
✓	✓	✓	✓	✓	✓	10.3			
✓	✓	✓	✓	✓	✓	10.4			
✓	✓	✓	✓	✓	✓	10.5			
✓	✓	✓	✓	✓	✓	10.6			
✓	✓	✓	✓	✓	✓	10.7			
✓	✓	✓	✓	✓	✓	10.8			
✓	✓	✓	✓	✓	✓	10.9			
✓	✓	✓	✓	✓	✓	10.10			

10.1 What is Production?

Production means creating goods and services which satisfy people's needs. It is sometimes used in the narrow sense of *manufacturing production* (making goods in factories). However, a bus-driver or a stand-up comedian are also involved in production.

Production involves converting *inputs* of materials, labour, capital and management into a good or service which can be marketed to the customer.

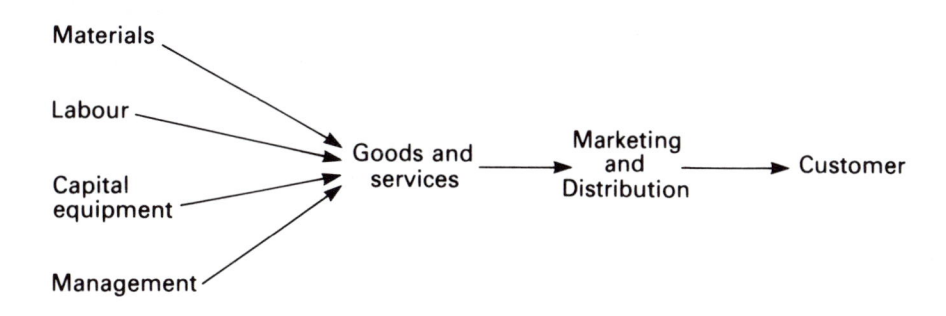

Figure 10.1 Processes in production

10.2 Methods of Production

(a) Job Production

Job production occurs when a single product is designed and made, e.g. a cruise liner or the Channel Tunnel. The product is designed and made to exact requirements for a special purpose. The main disadvantage of job production is that it is usually expensive because of the need for specialised attention. Large projects may be difficult to cost in advance.

(b) Batch Production

Batch production involves a number of identical items being produced. Equipment and labour is then switched to another product. A good example is the work of a bakery, which will make different loaves and cakes using the same equipment.

(c) Flow Production

Flow production is used to make thousands or millions of identical products. It is used to manufacture goods such as cars and baked beans. An *assembly line* may be used, with a product being transported along a conveyor belt or track. For example, a car will have various parts added to it as it is passed along the line (see Figure 10.2).

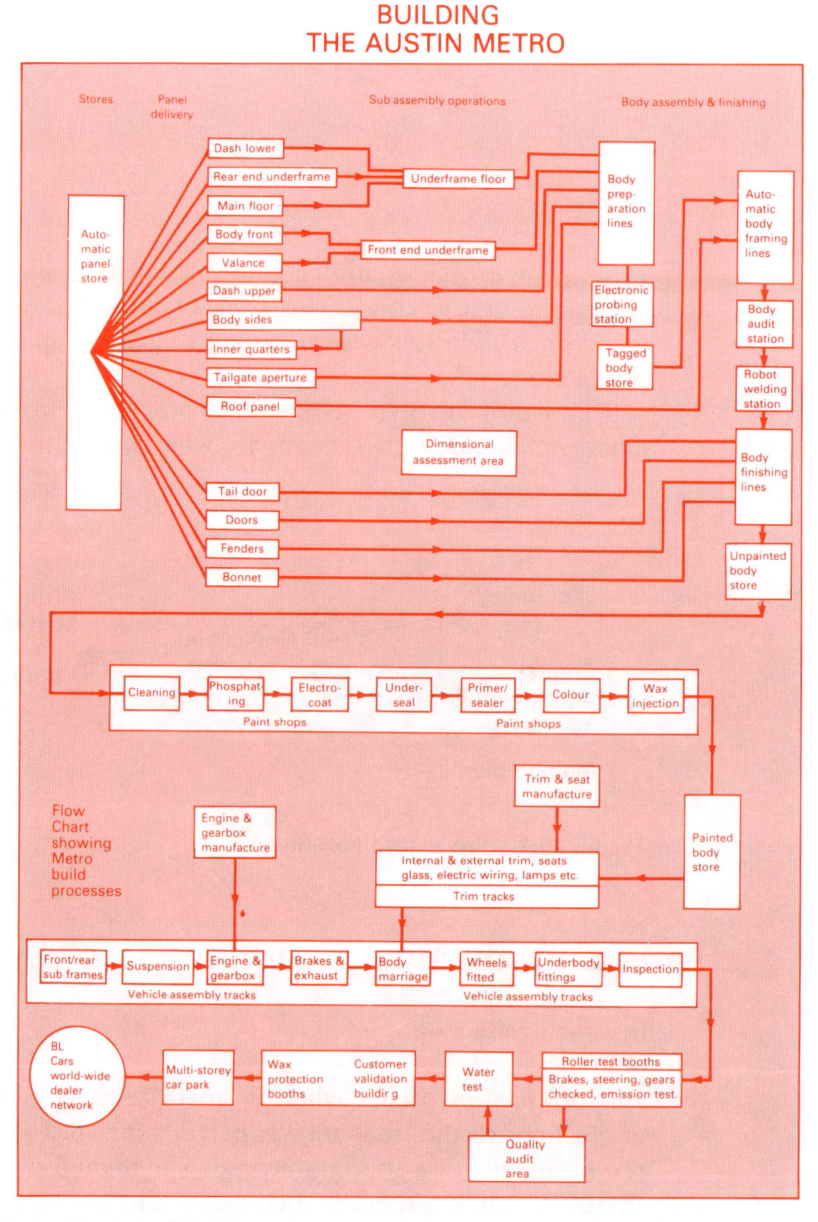

Figure 10.2 Car assembly line

Flow production is very cheap and can often use unskilled labour. However, it requires very high sales and suffers from the disadvantages of *division of labour*.

10.3 Division of Labour

Division of labour means that workers concentrate on doing one particular job. The simplest form of this is for a worker to concentrate upon producing one good or service such as making clothes or repairing cars.

Modern manufacturing frequently relies upon *division of labour by process*, which splits jobs up even further. Each worker carries out one or two very simple tasks, repeating the same operation hundreds of times a day.

A famous example of this was in the Ford car factory in Detroit during the early twentieth century, which was one of the first to use an assembly line. In his autobiography Henry Ford describes how the construction of the Model T was broken down into small stages:

> 'The chassis assembling line, for instance, goes at a pace of six feet; the front axle assembly line goes at one hundred eighty-nine inches per minute. In the chassis assembling are forty-five separate operations or stations. The first men fasten four mud-guard brackets to the chassis frame; the motor arrives on the tenth operation and so on in detail. Some men do only one or two small operations, others do more. The man who places a part does not fasten it – the part may not be fully in place until after several operations later. The man who puts in a bolt does not put on the nut; the man who puts on the nut does not tighten it. On operation number thirty-four the budding motor gets its gasoline; it has previously received lubrication; on operation number forty-four the radiator is filled with water, and on operation number forty-five the car drives out onto John R. Street.'

By breaking production down into such small stages Ford was able to produce the Model T in far greater numbers and much more cheaply than its competitors. Despite changes in technology, almost all large car manufacturers still use a similar system.

(a) Advantages of the Division of Labour

(i) Higher output

People can do what they are best at, and by doing the same job continuously, can get better at it. Jobs can be made very simple, requiring shorter training. Time is saved moving from one job to another.

(ii) Cheaper goods and services

By increasing workers' *productivity*, division of labour reduces the costs of production.

(iii) Higher standard of living

If the economy produces more goods and services at lower cost, its citizens should be better off.

(iv) More choice of work

Division of labour should allow people to choose work that they enjoy and have a talent for.

(b) Disadvantages of the Division of Labour

(i) Boring jobs

Division of labour can involve jobs which are very simple and repetitive. A typical assembly line operation, for example, lasts less than two minutes. This means that the worker is doing the same thing more than thirty times an hour. Boring jobs can cause problems such as poor quality work, absenteeism, stress and illness, strikes and high labour turnover (see Chapter 11).

(ii) Loss of skills

If workers are only trained in one job or part of a process they may have difficulty in adapting to new techniques of production. If their industry is declining they may find it difficult to find work elsewhere.

(iii) Risk of regional unemployment

Many industries are concentrated in particular areas. If a town depends heavily upon an industry which is declining, the result may be high unemployment. The fastest rise in unemployment during the 1980s was in the West Midlands, which depended heavily upon engineering and car manufacture.

10.4 Mass Production

Mass production means producing goods and services in large quantities. The main advantage of mass production is that it can lead to cheaper production because of *economies of large-scale production*, or *economies of scale* for short.

Economies of scale may be *internal* or *external*.

(a) Internal Economies

Internal economies of scale occur as the result of a *firm* growing larger.

(i) Technical economies

Technical economies occur because of the division of labour and better use of capital equipment. The more a machine or building is used, the lower the *average cost* of each good or service.

For example, if the fixed *costs* of running a factory are £1000 a week and the firm produces 500 units, the firm will have to pay costs of £2 per unit to pay for the factory. If output is 1000 per week, each unit will only take £1 in fixed costs.

Larger firms can also make use of specialised equipment such as machines or vehicles designed for a particular purpose, e.g. the Post Office uses machines which can automatically read typed addresses. These can only be afforded if the costs can be spread over a large output.

Research and development of new products are vital in industries such as chemicals, drugs and car manufacture. A product such as a new passenger plane costs several billion pounds to develop before even one can be sold. Only the very largest firms can afford to risk such large sums of money.

(ii) Managerial economies

Managerial economies occur when a large firm can afford specialist staff such as lawyers, accountants and personnel managers. This allows them to apply division of labour to management.

(iii) Commercial economies

Commercial economies can be obtained by large firms when they buy or sell. By buying in bulk they may receive discounts or better terms such as longer credit or goods made to their own standard.

Large firms also have advantages when selling goods and services. It is cheaper to sell and distribute products in large quantities. More can be spent on advertising and marketing products, and many large firms have their own retail outlets, e.g. breweries own pubs; petrol companies own garages. Some firms such as car manufacturers can offer cheap credit to their customers.

Figure 10.3 Co-op superstore – an example of large-scale production

113

(iv) Financial economies

Financial economies are available to large firms, who can usually borrow money at lower interest rates than small businesses. Public limited companies can obtain capital from sources such as international banks and the Stock Exchange.

(v) Risk-bearing economies

Risk-bearing economies occur when a firm is large enough to withstand business risks such as loss of orders or unpaid debts. Small firms often depend heavily upon a few customers or products. As they grow larger they usually aim to spread the risks by *diversifying* into new products or markets. The largest firms are *conglomerates* (producing many different products) and usually *multinational* (producing in countries all over the world). Figure 10.5 gives an example of a firm which is both conglomerate and multinational.

(b) External Economies

External economies occur as the result of an *industry* growing. They are especially likely to be found where an industry is *localised* in a particular area. In this case they are called *economies of concentration*.

The benefits of external economies are available to all firms within an industry, whatever their size. For example, even the smallest engineering firm can benefit from specialist courses at schools and colleges.

(i) Information and technology

Firms may benefit from research and publication of information relevant to their industry such as new materials or manufacturing techniques.

(ii) Education and training

Educational institutions such as colleges and universities run courses for many industries. If an industry is concentrated in a particular area the local college may run specialist courses, e.g. colleges in Leicester have departments which teach textile technology.

(iii) Specialised labour

Because of training and experience, many areas have workers who are skilled in particular industries or processes.

(iv) Ancillary firms

Most large industries have firms which specialise in supplying or servicing them. For example the car industry can buy components from firms such as Dunlop, Lucas and Girling. As well as supplies of parts and materials, ancillary firms may supply specialised services such as banking, marketing and insurance.

(v) Reputation

When an industry has been in an area for many years all firms in the region may benefit from its good reputation. For example, Scotch whisky and Sheffield steel have the advantage of a good name for quality.

(c) Diseconomies of Scale

It is possible for a firm's average costs to rise as it grows bigger because of *diseconomies of scale*. These are the disadvantages of growing large. The reasons are:

1. Large firms may have very high overheads and waste time and effort with excessive paperwork as communications within the business become more complicated.
2. In large firms labour problems such as strikes and absenteeism tend to occur more often.
3. Public limited companies have many different shareholders and are always vulnerable to being taken over by another firm. This does not always lead to efficient production.

(d) Small Firms

Despite the advantages of large firms, many small businesses are very successful. There are a number of reasons for this:

1. Small firms do particularly well in industries where specialised labour and personal service are important, e.g. garages, hairdressing, accountancy.
2. The production of many goods and services can be managed without a large investment of capital in buildings or equipment.
3. Small firms are often suppliers of goods or services to larger firms.
4. Some goods and services are too specialised for large firms, but can be quite profitable for a small business, e.g. hand-made jewellery; classic car restoration.
5. Many people who wish to become their own boss by starting a business are happy to run a small concern without the effort and worry involved in growing larger.
6. A small business depends heavily upon its owners, who may not have the business skills needed to make the firm grow.
7. The Government has special schemes to assist small firms (see Chapter 15).

10.5 Integration

Integration occurs when a business merges with or takes over another business. It can be divided into *horizontal*, *lateral* and *vertical* integration.

(a) Horizontal Integration

Horizontal integration occurs when two firms producing the same product merge, e.g. one car firm taking over another. This will usually occur in order to increase a firm's market share by making it larger.

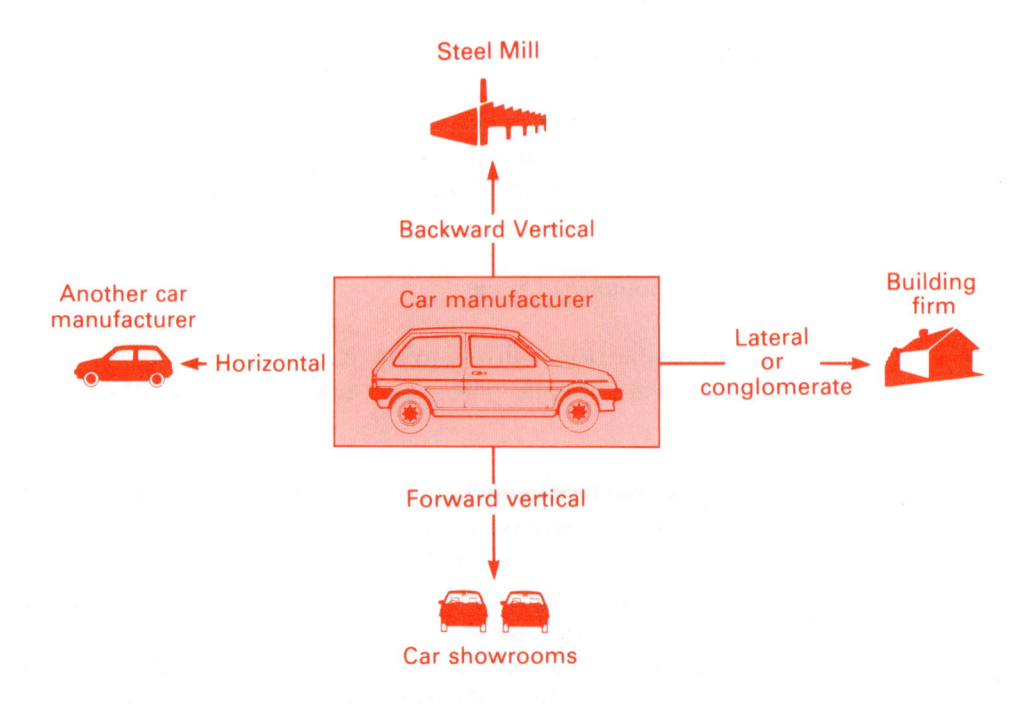

Figure 10.4 Integration by a car manufacturer

(b) Lateral Integration

Lateral or *conglomerate* integration is the merger or take-over of a firm producing a different product, e.g. a car firm taking over a building company. In some cases the two firms will produce similar products, such as a brewery taking over a chain of restaurants. However, a *conglomerate* such as Lonrho (see Figure 10.5) may own many completely different types of firm.

(c) Vertical Integration

Vertical integration means taking over a supplier or customer. It is *backward vertical* integration if a supplier is taken over, e.g. a car firm buying a steel mill. *Forward vertical* integration means buying an outlet for the firm's product, e.g. a car manufacturer buying car showrooms.

10.6 Computers in Business

Over the past 20 years computers have become smaller, cheaper, faster and more powerful. Because of these changes the number of businesses using computer systems has increased rapidly. Some of the main uses of computers are listed below.

(a) Word Processing

A computer can be used as a very sophisticated typewriter, with the advantage that mistakes can be quickly and easily corrected by changing one word rather than an entire document.

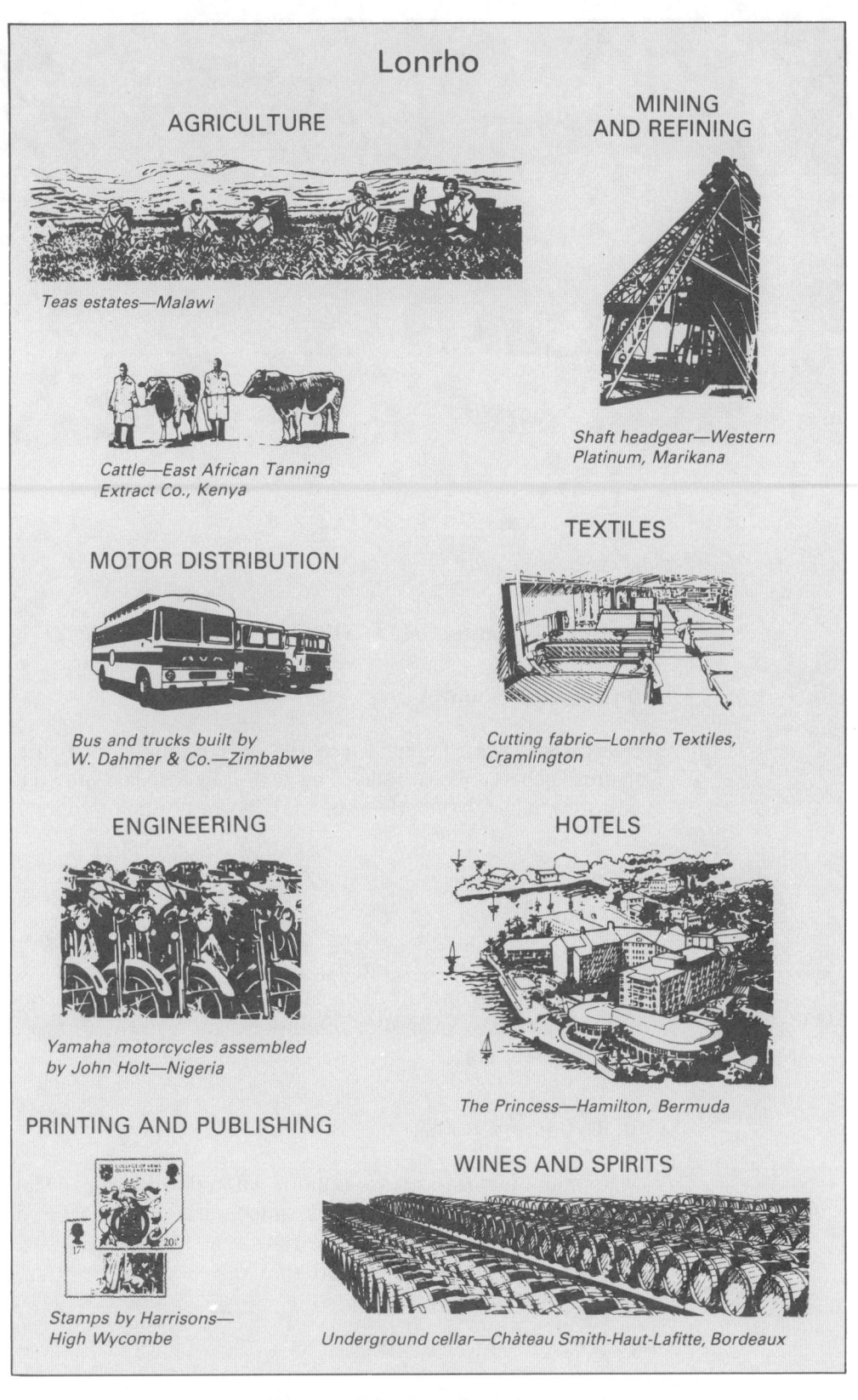

Figure 10.5 Lonrho – a multinational conglomerate

Word processors are particularly useful when the same list or letter is used many times for different people. A document can be altered each time by typing in the name and address, without the bother of retyping the same message every time. Longer documents such as reports or book manuscripts can be altered quickly and easily.

Figure 10.6 Amstrad PCW – a popular word processor

(b) Financial Control

Many firms keep financial records on computers, which can quickly calculate figures such as costs or sales. The cash-flow forecast shown in Figure 8.3 could be adjusted to check the effects of a fall in sales or an increase in costs.

(c) Data Processing

Businesses collect large volumes of data such as information on their customers. These can be kept in a *database*, which is a list of certain information about a customer. The computer can also be instructed to act automatically upon the information. For example, reminders can be sent to customers who have not paid their accounts.

(d) Design and Testing

Many manufacturers use computers when developing new products or testing the quality of their products. For example, cars can be tested for weak points by robots. The quality of a service can be tested by examining records to find out how many customers use it more than once.

(e) Assembly

Many factories use computerised robots to assemble goods, particularly where repetitive and heavy work is involved.

(f) Communications

An increasing proportion of communication in business uses computers. Some of these services are described in Chapter 14.

Figure 10.7 Computer-controlled robot assembly

10.7 Location of Industry

The choice of location for a firm or industry is affected by several factors.

(a) Raw Materials

Industries which rely upon particular materials may locate near to natural resources, e.g. Sheffield became a major iron- and steel-making area because it was near to sources of iron ore, coal and limestone. Modern steelworks are near the coast because most raw materials are imported. With improved transport many industries are now *footloose*, with their location having little effect upon transport costs.

(b) Power

The first major industries in Britain were located near to fast-flowing rivers because they used water-power. When steam-driven machines came into use factories were set up near coalfields. In twentieth-century Britain access to power is rarely a problem.

(c) Nearness to Markets

Until the twentieth century many industries had to be near their main markets. This was particularly important for heavy low-value goods such as beer and

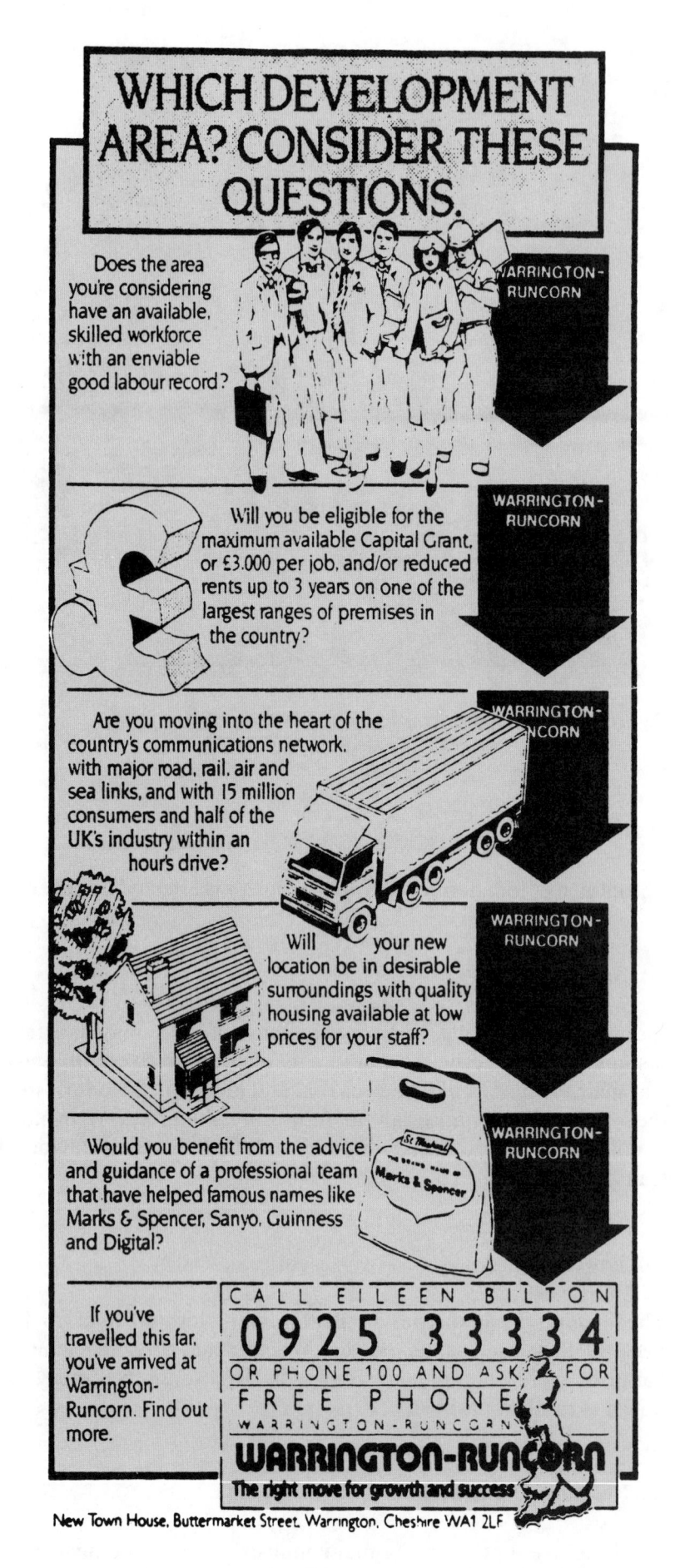

Figure 10.8 An example of Government regional incentives

bricks. This factor is no longer as important for firms producing goods, but service industries such as retailing and banking have to be convenient for their customers.

(d) Transport

Firms may choose an area because it has good transport links for their customers, suppliers and workers. Many towns have grown up around railways, airports and motorway junctions for this reason. The importance of transport is discussed in Chapter 16.

(e) Climate and Landscape

This is important for industries such as agriculture and tourism.

(f) Supply of Labour

Many areas have a ready supply of labour with particular skills, e.g. metal-workers in Sheffield or financial analysts in the City of London.

(g) Government Influence

The Government gives grants, loans and other assistance to firms locating in Assisted Areas (see Chapter 15).

(h) Industrial Inertia

An industry may remain in a particular area after its original advantages have disappeared. For example, the pottery industry remains in North Staffordshire although the deposits of china clay in that area ran out many years ago. Pottery manufacturers have stayed because of tradition and the area's reputation.

(i) Economies of Concentration

When an industry is well-established in an area, firms obtain benefits such as skilled workers, local school and college courses and a reputation for a particular product. These benefits are called *economies of concentration*.

10.8 Coursework Assignments

Assignment 1: What effect will new technology have upon an organisation?

Choose a local organisation which has introduced new machinery and/or computer systems recently (or one which is proposing to do so). It does not have to be a large firm – a small shop or office might be suitable.

Investigate the costs and benefits that new technology has brought or is expected to bring. These might include:

- Higher productivity.
- Lower costs.
- Loss of jobs.
- Changes in work.
- Alteration or moving of premises.
- Better service to customers.

Make a list of possible costs and benefits before you start collecting your data. The best method of collecting information is to interview people involved in the organisation, e.g. managers and supervisors, workers, trade union representatives etc.

List your potential advantages and disadvantages under headings such as 'production costs', 'effect upon workers', 'customer service' etc., explaining the effects of new technology.

Assignment 2: How can a small firm compete?

How does a small firm manage to survive against larger competitors? Choose a small local firm which has competition from national and international companies. Shops or small service companies such as garages, estate agents or printing firms are likely to be suitable examples.

Make a list of all the ways in which firms attract business, for example:

- Low prices.
- Customer service.
- Distinctive products.
- Convenient location.

It may be possible to obtain information by checking the prices of different firms. For example, if you are comparing a small grocery store with a supermarket, you could make a list of about 20 goods and compare their prices.

Explain in detail why your chosen small firm is able to survive against larger competition. Where possible use sources of information other than statements by owners and managers, e.g. price surveys and newspaper articles.

10.9 Worked Example

Look at the diagram of a car assembly line in Figure 10.2.

(a) What are the advantages of making cars using this type of system? (10)
(b) What problems might be caused by using this method of production? (8)

Answer

(a) Simple statement e.g. cheaper, can make a lot. (4)
Explain in more depth e.g. speed, specialist equipment, division of labour, higher productivity, lower costs. (6)
(b) Labour problems e.g. boring jobs, absenteeism, strikes. (4)
Production problems e.g. co-ordination of processes, quality control, need to sell in large numbers. (4)

10.10 Self-Test Question

Study the following carefully, and answer the questions.

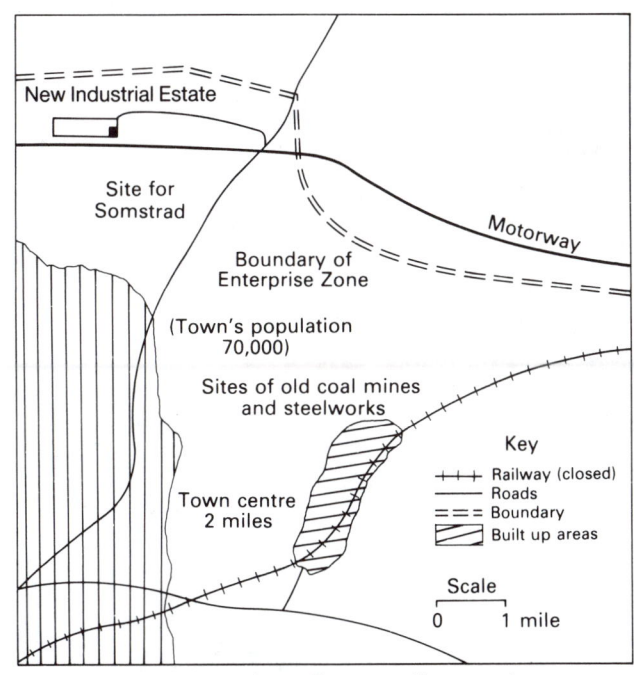

A map to show Somstrad's new site

Somstrad, a multinational, has now agreed to site its European microelectronics plant in Wales. The Japanese head of the firm is delighted with the new site, and very pleased with the financial help received from the Government.

The town's mayor has welcomed the news saying that the 700 new jobs will add a much needed boost to a depressed region which has suffered from the decline of heavy industry. The locals are happy, although a few people are worried about the impact of the plant on what is an area of outstanding beauty.

The new micro chips will be sold through Europe.

(a) In what ways do you think the region will have suffered from the decline of heavy industry in the area? (8)
(b) A pressure group was formed to oppose the building of the new plant. What points might they have raised against the siting of the plant at this particular location? (4)
(c) Explain why **each** of the following will have been important in deciding where to site the new plant:
  (i) being close to a motorway; (4)
  (ii) financial aid from local and central government. (6)
(d) One of the many new jobs at Somstrad will be a secretarial/clerical post in the firm's computerised office.
  Suggest ways in which the firm would advertise, and recruit, for this post. (10)
(e) How will membership of the EC help Somstrad to sell its products throughout Europe? (3)

(WJEC)

11 Managing People

SEG	LEAG	NISEAC	WJEC	NEAB	MEG	Topic	Date attempted	Date completed	Self Assessment
✓	✓	✓	✓	✓	✓	11.1			
✓	✓	✓	✓	✓	✓	11.2			
✓	✓	✓	✓	✓	✓	11.3			
✓	✓	✓	✓	✓	✓	11.4			
✓	✓	✓	✓	✓	✓	11.5			
✓	✓	✓	✓	✓	✓	11.6			

11.1 Motivating Workers

(a) The Need to Motivate Workers

The quality of a business's workforce is vital to its success. If workers are happy and interested in their work they will tend to do it better, and the firm's products will be of higher quality.

In most large firms, motivating employees is the responsibility of the Personnel Department, although all managers must motivate their workers. The Personnel Department's responsibilities will include matters such as:

1. Recruitment and training.
2. Pay and working conditions.
3. Industrial relations.
4. Welfare of workers.

The advantages of successful personnel management are summarised in Figure 11.1.

Benefits of good personnel management

Some of the particular advantages of operating a sound personnel management policy can be highlighted:

- People suited to their jobs.
- People trained to do their jobs most effectively.
- People motivated to contribute to business success.
- People rewarded appropriately for their efforts.
- People satisfied with their employment.
- People staying with the company.

All of these come together to mean that the company is better run, the customers receive a better service and the business itself is more successful.

(*Source:* National Westminster Bank *Small Business Digest*)

Figure 11.1 Benefits of successful personnel management

(b) Labour Problems

The following are usually regarded as signs of dissatisfied employees:

1. High or increasing *labour turnover*, i.e. a high proportion of workers leaving compared to the past or to similar types of work.
2. People leaving after a short time with the firm. This shows that the firm is choosing the wrong type of people or failing to train them properly.
3. Workers leaving for jobs of the same or lower status, rather than for promotion.
4. Employees leaving soon after completing their training or becoming effective at their jobs. This may be a sign that the firm is not providing enough opportunities for promotion.
5. High or rising rates of sickness or absenteeism.

These problems may be concentrated in particular jobs or departments. This may be due to work being boring or a department being badly managed.

(c) Factors which Motivate Workers

There are many theories about how firms can motivate their workers to work well. The following are generally thought relevant, although workers may disagree about which are the most important:

1. Pay and fringe benefits.
2. Promotion prospects.
3. Working environment, e.g. physical surroundings, noise and dirt.
4. Security of employment.
5. Status and prestige at work.
6. Interesting and challenging work.
7. Personal relationships with other workers.
8. Style of management.
9. Hours of work and holidays.
10. Social life, e.g. works outings or office parties.

11.2 Payment Systems

(a) Time-rates

Under *time-rate* payment a worker is paid a fixed amount per hour, week or month. *Overtime rates* may be paid for work outside the normal hours, e.g. at night or weekends. Common overtime rates are *time-and-a-half* for nights and *double-time* for weekends or bank holidays. A worker whose normal rate was £5 per hour would be paid £7.50 for time-and-a-half and £10 for double-time.

The advantages of time-rates are that they are easy to calculate and the worker is guaranteed a certain wage provided the hours are worked.

The main disadvantage of time-rate is that the worker gets paid the same amount no matter how much is done. There is no monetary incentive to work hard.

(b) Piece-rates

Piece-rate or *payment-by-result* systems reward the employee according to the work done. Examples include commission on sales and payments to a bricklayer for the number of bricks laid.

The advantage of piece-rate systems is that they encourage effort by providing higher wages to successful workers.

The disadvantages of piece-rates are that the worker's wage is uncertain, and essential tasks such as paperwork or cleaning of machines may be ignored if there is no extra payment. Work may be rushed, resulting in poor-quality goods and services. Many jobs are difficult to measure, e.g. it would be difficult to assess the work done by a teacher or police officer, because so many different tasks are involved.

Because of these disadvantages, very few workers are paid completely by piece-rates.

(c) Incentive Schemes

Many employers try to obtain the advantages of time- and piece-rates by paying a basic wage, but giving workers the opportunity to earn extra money by working harder. Typically the incentive will account for up to 25 per cent of the total wage.

(i) Bonuses

Bonuses are extra payments for workers who reach a set target for production or sales.

(ii) Profit-related pay schemes

Profit-related pay schemes give workers a share in the company's profits. The Conservative Government has tried to encourage these because of the belief that they make workers more aware of the business's need to make profits.

(iii) Merit payments

Merit payments are given to workers and managers who are believed to have performed exceptionally well. They are sometimes given in the form of *fringe benefits*, e.g. successful sales representatives may be given cars or exotic holidays.

(d) Fringe Benefits

These are given in addition to a salary, and are also called *perks* or *non-monetary benefits*. Common examples include:

- Company cars.
- Discounts on company products.
- Cheap mortgages or personal loans.
- Subsidised canteen and sporting facilities.
- Free or cheap health insurance.

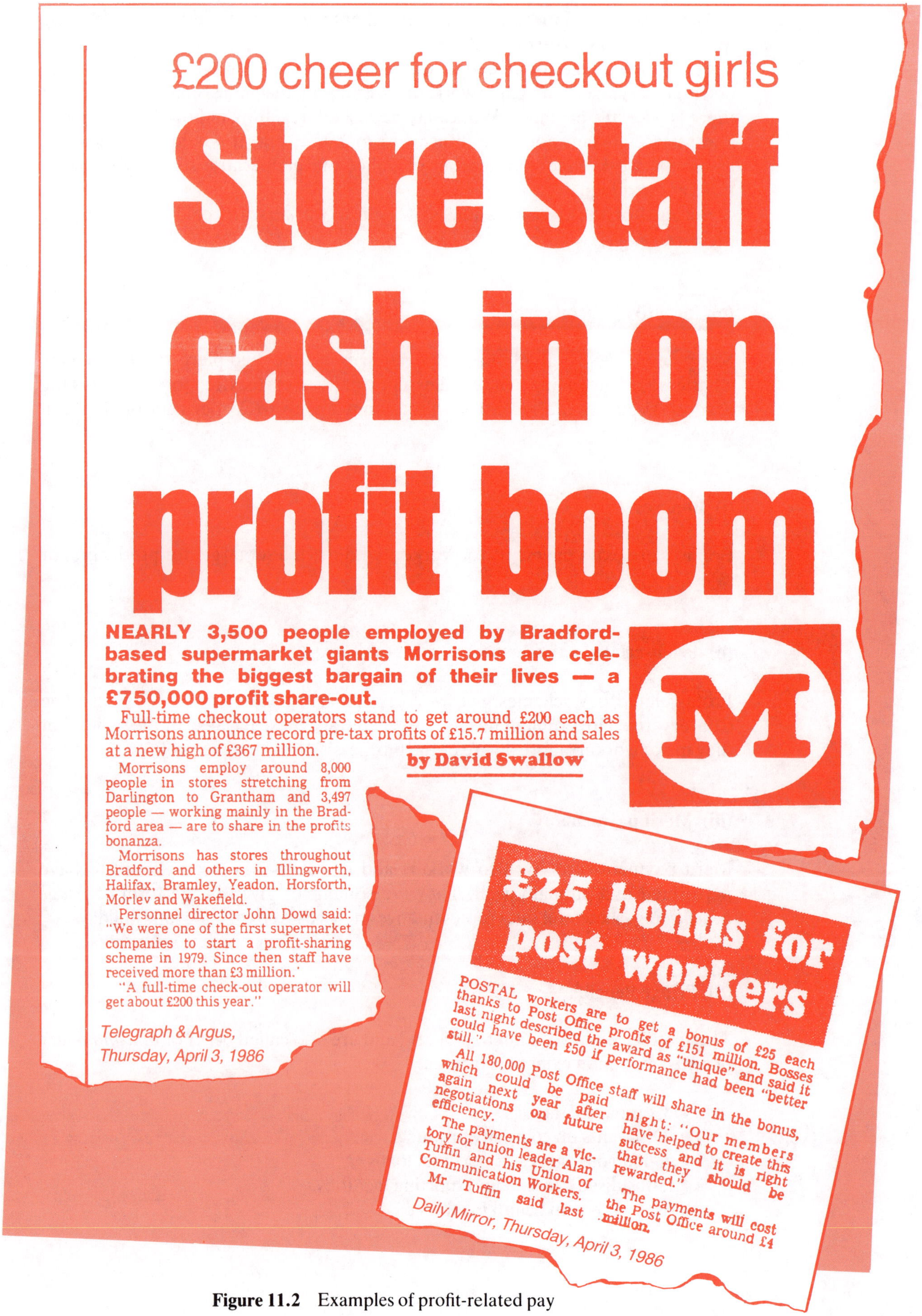

£200 cheer for checkout girls

Store staff cash in on profit boom

NEARLY 3,500 people employed by Bradford-based supermarket giants Morrisons are celebrating the biggest bargain of their lives — a £750,000 profit share-out.

Full-time checkout operators stand to get around £200 each as Morrisons announce record pre-tax profits of £15.7 million and sales at a new high of £367 million.

by David Swallow

Morrisons employ around 8,000 people in stores stretching from Darlington to Grantham and 3,497 people — working mainly in the Bradford area — are to share in the profits bonanza.

Morrisons has stores throughout Bradford and others in Illingworth, Halifax, Bramley, Yeadon, Horsforth, Morley and Wakefield.

Personnel director John Dowd said: "We were one of the first supermarket companies to start a profit-sharing scheme in 1979. Since then staff have received more than £3 million."

"A full-time check-out operator will get about £200 this year."

Telegraph & Argus, Thursday, April 3, 1986

£25 bonus for post workers

POSTAL workers are to get a bonus of £25 each thanks to Post Office profits of £151 million. Bosses last night described the award as "unique" and said it could have been £50 if performance had been "better still."

All 180,000 Post Office staff will share in the bonus, which could be paid again next year after negotiations on future efficiency.

The payments are a victory for union leader Alan Tuffin and his Union of Communication Workers. Mr Tuffin said last night: "Our members have helped to create this success and it is right that they should be rewarded."

The payments will cost the Post Office around £4 million.

Daily Mirror, Thursday, April 3, 1986

Figure 11.2 Examples of profit-related pay

11.3 The Pay-Slip

BALLYGOWEN METALS LTD
Pay Advice
TAX WK/MTH 05   PAY DATE 31/08/88
EMPLOYER NO 70850

EARNINGS	HOURS	AMOUNT
① GROSS PAY		1,111.75

DEDUCTIONS	AMOUNT
② INCOME TAX	175.25
③ NAT INS	81.38
④ UNION SUBSCRIPTION	6.16
⑤ SUPERANNUATION	66.71

TOTAL DEDUCTIONS 329.51 ⑥

⑦ 782.25   NET PAY

PAY CERTIFICATE AND TOTALS			
TAXABLE PAY PREV EMPLOYMENT	TAX PAID PREV EMPLOYMENT	TAX CODE 0409H	BASIC HOURLY RATE ⑧
TAXABLE PAY THIS EMPLOYMENT 5225.20	TAX PAID THIS EMPLOYMENT 876.00		
GROSS PAY TO DATE 5558.75	EMPLOYEES SUPERANNUATION 333.55	EMPLOYERS SUPERANNUATION 525.31	
NI CATEGORY D	NI NUMBER YZ116403B	EMPLOYEES NI CONTRIBUTIONS 406.90	EMPLOYERS NI CONTRIBUTIONS 403.46
NI EESCO 326.80	NI EARNINGS 5558.75	NI EARNINGS RATE? 4668.75	PAY METHOD

KEEP THIS SLIP IT WILL HELP YOU TO CHECK YOUR INCOME TAX

CASH MUST BE EXAMINED IMMEDIATELY OTHERWISE ANY CLAIM OR ERROR CANNOT RE ADMITTED

Figure 11.3 A pay-slip

Figure 11.3 illustrates a typical pay-slip for a worker who is paid a monthly salary. This might be paid in cash, but is more likely to be paid by the firm into the employee's bank or building society account.

Gross pay (1) is the total amount paid before *deductions* (6). The main deductions paid by this worker are:

1. *Income tax*. This is paid upon all earnings above the employee's *personal allowance*, which is the amount he or she can earn before paying income tax. This worker has a personal allowance of £4095 per year, which was the married man's personal allowance for 1988–89.

129

The *tax code* (8) is the personal allowance with the last figure knocked off. The 'H' shows a married man; a single person's or married woman's code usually ends in the letter 'L'.

Most employees pay income tax through the *pay-as-you-earn* system (PAYE). The employer deducts the tax due and pays it to the Inland Revenue on the worker's behalf.

2. *National Insurance* (3) is paid to the Department of Social Security (DSS) towards the cost of benefits such as state pensions, sickness and unemployment benefit. The employer also pays contributions to National Insurance.
3. *Superannuation* (5) payments may be made to a company pension scheme, in addition to the state pension. Unlike income tax and National Insurance, superannuation payments are often voluntary.
4. *Union subscriptions* are often paid through the employer.

Net pay (7) is the amount that the worker actually receives after deductions. It is sometimes called *take-home pay*. In the example given it will be:

	Gross pay	1 111.75
Less	Deductions	329.50
=	Net pay	782.25

11.4 Coursework Assignment

Make a comparison of the training opportunities and workload of two different types of employees, such as an office worker, a manual worker or an apprentice technician.

Suggested approaches to this task are:

1. Select two businesses that you will be using to present the information.
2. From information obtained from each of the chosen businesses identify:
   - the place of the specified worker within the business;
   - the type of work done by him/her;
   - terms of employment;
   - remuneration.
3. State the training and retraining opportunities provided by schemes such as YTS, apprenticeship and day-release.
4. Give the sources of advice available to the young person seeking employment for the first time.
5. Draw up an advertisement for submission to a local newspaper, asking people who are interested to write for an application form.
6. Write a letter requesting the application form.
7. Draft an application form suitable for the position.
8. Prepare a list of points to be taken into consideration before and at an interview for the job in the advertisement.
9. Give your opinion on how good relationships between employer and employee can be established and retained.
10. How could the use of technological developments help the employees in their work?

(SEG Specimen)

11.5 Worked Example

The monthly pay slip of John Brown, an office worker, is shown below. Unfortunately the computer has left out the figure for net pay.

PAY SLIP

Location	Pay No.	Name	Month	N.I. Number
247	9090021	J BROWN	SEP 1982	ZT128578C

Pay to Date (excl. Supn.)	Pay with other Employment	Tax to Date	Tax with other Employment	Supn. to Date	N.I. to Date	Tax Code
3668.09		804.90		234.16	124.86	156L

Gross Pay	Overtime etc.	Sick Benefit Adjustment	Supn. Addit Pay	Gross Pay After Adjustment	Superann.	Income Tax	Nat. Ins.
671.00				671.00	40.26	150.00	21.47

Advances	Other Deductions	Round up last month	Non Taxable Allowances	Net Pay	Round up this month
	20.00				

(a) What is John Brown's Pay Number? (1)
(b) What do the initials N.I. on the pay slip stand for? (1)
(c) State how much John Brown paid in September towards his pension scheme. (1)
(d) How much tax had John Brown paid BEFORE receiving his September pay slip? (1)
(e) Calculate John Brown's net pay for September. (2)
(f) State:
  (i) John Brown's tax code number. (1)
  (ii) How this number is arrived at. (2)
  (iii) How John Brown is informed each year of his tax code. (1)

(LEAG Specimen)

Answers

(a) 9090021 (1)
(b) National Insurance (1)
(c) £40.26 (1)
(d) £804.90 (1)
(e) £439.27 (2)
(f) (i) 156L (1)
  (ii) Consideration of entitlement to personal allowances (2)
  (iii) By the Inland Revenue (1)

11.6 Self-Test Question

Read the advertisement below which is to appear in a local newspaper.

> Wanted for small office in the town centre
> **TRAINEE CLERK**
> **TO UNDERTAKE GENERAL OFFICE DUTIES**
> She must be aged 16–18
> have good English and Maths GCSE grades
> and RSA Typewriting Skills Stage 1 or Joint RSA/GCSE grade C
> **SALARY £6000 per annum**
> Hours – 35 per week on flexitime – no Saturday working
> Luncheon Vouchers

(a) What is the meaning of the terms:
   (i) 'luncheon vouchers'
   (ii) 'flexitime' (4)
(b) How does the advertisement break current laws on discrimination? (2)

Julie lives on the outskirts of town. She is qualified for the job advertised above. She is also interested in a job in her local hypermarket as a checkout operator. It pays £100 per week for 39 hours on shifts Monday–Saturday.

(c) (i) What are the advantages for Julie of the hypermarket job?
    (ii) What are the disadvantages for Julie of the job in town? (12)
(d) Julie is offered both jobs. She decides to take the job in town. She makes her decision because of what she learned about the firms at the interviews. What kind of things may have persuaded her to take the town job? (12)
(e) What qualities other than those mentioned in the advertisement will interviewers be looking for in the applicants? (10)

(SEG)

12 Recruitment and Training

SEG	LEAG	NISEAC	WJEC	NEAB	MEG	Topic	Date attempted	Date completed	Self Assessment
✓	✓	✓	✓	✓	✓	12.1			
✓	✓	✓	✓	✓	✓	12.2			
✓	✓	✓	✓	✓	✓	12.3			
✓	✓	✓	✓	✓	✓	12.4			
✓	✓	✓	✓	✓	✓	12.5			
✓	✓	✓	✓		✓	12.6			
✓	✓	✓	✓	✓	✓	12.7			
✓	✓	✓	✓		✓	12.8			
✓	✓	✓	✓	✓	✓	12.9			
✓	✓	✓	✓	✓	✓	12.10			

12.1 Stages in Recruitment

Almost all businesses occasionally have to recruit new workers. The recruitment process is summarised in Figure 12.1.

```
Decide number and type of workers needed
                    ↓
         Drawn up Job Description
                    ↓
             Advertise vacancies
                    ↓
            Application received
                    ↓
      Select some applicants for shortlist
                    ↓
           Interview text applicants
                    ↓
              Take up references
                    ↓
              Select candidates
                    ↓
                 Job Offer
                    ↓
            Induction and Training
```

Figure 12.1 Stages in recruitment

12.2 The Job Description

The person responsible for recruiting employees should decide upon a *job description*. In a small business such as a corner shop the owner may simply decide that he or she wants a part-time assistant 'to serve customers' and not bother to draw up a detailed specification. Larger organisations may set out a formal written job description. In either case certain details will need to be decided in order to attract and interview applicants. These might include as a basic minimum:

- Title of job.
- Type of work.
- Place and hours of work.
- Pay and other benefits.
- Person to whom the employee will be responsible.
- Workers who will be supervised by the successful applicant.

An example of a job description for a hotel reception supervisor is given in Figure 12.2.

> Job Title: **Reception Supervisor**
> Victoria Hotel, Chillingsworth
>
> Responsibilities
>
> 1. Overall responsibility for supervision of reception area, under the direction of the General Manager.
> 2. Supervision of staff, including allocation of tasks, drawing up work rotas and basic training and instruction.
> 3. Dealing with customer enquiries and requests.
> 4. Completion of records including reservations, payment of bills, requests for services and accounts.
> 5. Maintaining in self and subordinates a standard of service and dress which reflect the good name of the Company.
> 6. Attending training courses as and when directed by the General Manager.
> 7. Being aware of and implementing the Company's Health and Safety procedures.
> 8. Other duties as may be reasonably required by the General Manager.

Figure 12.2 Job description

12.3 Personnel Description

Having described the duties, the recruiter will have to think about the type of person who will be suitable to fill the post. Again, this may be very simple, e.g. 'able to carry sacks of fruit and count change', or it may be based on a detailed checklist of the skills and personal qualities desired. The most famous is the 'Seven Point Plan' of the National Institute of Industrial Psychology, which lists requirements under seven headings.

Figure 12.3 shows these headings, together with an example of how they might be applied to the job description in Figure 12.2. The requirements must comply with the law. For example, with certain exceptions, it is illegal to specify qualities which automatically exclude a particular sex or racial group.

1. Physical make-up	–	The receptionist should be presentable to customers, e.g. dress smartly.
2. Attainments	–	Evidence of a good education and supervisory experience would be desirable.
3. General intelligence	–	A reception supervisor would have to think quickly when dealing with hotel guests.
4. Special aptitudes	–	Ability to write in clear English and work with figures would be essential. Knowledge of a foreign language might be useful.
5. Interests	–	An applicant's hobbies may show their ability to work in a team.
6. Disposition	–	The reception supervisor would need to be pleasant to customers and remain calm even when problems occur.
7. Circumstances	–	Night and weekend work would be essential, so the successful applicant would have to be able to work these hours.

Figure 12.3 Seven-point plan for assessing candidates

12.4 Attracting Candidates

There are two basic ways of finding applicants.

(a) Internal Recruitment

The job may be advertised through a staff notice board or bulletin, or even given to a particular person without allowing other staff to apply. There are some advantages to internal recruitment:

1. The candidates' strengths and weaknesses are already known.
2. The person appointed will be familiar with the work of the organisation.
3. Internal promotions are good for staff morale.
4. It is quicker and cheaper than external recruitment.

The disadvantages are:

1. Restricted choice, which may lead to unsuitable people being appointed.
2. Internal promotion can cause jealousy and resentment amongst people passed over.
3. The organisation does not benefit from people with new ideas.

(b) External Recruitment

The advantages and disadvantages of external recruitment are basically the opposite of those of internal selection. Amongst the possible methods of recruiting people from outside the organisation are the following.

(i) Personal recommendation

Recommendations may come from employees, friends and business contacts.

(ii) Unsolicited applications

People often write in to enquire about employment, even where no specific job is available at the time. Some firms keep suitable applications 'on file' until a post becomes available.

(iii) Schools, colleges and universities

A firm may have personal contacts with local schools or colleges providing particular types of courses.

(iv) Recruitment agencies

There are a large number of these, some general, others specialising in particular types of work.

(v) Professional journals

These are important for specialist workers who may have to be recruited from a wide geographical area. Examples include *Personnel Management* and *The Times Educational Supplement*.

(vi) Local and national newspapers

Local papers will tend to be used for most unskilled and semi-skilled jobs. For professional workers national papers may be used. Most 'quality' papers such as the *Guardian* and *Independent* have specialist sections on certain days of the week for particular groups of advertisement, e.g. 'Public Sector' or 'Computer Appointments'.

(vii) Government agencies

These include Job Centres, Careers Service and Professional and Executive Recruitment (PER).

(viii) Display boards

Some firms advertise vacancies outside their premises, e.g. in windows or on special display boards.

12.5 Selection of Employees

(a) Job Advertisements

However a post is advertised, certain details will need to be made known to potential applicants. Some of these will be taken from the job description. Typical information included might be

- Job title.
- Description of work involved.
- Earnings or salary grade.
- Fringe benefits.
- Hours of work.
- Holidays.
- Place of work.
- Qualifications or experience needed.
- Training and future prospects.
- How to apply for the post.

Some of this information may be omitted to save advertising costs, but the advertisement should be designed so as to contain enough information to attract the right type of person to apply.

(b) Application Form

This is the most commonly-used means of collecting information about applicants. The information requested will vary, but the basic minimum needed would usually include the following:

- Name.
- Address and telephone number.
- Date of birth.
- Education and qualifications.
- Work experience.
- Personal interests.
- Health record, e.g. details of serious illnesses.
- National Insurance number.
- Referees who will provide information about the applicant's character and work record.
- Other information showing the applicant's suitability, e.g. for positions of responsibility it is common to ask how the applicant would organise his or her department if given the job.

(c) Curriculum Vitae

A *curriculum vitae* gives similar information to that asked for in an application form, but is set out by the applicant rather than the recruiter. From the company's point of view there is the problem that essential information may be omitted.

(d) Selection Methods

(i) Interviews

Interviews are the most commonly-used methods of selection. They are cheap and easy to arrange but have some disadvantages:

- They depend very much upon personal impressions.
- Many good and capable workers suffer from nerves and do badly.
- Interviewers are rarely trained in interview techniques.
- They don't necessarily give much information about the applicant's ability to do the job.

(ii) Aptitude tests

Aptitude tests can, if well-designed, provide useful information about applicant's abilities. They include tests of general intelligence and specific skills such as mental arithmetic and typing.

(iii) Psychological tests

Psychological tests have to be administered by experts and are therefore expensive. However, the Armed Forces have found them to be the most accurate method of forecasting a recruit's success in the job.

(iv) Group selection

Group selection is often used for professional jobs and the Forces. Applicants are asked to lead and participate in group exercises such as discussions and practical tasks.

12.6 Induction

Induction is the process of introducing a new worker to the organisation.

(a) Contract of Employment

By law an employee must be given a contract of employment within three months. This must contain certain basic information:

- Employer's name and place of work.
- Date employment started.
- Title of job.
- Rate of pay.
- Hours of work.
- Holiday entitlement.
- Amount of notice to be given by worker or employer.
- Procedures for disciplinary matters.
- Arrangements for sick pay.
- Pension rights.

Some of these items may not be described in detail, but may refer the employee to documents such as national union agreements or pension fund conditions.

(b) Information Needed by the New Employee

An induction programme, which may take anything from a couple of hours to several months, has three basic purposes:

1. To familiarise the new employee with the job and place of work.
2. To encourage him or her to become committed to the job and therefore likely to stay.
3. To make the employee a useful and efficient part of the organisation as quickly as possible.

For example, a person appointed to the job of hotel reception supervisor described in Figure 12.2 would want answers to questions such as:

- To whom should I report on the first day?
- Where do I take documents such as income tax forms?
- When and are where are tea- and lunch-breaks taken?
- Where are the toilets?
- Whom do I ask for help if I am not sure what to do?
- How do the switchboard, computer and other items of equipment work?
- What authority do I have over my staff, e.g. can I allow them time off or does someone else do this?

Most of these are very simple questions, and the answers may seem obvious to a person already working at the hotel. However, not knowing what to do can cause terrible embarrassment to a new employee and may push them into leaving very quickly.

12.7 Training

(a) Why Employees need Training

A new employee will often need training for the job, particularly if he or she has little or no experience of the type of work. Training may be concerned with matters such as:

- The business's organisation and methods.
- Operating equipment.
- Handling accounts and other records.
- Dealing with customers and suppliers.
- Company products and services.
- Health and safety procedures.
- Training for promotion to the next grade.

Obviously, even existing employees may need training about items such as these to enable them to adapt to change in the business.

(b) Types of Training

There are two basic types of training:

1. *On-the-job*, with the worker learning as he or she goes along from an experienced fellow-worker, supervisor or trainer.
2. *Off-the-job*, on courses at the company training centre or local college.

Many training programmes use both methods, paying workers to attend courses on day- or block-release.

(c) The Training Commission

This was established in 1988, but is actually a section of the former Manpower Services Commission (MSC). Its management is appointed by the Government. The Training Commission is responsible for supervising vocational training and some educational programmes. It is due to become a Government Department under a new name in 1989.

Government training schemes include the *Youth Training Scheme* (YTS) for 16–17-year-olds, and programmes for the unemployed such as the *Community Programme* and *Job Training Scheme* (JTS). YTS runs Skillcentres for retraining workers, and is involved in school education of 14–16-year-olds through the *Technical and Vocational Education Initiative* (TVEI).

12.8 Coursework Assignment

What job opportunities are available in _____ for school/college-leavers?

This assignment involves setting up a computer database listing the job opportunities available in a local area. It is best approached as a group exercise because of the time involved in collecting information.

You will need to plan the type of information to be collected, and the methods to be used. You could concentrate upon a particular type of work, or on a particular area such as a town or county.

Setting up a database involves choosing headings such as:

- type of jobs, e.g. banking, coal-mining, tourism.
- age of entry, e.g. 16, 17, 18.
- type of entry, e.g. apprenticeship, permanent job, YTS.
- qualifications, e.g. GCSE, A-Level, degree.

When deciding upon the classifications to be used, consider the type of questions a user might wish to ask e.g. 'What opportunities are available in banking in Belfast for a 16-year-old with four GCSE grade Cs?'

The database should be as easy to use as possible. Information can be collected by using letters, telephone calls, careers leaflets, advertisements and personal interviews.

If the assignment is to be used for the examination, you will probably have to submit a written report upon your work. This should describe any problems you have encountered in collecting information and in using the database. Test the database by asking other students to use it, and suggest solutions to the difficulties that they point out.

12.9 Worked Example

Barbara Green has been left £10,000 in a relative's will. She would like to set up a hairdressing business and employ three assistants. Explain to Barbara:

(a) How a bank current account would be useful for making business payments. (3)
(b) **Two** possible ways of recruiting staff for Barbara's business. (2)
(c) Brief details of **two** laws which Barbara must be aware of when appointing staff. (2)
(d) A form of training suitable for the school leaver appointed as an assistant for Barbara. (2)
(e) How a good training programme benefits both employer and employee. (3)
(f) Reasons why employees are likely to be contented in their work. (3)

(LEAG Specimen)

Answers

(a) Cheques – crossings and safety. (3)
(b) Advertisement, Job Centre, employment agency. (2)
(c) Equal Pay Act 1970, Sex Discrimination Act 1975, etc. (2)
(d) Day release to Further Education: apprenticeship. (2)
(e) Employee: increases skill and hence employability. Employer: improves quality of staff, brings in new skills and ideas, etc. (3)
(f) Incentives may be financial and non-financial, e.g, job satisfaction through provision of personal service to customers. (3)

12.10 Self-test Questions

Question 1

(a) Read the information given in the two advertisements and answer the questions which follow.

Advertisement A

ALTAMY LTD

require a hardworking, energetic young person to work in the challenging world of double glazing sales.

The successful applicant will be smart, lively and able to get on well with people.

Training will be provided.

The pay is based on commission, and earnings of up to £300 per week are possible.

Advertisement B

Weltex Limited

SALES ORDER ADMINISTRATOR/ RECEPTIONIST/ SECRETARY

We are looking for someone to do all three functions!

We are a busy, friendly company selling food ingredients to manufacturers and have recently moved to Leeds.

The individual appointed will be mainly responsible for dealing with orders, but there will be a wide variety of other duties.

This is an interesting position, involving direct contact with many household names in the food industry.

An ability with figures and some secretarial skills are essential, but good personality, charm, tact and a pleasant telephone manner are important. The pay reflects the high standard and experience we are looking for.

(i) In **advertisement A** above, state with reasons what kind of training might be given to the successful candidate. (10)

(ii) In **advertisement B** above, what is meant by 'dealing with orders'? Use examples to illustrate your answer. (10)

(iii) Explain what a firm should consider about a job before employing new people. Use examples from the advertisements above to illustrate your answer. (15)

(iv) Apart from good pay, say what there is about these two jobs that might motivate the successful applicants, and explain why you think so. (15)

(b) The following is an internal memo from the Personnel Officer in Altamy Ltd (see advertisement A above).

MEMO Date: 05.05.88
From: Personnel Officer To: Head of Sales

Below is a summary of the number of staff who left and were replaced last year. It is fairly obvious that a problem exists in your department. I should like to discuss your views on this at our next meeting. Please come prepared with a short report, saying why your department has this problem, and outlining any action you feel we might take to improve matters.

Staff Turnover

Department	Total number employed	Left and replaced
Assembly	150	10
Maintenance	10	1
Office	12	2
Sales	5	4

Answer the memo with the kind of report you would expect the Head of Sales to write, including the following points.

1. The nature of the main problem.
2. Why it is a problem to the firm.
3. What might be done about it. (15)

(NEA)

Question 2

Read carefully the information given and use it to help answer the questions that follow.

James & Cartwright are an '**up-market**' store whose **turnover** has increased in the last five years. Recently they put up the following advertisement in a local **job centre**.

JOBCENTRE

JOB	FULLTIME SALES ASSISTANT MAN OR WOMAN
DISTRICT	HIGHCROSS
SALARY	£3.00 per hour. Annual staff bonus. Fringe benefits.
HOURS	40-hour week, 6-day flexible work pattern.
DETAILS	Ladies fashion department. Age 25–45. Experience essential.
JOB NO.	15

(a) How is the basic rate of pay calculated? (2)

(b) How much would the sales assistant earn each week? (2)

(c) Give **two** examples of fringe benefits that the store might offer its employees. (2)

(d) If the store is open six days a week, how would you expect the 40-hour flexible work pattern to operate? (4)

(e) The job is in the ladies fashion department. Why does the advertisement say 'man or woman'? (2)

(f) The advertisement was not successful. Only three people applied and none of them had experience of working in a shop. By what other means might James & Cartwright find the staff they need? (2)

(g) If they have to employ staff who lack experience, what kind of training would be most suitable? (2)

(h) Design a job application form for the Personnel Manager to send to applicants for the job at James & Cartwright. Your completed form should invite applicants to give the **ten** most important pieces of information. Set out your form neatly and clearly within the outline given.

(One piece of information you would require is the name of the applicant, so the word **'name'** and a space for the applicant to write his/her name in has already been put on form.

Now complete the form to obtain **nine** more important pieces of information.) (20)

(i) Explain briefly why you have asked for any **six** of the pieces of information. (8)

(j) When recruiting staff, the firm often uses a job description which states exactly what the job involves. Write a job description that you think would be appropriate for this job. (10)

(k) State **two** other uses that the firm might have for its job description. (2)

(l) The Personnel Manager listed the qualities he was looking for:

Helpful	Honest
Physically Strong	Ambitious
Humorous	Imaginative
Serious	Responsible
Highly Intelligent	Numerate
Well-motivated	Punctual
Clean Driving Licence	Well-groomed
Reliable	

1887 J&C 1987 JAMES & CARTWRIGHT plc

APPLICATION FOR THE POST OF FULL-TIME SALES ASSISTANT

Name _____

Completed forms must be returned to the Personnel Manager,
James & Cartwright plc, Grand Parade, Highcross HS1 1DS
no later than 30 September 1987.

Group the 15 qualities in the list under the following headings:

ESSENTIAL   **DESIRABLE**   **NOT APPLICABLE**   (5)

(m) Briefly state why you have chosen the qualities listed as essential. (4)
(n) Give another desirable quality not listed above which should be included. Give reasons for your choice. (3)
(o) James & Cartwright need the experienced staff because they are an up-market and expanding store. Give **three** reasons why their turnover might be increasing. (6)

(MEG Specimen)

13 Industrial Relations

SEG	LEAG	NISEAC	WJEC	NEAB	MEG	Topic	Date attempted	Date completed	Self Assessment
✓	✓	✓	✓	✓	✓	13.1			
✓	✓	✓	✓	✓	✓	13.2			
✓	✓	✓	✓	✓	✓	13.3			
✓	✓	✓	✓	✓	✓	13.4			
✓	✓	✓	✓	✓	✓	13.5			
✓	✓	✓	✓	✓	✓	13.6			
✓	✓	✓	✓	✓	✓	13.7			
✓	✓	✓	✓	✓	✓	13.8			

13.1 What is Meant by Industrial Relations?

Industrial relations is a general term for the processes by which the managers of an organisation discuss pay and working conditions with its workers and their representatives.

Issues which would be considered under this heading include:

- Pay and fringe benefits.
- Hours of work and holidays.
- Health and safety.
- Redundancy and dismissal.
- Training and promotion of workers.

Industrial relations is sometimes thought of as being concerned with negotiations with trade unions, but in many cases this may not be true. More than half of all workers are non-union members, but they are still concerned with matters such as those described above.

13.2 Trade Unions

A trade union is a collection of workers who agree to negotiate with employers as a group of employees rather than individually. This process is called *collective bargaining*. The size of trade unions varies from the Sheffield Wool Shearers Union (17 members) to the Transport & General Workers Union (TGWU) with over one million members.

(a) Functions of Trade Unions

As Figure 13.1 shows, trade unions are not concerned only with strikes and negotiating wage rises.

(b) Organisation of Trade Unions

The organisational structure of a typical trade union is illustrated in Figure 13.2.

Members pay a subscription to the union in return for its services. If a workplace has a *closed shop* agreement all workers must belong to a recognised union. Many firms now have *single-union* agreements, where the firm will only deal with one particular union.

Shop stewards are the union's representatives at the individual workplace. They are elected by the members, and are in daily contact with their fellow workers. The shop steward does not work full-time for the union, but may be

Figure 13.1 Functions of trade unions

```
                        President
                            |
                   National executive
                            |
                      Head Office
                       / | | \
                    Regional Offices
                      / | | \
                      Branches
                    //// |||| \\\\
                    Shop Steward
                  ///// |||||| \\\\\
                 Individual   Members
```

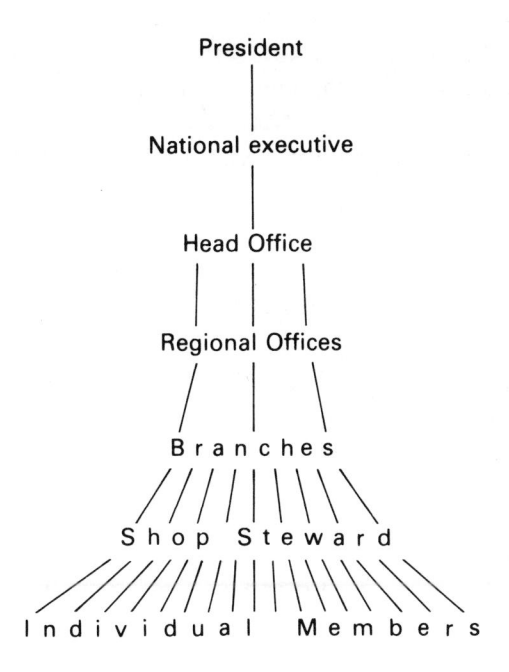

Figure 13.2 Organisation of a typical trade union

given time off from his or her work to carry out union duties. In large factories or offices there may be several shop stewards who will in turn elect a *convenor*.

The *branch* is usually based upon a local area, although it may consist of members from a single firm. The branch may have a full-time official employed by the union.

Larger unions often have *regional offices* covering a number of branches. For example, the TGWU has eleven regions covering the whole of the United Kingdom.

The *head office* contains the most senior officials, and usually employs specialists such as solicitors and accountants to provide a service to branches.

The *National Executive* is an elected committee, typically of around 40 members who represent different areas. Executive members are not usually paid officials of the union.

The *President* or *General Secretary* is responsible for overall co-ordination of the union's activities. By law senior officials must now be elected by ballot every five years.

(c) Types of Trade Union

```
                        Types of Trade Union
           ┌─────────────┬─────────────┬─────────────┐
         CRAFT         GENERAL       INDUSTRIAL    WHITE-COLLAR
           |             |              |              |
      workers with a  workers from a  all types of   non-manual workers
      particular skill variety of trades workers in a     |
           |          and industries   particular    eg National Union of
      eg Musician Union (often unskilled) industry   Teachers (NUT) Civil
      (MU),              |                 |          and Public Services
      Amalgamated    eg Transport and  eg National Union of  Association (CPSA)
      Engineers      General Workers   Mineworkers (NUM)
      Union (AEU)    Union TGWU
```

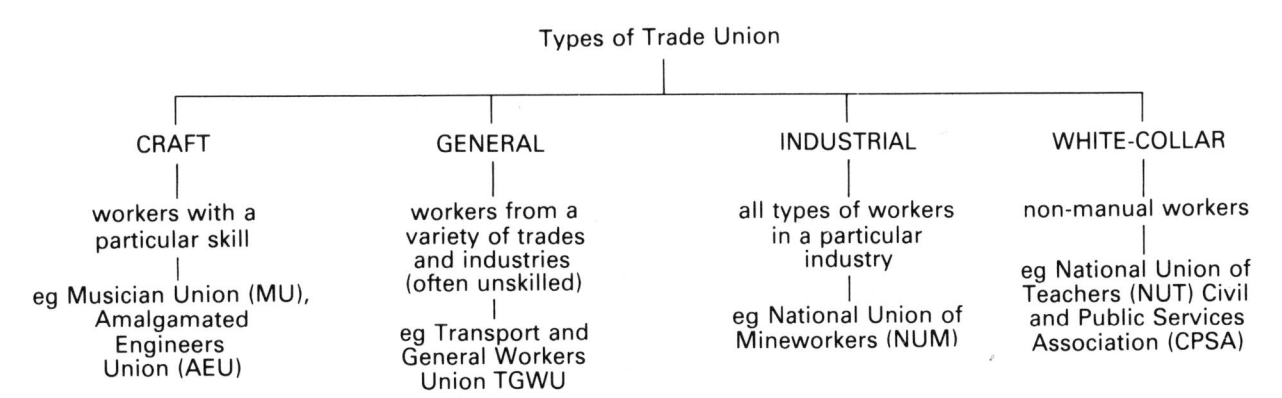

Figure 13.3 Types of trade union

Unions are often divided into four types, as shown in Figure 13.3. However, the distinction between each type is not complete. Many unions have merged in recent years and united different types of workers. For example the Amalgamated Engineering Union (AEU) now has unskilled members.

13.3 Trades Union Congress (TUC)

Most unions belong to the Trades Union Congress (TUC), which campaigns on behalf of all workers, and is represented on Government bodies such as the Health and Safety Commission and the Advisory, Conciliation and Abitration Service (ACAS).

TUC policy is decided at the annual Conference, which is attended by delegates from all unions. The TUC has no power over its member unions, although it is often asked to settle disputes between unions.

13.4 Employers' Associations

Many industries have employers' associations which represent firms' interests. The Engineering Employers Federation is one example. The largest employers' association is the Confederation of British Industry (CBI), which has over 250,000 members. Like trade unions, employers' associations campaign for their members on issues concerned with industry and employment.

13.5 Collective Bargaining

(a) Stages in Collective Bargaining

Collective bargaining is the process of negotiation between employers and trade unions. Most cases are settled without the need for *industrial action* or *arbitration*, but as Figure 13.4 shows, industrial disputes may go through several stages before agreement is reached.

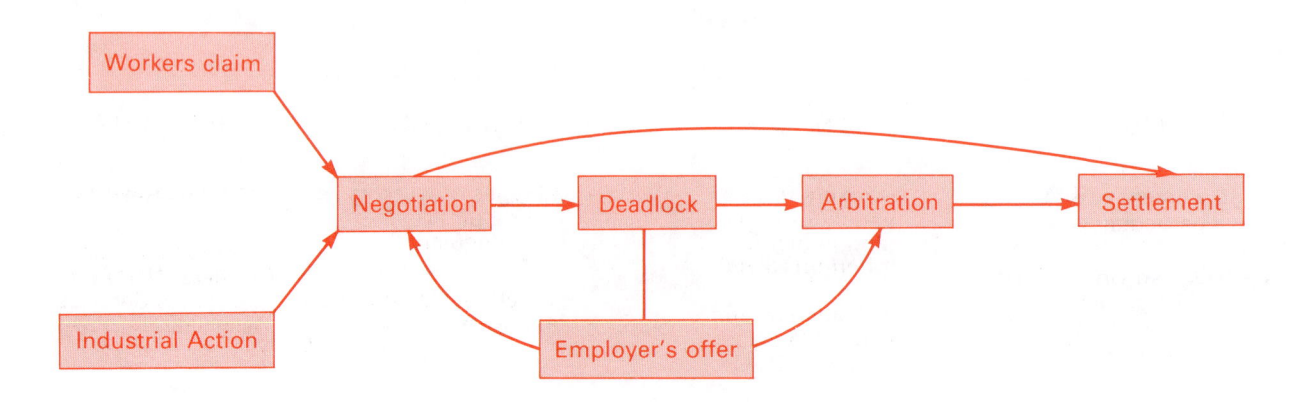

Figure 13.4 Stages in collective bargaining

(b) Types of Industrial Action

If employers and trade unions cannot reach agreement by talking, either may use industrial action to try to force better terms. Union action may be *official*, which means that the union's full-time officers agree that it should be taken. Sometimes, however, members may take *unofficial* action against their union's advice.

Under the terms of various Acts of Parliament passed during the 1980s, most industrial action now has to be approved by members in a secret ballot. If this is not done the employer can sue the union for damages caused by the action. In extreme cases a court may *sequestrate* the union's assets, i.e. hand over financial control of the union to an independent person until it agrees to call off industrial action.

Strikes are the most serious form of union action, with workers refusing to work at all. Members may *picket* their employers' premises by asking fellow workers, customers and suppliers not go go in or out of the work-place. However, picketing another firm's premises is called *secondary action* and is illegal.

Overtime bans are common in certain industries such as transport, the postal services and coal-mining, which rely heavily upon overtime to maintain production. By working only the basic hours, workers can create shortages of the good or service.

Sit-ins involve the workers occupying the employer's premises and preventing goods and other items going in or out. They are often used when a firm is planning to close a particular factory or office.

Employer's action may include sacking or suspending workers who are taking industrial action. This is legal as long as all the workers involved are sacked. Another employer's weapon is a *lock-out*, with workers being told to stay at home.

(c) Arbitration

If employers and unions cannot agree, they may ask an independent person or body to *arbitrate* by suggesting a solution to the dispute. The main arbitrating agencies in the United Kingdom are the Advisory, Conciliation and Arbitration Service (ACAS) in England, Scotland and Wales and the Labour Relations Agency (LRA) in Northern Ireland. These consist of independent members and representatives of employers and trade unions.

An increasingly common form of arbitration is *pendulum arbitration*. The arbitrators cannot simply 'split the difference' between offer and claim, but must decide for one or the other. This is designed to prevent unrealistically low offers by employers and over-ambitious claims by unions.

13.6 Coursework Assignment

What effect will a change in work have upon an organisation?

Investigate the likely effects of a change in the way in which work is organised in a firm or other organisation. Possible situations might include:

- Introduction of new machinery.
- An extra shift, e.g. 24-hour working.
- An increase in casual or part-time working.

Choose an example which is currently in the news. Assess the likely effects of the change upon the organisation and its workers. Sources of information will vary, but could include the following:

- Newspaper and magazine articles.
- Firms and other organisations.
- Trade unions.
- MPs and local councillors.

If you have newspaper or magazine articles, you may be able to use them as leads, as shown in Figure 17.6.

Don't simply copy or list newspaper articles or statements made by people involved. If there is disagreement about the issue, much of the 'evidence' is likely to be biased. Try to sort out any points upon which different people agree. Give your own opinions, backing them up with facts wherever possible.

13.7 Worked Example

> The following article appeared in the *Daily News*.
>
> ### Possible Layoffs at XYZ
>
> "We are facing increasing competition from home and abroad", Bob Smith, managing director of XYZ Engineering told our reporter yesterday.
>
> "We must get more up to date machinery and reduce our labour costs. Productivity must improve and we need to become more competitive".
>
> Immediately after the article appeared, Arthur Jones the senior shop steward said, 'This is the first the Union has heard of any changes. I will be calling a meeting of my members tomorrow, and we shall be seeking a meeting with the management as soon as possible. We will resist plans for redundancies.' Bob Smith, when he read the article, said, 'They have blown this up out of all proportion. I should have spoken to the unions before letting the press interview me'.

(a) Even before the meeting called by Arthur Jones, many of the members were pressing for immediate strike action. Why might they be suggesting this?
(16)

(b) Some members thought that other methods of solving the problem should be tried before taking strike action. What might these methods be and why should the union consider them?
(18)

(c) Why do changes at work usually worry the people who will be affected by them?
(16)

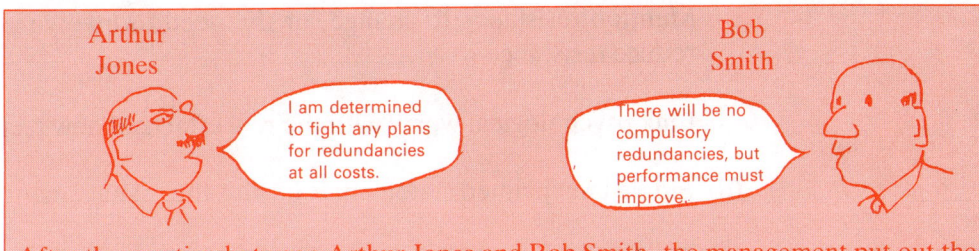

> **Arthur Jones:** I am determined to fight any plans for redundancies at all costs.
>
> **Bob Smith:** There will be no compulsory redundancies, but performance must improve.
>
> After the meeting between Arthur Jones and Bob Smith, the management put out the following statement.
>
> 'The management at XYZ is thinking of buying new machinery for the factory. This may lead to some reduction in manning levels. There will be full consultation with the union at all stages. There will be no compulsory redundancies.'

(d) What does the management mean by 'there will be full consultation with the union at all stages'? What do you think will be the main points in their discussion? (16)

(NEA Specimen)

Answers

(a) Single reason, no explanation e.g. threat of job losses. (0–4)

As above but with explanation/development. (5–8)

Acceptance that worker confidence may well be low and not only the threat but also the likely/expected failure of negotiations would cause desire for action. (9–12)

Awareness of other possible causes e.g. poor communication, press discovery before Unions, failure to explain possibilities beforehand, desire to show their strength. (13–16)

(b) Single suggestion, no explanation e.g. talk with management. (0–2)

More than one suggestion, no explanation e.g. talk and threaten action. (3–4)

As above with an attempt to explain why e.g. talks may lead to layoffs being avoided, action may be damaging to their members. (5–10)

Showing an awareness that all courses are likely to be explored before taking action because it is so damaging to the firm and the members. (11–14)

Show an awareness of current reality e.g. unions are now weaker than in the past, the engineering industry is notoriously weak and facing competition, this particular management are willing to consult. (15–18)

(c) Simple response, single factor e.g. people don't like change. (0–4)

Awareness of the needs of people for security/predictability. (5–8)

Mention resistance to change, or the need to involve people in planning to reduce resistance. (9–12)

Link psychological worry with the real effects of new technology. (13–16)

(d) Single unexplained statement e.g. with the management. (0–2)

Explain statement above e.g. in order to come to a decision, they must talk with each other. (3–4)

Mention specific type of body e.g. Joint Consultative Committee. (5–6)

Explain that some of the reasons for this consultation e.g. non compulsory redundancies, can be negotiated through e.g. natural wastage, reduced trainees, negotiated redundancies, increases in productivity. (17–12)

Show an awareness of a broad range of possibilities to avoid compulsory redundancies, increase productivity and avoid layoffs. (13–16)

13.8 Self-Test Question

Read the extract from a newspaper and answer the questions below.

VICTORY FOR VENETTA WORKERS

A group of 40 workers are celebrating victory in a long running battle with VENETTA TEXTILES PLC.

The workers, who operate packing machinery, have been fighting for four years to have their jobs classified as skilled. Now an independent arbitrator has ruled in their favour.

The decision means an extra £8 on top of their *basic pay* of £110 per week, and will be backdated to January of this year.

Yesterday's verdict by the *Labour Relations Agency* comes as the climax to a campaign which began with a *work-to-rule* and ended in a six-week strike in the early months of this year.

The strike at three of Venetta's factories led to 1500 other workers being laid off.

(a) Explain the three terms in italics. (3)
(b) What other forms of industrial action could the workers have used to get more pay? (2)
(c) Why did the packing machinists at Venetta want a pay rise? (3)
(d) Give **three** ways in which their Trade Union could have played a part in this dispute. (3)
(e) Why were the 1500 other workers laid off? (3)

(NISEC)

14

Communication

SEG	LEAG	NISEAC	WJEC	NEAB	MEG	Topic	Date attempted	Date completed	Self Assessment
✓	✓	✓	✓	✓	✓	14.1			
✓	✓	✓	✓	✓	✓	14.2			
✓	✓	✓	✓	✓	✓	14.3			
✓	✓	✓	✓	✓	✓	14.4			
✓	✓	✓	✓	✓	✓	14.5			
✓	✓	✓	✓	✓	✓	14.6			
✓	✓	✓	✓	✓	✓	14.7			

14.1 What is Communication?

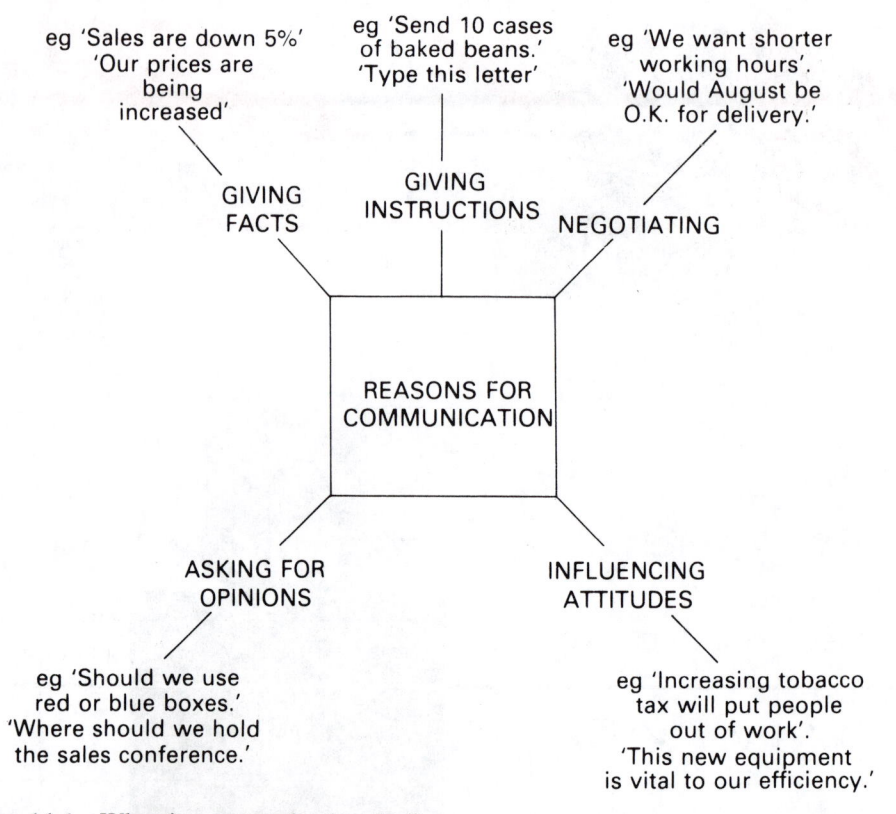

Figure 14.1 What is communication for?

Good communication is vital to the effective running of a business. Figure 14.1 gives some examples of the ways in which people within a business will communicate with each other (*internal* communication) and people and organisations from outside (*external* communication).

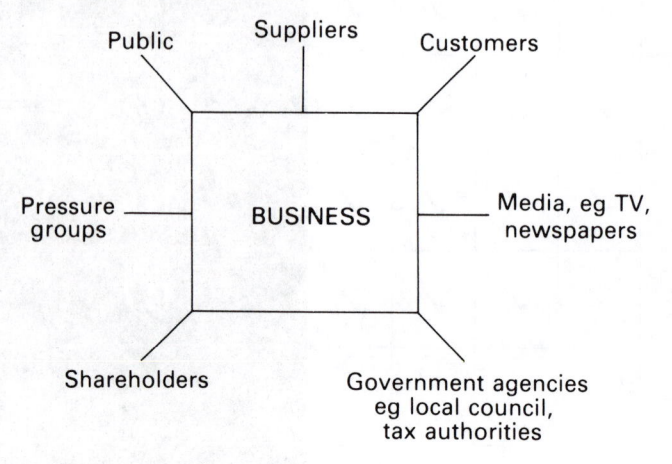

Figure 14.2 External communication

14.2 The Four Elements of Communication

Any form of communication has four elements:

1. *Transmitter*. This is the person who sends a message.
2. *Message*. All the statements in Figure 14.1 are messages. A message may be a simple sign saying 'No Entry' or a complex document such as a financial report or a book.
3. *Medium*. This is the method used to send the message, e.g. spoken, visual or electronic.
4. *Receiver*. This is the person or group of people to whom the message is sent.

An example of these four elements combined is given in Figure 14.3.

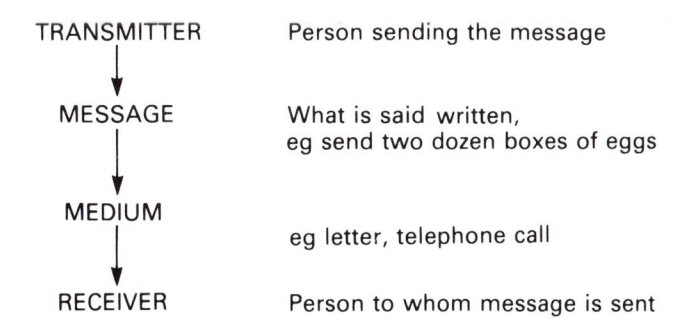

```
TRANSMITTER      Person sending the message
     ↓
  MESSAGE        What is said written,
     ↓           eg send two dozen boxes of eggs
  MEDIUM
     ↓           eg letter, telephone call
  RECEIVER       Person to whom message is sent
```

Figure 14.3 The four elements of a message

14.3 Barriers to Communication

Problems in communication can occur for several reasons:

- Complex language or jargon is used.
- The message is too long.
- Essential information is missed out because of poor planning.
- The 'lines of communication' (see Chapter 7) are too long, e.g. a message is passed through too many people.
- The medium used is unsuitable, e.g. complex messages sent by phone.
- The receiver is distracted by noise or work.
- The tone of the message is wrong, e.g. a manager 'talking down' to workers.
- The message is sent too late for the receiver to act on it.

14.4 Methods of Communication

(a) Oral Communication

Oral communication is ideal when it is necessary to pass on a short message or find information quickly. It is unsuitable for communicating complex information.

(i) Face-to-face contact

Face-to-face contact is the most widely-used form of communication in business. It may be *informal* e.g. simple requests or orders, or *formal*, e.g. meetings and interviews.

(ii) Interviews

Interviews are formal and are commonly used to select employees or for purposes such as grievance or disciplinary procedures.

(iii) Meetings

Meetings usually follow a particular procedure which is used by organisations of all types. An *agenda* listing the points to be discussed is sent to the people who will be attending. The main arguments and decisions taken are summarised in the written *minutes* of the meeting.

(iv) Telephones

Telephones enable quick conversation with people in other rooms or outside the premises.

(b) Non-verbal Communication

People's actions or *body language* are a form of communication which is as important as any other type. For example, a supervisor may annoy workers by staring round the room while they are asking for help or making a complaint.

(c) Written Communication

Written forms of communication are used for situations where:

- Speed is not particularly important.
- Long or detailed messages are sent.
- The message is to be recorded for future use.
- It is necessary to contact several people at the same time.
- People cannot be contacted in person or by telephone.

(i) Letters

Letters are used mainly for external communication.

(ii) Memoranda

Memoranda or 'memos' are short notes sent to people within the same organisation.

(iii) Brochures and advertisements

Brochures and *advertisements* are designed to sell a firm's goods and services to outside people and firms.

(iv) Reports

Reports are collections of facts, often listing alternative solutions to a particular problem, e.g. a Health and Safety report may give details of accidents and illness, together with recommendations for reducing them.

(v) Manuals

Manuals give employees instructions about company products or procedures, e.g. on handling machinery or dealing with customers.

(vi) Notices

Notices are used to display information or instructions throughout the premises.

(vii) Annual reports

Annual reports detailing the company's financial performance and plans must be sent to shareholders every year.

(viii) Press releases and public relations material

Press releases and *public relations material* are used by firms to inform the public and mass media about company affairs such as new products and orders.

(ix) Micro-film

Micro-film can store large amounts of data in a very small space. It is used by organisations such as credit card companies, libraries and retailers of motor spares.

(d) Electronic Communication

During the last 20 years the cost of using computers has fallen dramatically, and electronic communication has become increasingly important. The speed and cheapness of electronic communication make up for the cost of buying special equipment. For example, a small business can buy a sophisticated computer system for under £10,000, which is less than the cost of employing a worker for a year.

(i) Electronic mail

Electronic mail uses the telephone system to send messages from one computer to another. A *modem* is needed to connect a computer to the telephone network. The receiver's computer stores the message until he or she has time to read it.

(ii) Telex

Telex is one of the oldest forms of electronic communication. A message is typed into a special machine and transmitted to a telex printer via a telephone line. Telex cannot transmit drawings or graphics.

(iii) Facsmile transmission

Fascimile transmission sends a copy of a document or drawing through a telephone line without the need to type a message in. It is therefore faster and more flexible than telex, which it is gradually replacing.

(iv) Teletext

Teletext services such as Prestel link television screens, telephone lines and keyboards to send information of different types. The Stock Exchange's SEAQ system (Figure 6.2) is one example of this kind of service.

14.5 Coursework assignment

How could a firm improve its external communications?

Investigate the methods used by a firm to communicate with other people and organisations such as customers and suppliers. A full list is given in Figure 14.2.
　　Look at the methods used e.g. face-to-face, written and electronic. Are there any ways in which communication could be improved e.g. better notices in offices, more imaginative advertising or use of electronic communication. You may wish to concentrate upon one aspect, e.g. would ordering of goods and services be improved by the use of computers; does the layout of a shop or reception area discourage callers.
　　If possible compare two firms in the same type of business, such as shoe shops or travel agents. Look for signs of poor communication, such as customers not knowing where things are, or people trying to use phones in noisy areas. Prepare a report to suggest how these problems might be overcome.

14.6 Worked Example

Bantock's Ltd is a chain of shops selling a range of electrical goods such as televisions, stereo equipment and computers.

Bantock's shops are in various towns in the North and Midlands. The Head Office is in Oxford, with some of the shops, such as that in Barton-on-Tyne, being over 200 miles away.

Management of the company is highly centralised, with store managers being told which goods to stock and what prices to charge.

The manager of the Barton store, Ann Davies, receives the following letter from Sarah Jones, Stores Controller, who works from the Head Office.

BANTOCK'S LTD

Head Office
Large Lane
Oxford

7.7.89

Ann Davies
Bantock's
Northern Road
Barton-on-Tyne

Dear Mrs Davies,

My records show that you were sent 100 A264T stereo systems in January, but have only sold ten of them. Our stores in other areas have sold their stock and ordered more of the units.

Will you please instruct your staff to make more effort to sell the A264T. I would like an order for at least 50 more by the end of the month.

Yours sincerely

Sarah Jones

Sarah Jones
Stores Controller

Ann Davies is annoyed by the letter. Sales in her shop have been hit by increased unemployment in the town because of the closure of two large firms. An independent store in the same street is selling the A264T for £50 less than Bantock's.

(a) Describe two methods of communication that Ann could use to reply to this letter, explaining possible advantages and disadvantages of each method. (8)
(b) What criticisms could be made of Sarah Jones' letter? (6)
(c) How does this case illustrate possible problems of centralised management? (6)

Answer

(a) Telephone – quick, easier to explain in detail, can discuss what to do next, but no written record of what is said, tempers may be lost.
Letter – written record of message, can be referred to later, but impersonal and slower than telephone. (4 each)

(b) Tactless, may upset staff, no explanation of poor sales is asked for, pointless to ask for further orders if A264T not selling. (6)

(c) Communication can be difficult, management may be unaware of local conditions, store managers have little power to make decisions, e.g. about prices. (6)

14.7 Self-Test Questions

Question 1

» ANGEL FASHION STORES LTD »

11 HASTINGS WAY
BELFAST
BT7 4QW

The General Manager
Norton Fabrics
43 Club Road
CARRICKFERGUS
Co Antrim
BT45 9RY

TEL 856435
TELEX 64534

Our ref LD/js

13 June 1988

Dear Sir

In January of this year I had a visit from your Sales Representative, Mr Bob Allan. I was impressed with your range of goods, and placed an order which was delivered very promptly.

Mr Allan indicated that he would call every month to keep me informed of any new ranges, and to collect any orders, but to date he has not done so.

I would appreciate it if you could enquire as to why he has not called, as I may have to consider taking my custom elsewhere.

Yours faithfully

Lesley Durham

Lesley Durham
HEAD BUYER

---

1. You are the General Manager of Norton Fabrics, and have just received the letter shown above.

   (a) (i) Give **two** methods by which your organisation could reply to Angel Fashion Stores Ltd. (2)
   (ii) Give one advantage and one disadvantage of using each of the methods you have identified. (4)
   (b) Efficient, effective communication with other organisations is important to your firm. What three factors would you take into account before deciding on your method of reply to Angel Fashion Stores Ltd? (6)
   (c) Your Sales Manager, Arnold Kerr, will be out of his office until late afternoon. Lay out a memo form and use it to write a memo to him, drawing his attention to the matter and requesting action. (8)

(NISEC)

Question 2

*Read the following material and answer **all** questions.*
Wherever possible you should illustrate your answer with evidence of your own research or knowledge of business gained prior to taking this examination.

*It is recommended that at least **15** minutes should be spent reading the material and absorbing the information it contains.*

The firm which employs you is moving to new offices. The senior managers have not yet decided on either the layout of the office or on the means of communication within the business. They have decided that they should consult the staff on these matters.

A questionnaire is issued which asks staff opinions on:

   (i) The benefits of the open-plan office for both themselves and the firm.
   (ii) How to organise communications to the best effect.

As far as the open plan office is concerned they find a number of different responses:

   (a) "I like open plan. All my friends work with me. We can talk about work and other things. Most of the others I know would not want to be shut up in a small office, especially with people you don't know."

   (b) "I work with my best friend. We went to school together and we get on very well. We help each other. If she needs something and I am not too busy, I will get it for her. She will do the same for me and there are a lot of us who work like this. Most of the equipment we need is in the office at present – like the photocopier – and we can see when it's not being used."

   (c) "I find it very hard to work in a large office. I can't seem to concentrate like I used to. When I'm doing confidential work it's not easy to keep it private and I'm making more mistakes. In my last job I worked in a small office with one or two other people who did the same kind of job and that was far better."

(d) "As a supervisor of the accounts staff I used to think that it was important for them to be separate from the others. Now that we are computerised it is easier to work in a large office because we can use all the equipment. It seems easy enough for us to concentrate when watching the VDUs. There were one or two 'office Romeos' when we first started but this has now stopped. Most of the staff prefer to work in a large office. I would, of course, still need a small separate office to see them privately and do my work quietly."

(e) "I'm a clerical supervisor and I can always see what my staff are doing in a large office. We meet together at the start of the day and I can give out the day's work and answer any problems. We all know what we are doing and how it fits into the whole picture. I find it difficult to have confidential chats at my desk in the middle of the office. Sometimes I have not said what I would like to say because others might overhear. I wish staff wouldn't interrupt when I am on the telephone and I dislike having to stop them gathering around the coffee machine and photo-copier for a chat."

(f) "Frankly I don't know why we are paying half the staff. I'm sure that we could do all the work with fewer of them, particularly the accounts people. A bit of the new technology in other areas would do the firm the world of good. Also, as one of the senior management in the firm, I believe that the behaviour of some of the girls is totally unacceptable. They call me by my first name, make rude remarks and hang around the photocopier for what seems like hours. I have just sacked one girl for flirting and more will follow unless they get their heads down and do some work. Whatever system people prefer we are going to have the one that gets the most work done at lowest cost."

1. What is meant by the term 'open-plan'? (2)
2. Briefly outline four points made by the staff in favour of the open-plan office. (8)
3. What recommendations would you make to management about the organis-ation of the office? (10)
4. The managing director is considering a complaint by the shop steward regarding the attitude of the manager whose comments appear in paragraph (f). The complaint makes two points:
   (i) The girl who was sacked will claim for unfair dismissal unless she gets her job back.
   (ii) The manager's attitude upsets the girls.

   Write answers to the following questions posed to you by the managing director.
   (a) Would the girl have a reasonable claim for unfair dismissal? Give one reason. (2)
   (b) What would be the advantages and disadvantages of moving the manager to a different department? (6)
5. The management have asked you to produce a report outlining the need for good communications and how modern technology can be used to achieve this.
   Produce this report. (12)

(SEG)

15

The Government and Business

SEG	LEAG	NISEAC	WJEC	NEAB	MEG	Topic	Date attempted	Date completed	Self Assessment
✓	✓	✓	✓	✓	✓	15.1			
✓	✓	✓	✓	✓	✓	15.2			
✓	✓	✓	✓	✓	✓	15.3			
✓	✓	✓	✓	✓	✓	15.4			
✓	✓	✓	✓	✓	✓	15.5			
✓	✓	✓	✓	✓	✓	15.6			
✓	✓	✓	✓	✓	✓	15.7			
✓	✓	✓	✓	✓	✓	15.8			

15.1 Government Influence on Business

As explained in Chapter 1, the Government has considerable influence over the running of business. It does this in three main ways:

1. Economic policy such as public spending, taxation and changes in interest rates.
2. Assisting business through advice and financial aid.
3. Regulating business activity through consumer, employment and competition laws.

15.2 Economic Policy

The Government spends about 40 per cent of the national income, amounting to £185 billion in 1988–89.

(i) Income tax

Income tax is paid upon wages and other income. In 1988–89 the basic rate was 25%, with a rate of 40% for higher earners.

(ii) National insurance

National insurance is paid by workers and their employers as a proportion of their wages.

(iii) Value added tax

Value added tax (VAT) is the major spending tax in Britain. Certain goods and services such as food, housing and electricity are exempt from VAT.

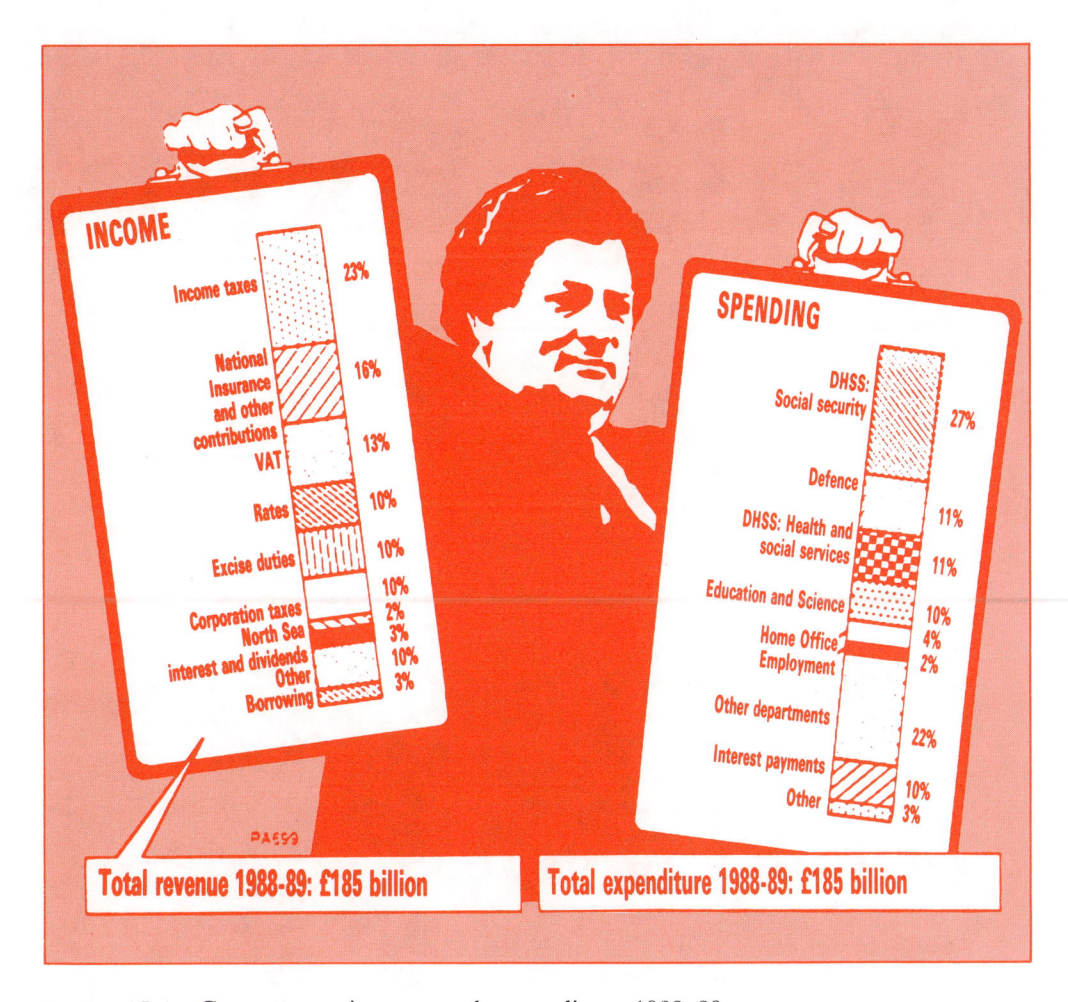

Figure 15.1 Government income and expenditure 1988–89

(iv) Rates

Rates are paid upon property such as housing and business premises. In the early 1990s they are due to be replaced by the *community charge*, better known as the *poll tax*.

(v) Excise duties

Excise duties are paid upon selected goods and services such as alcohol and tobacco.

(vi) Corporation tax

Corporation tax is paid by firms as a percentage of their profits.

(b) How Tax and Government Spending Affect Businesses

Changes in taxes and Government spending can have significant effects upon the running of a business. Figure 15.2 shows the major changes in the 1988 Budget.

Figure 15.2 1988 Budget

15.3 Government Assistance to Business

(a) Advice

Firms can obtain advice from several Government Departments. The most important is the Department of Trade and Industry, whose *Enterprise Initiative*, announced in 1988, pays part of the cost of advice and consultancy for marketing, design, quality control, manufacturing technology, business planning and financial and information systems.

what are BUSINESS MONITORS?

Business Monitors are designed especially for businesses. They provide statistics on manufacturing, energy, mining, service and distributive industries, compiled by the government's Business Statistics Office (BSO). The BSO regularly questions thousands of UK businesses on their output and performance. Some 400,000 inquiry forms are sent out each year, and the statistics are collated and presented by expert government statisticians using accepted statistical techniques.

Variously published at monthly, quarterly or yearly intervals, **Business Monitors** are the primary — and often the only — source of the information they contain. They tell you what you need to know — and what you ought to know.

how can BUSINESS MONITORS? help you?

Business Monitors can help you to plan and organise your business efficiently and effectively. They are a valuable package of statistics both for those starting up in business and for established companies. They can help you to

Monitor business trends — not only in your own industry, but also in your suppliers' and customers' industries

Identify successful products — by following the performance of different products to determine where sales are increasing

Assess your efficiency — by comparing your performance with that of your industry as a whole

Identify new markets — by determining which product sales are on the increase and what new retail outlets are opening

Pinpoint seasonal factors in your business — by studying the trends of monthly and quarterly surveys

Market your products — by reference to a list of manufacturers' names and addresses

Figure 15.3 Government information for firms

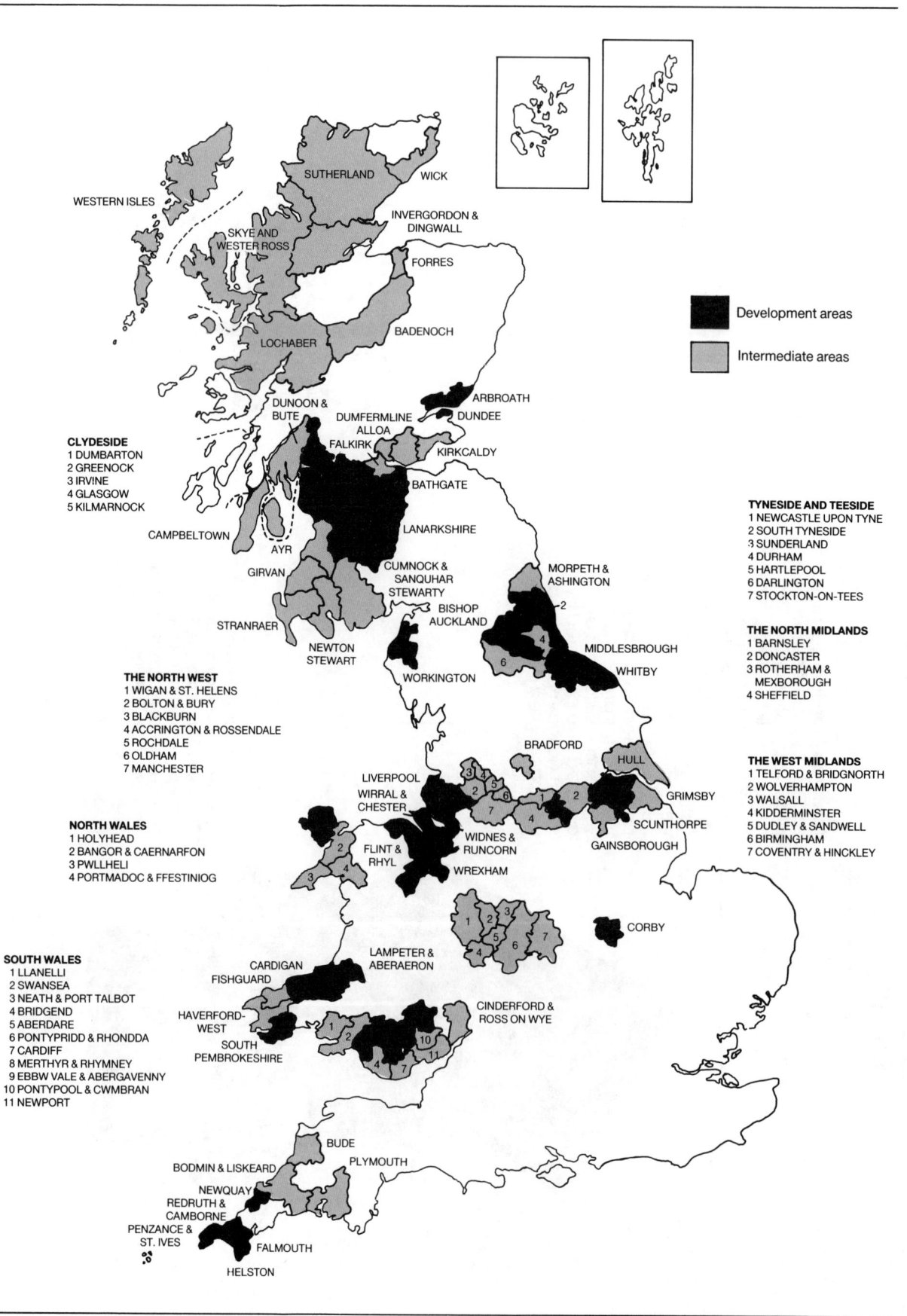

Figure 15.4 Assisted areas

(b) Information

The Government publishes vast amounts of information for firms (see Figure 15.3).

(c) Regional Assistance

Firms creating jobs in the assisted areas can obtain grants and tax reliefs.

(d) Help for Small Firms

The *Small Firms Service* provides free information and advice to new and expanding small businesses.

The *Business Expansion Scheme* gives tax relief to people investing in small businesses.

The *Loan Guarantee Scheme* guarantees bank loans to small firms.

The *Enterprise Allowance Scheme* pays unemployed people an allowance to set up in business.

Local Enterprise Agencies have been established for certain areas to advise local firms.

(e) Export Aid

The Department of Trade and Industry provides assistance for exporters, mainly through the *British Overseas Trade Board* (BOTB). This assistance includes:

- Information and advice on foreign markets.
- Introductions to business contacts and distributing agents.
- Specialist library of statistics and intelligence.
- Export market research.
- Technical advice about foreign standards.
- Advice on preparing documents.
- Trade missions and special promotions in other countries.

The Export Credits Guarantee Department (ECGD), a Government Department, arranges insurance for exporters against the risk of not being paid by their customers for reasons such as:

- Bankruptcy or refusal to pay.
- Failure to pay within six months.
- Wars or political difficulties preventing trade.
- A foreign Government preventing payments abroad, e.g. through exchange controls.
- Cancellation of orders.

(f) Training

Firms can obtain financial assistance and advice for training their workers (see Chapter 12).

15.4 Regulation of Business

Many laws affect the activities of businesses, particularly in three areas:

1. Consumer law.
2. Employment law.
3. Competition law.

(a) Consumer Law

(i) Sale of Goods Act 1979

This replaced and combined the Sale of Goods Act 1893 and the Supply of Goods (Implied Terms) Act 1973. All goods must be:

- *'Of merchantable quality'*, i.e. capable of doing what would be expected in normal use, and lasting for a reasonable length of time.
- *'As described'*, i.e. they must be what they are said to be. A 'solid gold' ring must not be made of some other metal.
- *'Fit for the purpose'*. If a seller gives incorrect advice, he or she can be held responsible, e.g. wallpaper described as suitable for a bathroom should be resistant to water.

The provisions about 'implied terms' make it illegal for a seller to attempt to take away the consumer's legal rights. Before they were made illegal some sellers tried to include *exclusion clauses* or notices such as 'no refunds' or 'no guarantee'. If the buyer is given extra rights such as 'your money back if not satisfied' the seller must point out that 'statutory rights are not affected'.

(ii) Unfair Contract Terms Act 1977

Sellers of services cannot use exclusion clauses to take away customers' statutory rights. For example, a launderette notice saying 'we accept no responsibility for damage however caused' would be illegal.

(iii) Supply of Goods and Services Act

This applies to services such as meals out and home improvements. The supplier must provide a reasonable standard of work within a reasonable time and at a reasonable price (assuming that the time and price are not agreed in advance).

(iv) Trade Descriptions Act 1968

It is a criminal offence to tell lies about a good or service such as the size, weight, materials and methods used.

(v) Unsolicited Goods and Services Act 1971

Consumers who are sent goods that they have not requested can give the sender notice to collect the goods, and keep them if they are not collected within 30 days. If the consumer does not inform the company, they become his or her property if the sender does not collect them within six months.

(vi) The Weights and Measures Act 1979

This is one of a series of Weights and Measures Acts which make it an offence to give 'short weight' or 'short measure', even by accident. Equipment such as scales or petrol pumps must also be tested and approved by the Trading Standards Department.

(vii) Consumer Protection Act 1987

This gives the Government the power to prevent the sale of unsafe goods and make rules about products. Manufacturers are also responsible for damage or injury caused by defective products (not including food) unless they can prove that the danger could not be foreseen.

(viii) Consumer Credit Act 1974

A business which offers credit to customers must be registered as a licensed credit broker. The annual percentage rate of interest (APR) must be shown on all advertisements and documents. The provider of credit is also jointly responsible with the supplier for faulty goods or services for transactions between £50 and £30 000 (with some exceptions).

(ix) Food and Drugs Act

This sets rules about the sale and service of food in shops and catering premises.

(x) Fair Trading Act 1973

This established the Office of Fair Trading (OFT), a government agency, to protect consumers against unfair practices by firms. The OFT's functions include:

- Publishing leaflets to help people to know their rights.
- Encouraging trade organisations to prepare voluntary *codes of practice* for dealing with customers.
- Suggesting new consumer laws and regulations.
- Prosecuting traders who break the law.
- Issuing licences under the Consumer Credit Act.
- Recommending to the Monopolies and Mergers Commission that certain firms or markets should be investigated.

Most consumer legislation is enforced by local councils, particularly by the *Trading Standards Department* or *Consumer Protection Department* and the *Environmental Health Department*.

The Trading Standards Department enforces laws such as the Weights and Measures Act. Trading standards officers carry out tests and surveys to check that traders are giving full weight and full measure, investigate complaints from the public and traders and often run Consumer Advice Centres.

Environmental Health Departments' responsibilities include checking that food is sold and served in clean and hygienic conditions. They inspect shops, cafes and restaurants and prosecute traders who break food regulations.

(b) Employment Law

(i) Health and Safety Act 1974

Employers must take all reasonable care to ensure the safety of their employees. Employees also have a duty to cooperate with the employer to ensure the safety of all workers. Employers with five or more staff must have a written statement of their health and safety policy.

(ii) Employment Protection Act 1978

This gives employees rights such as compensation for unfair dismissal and the entitlement to return to their jobs after having a baby.

(iii) Sex Discrimination Acts 1975, 1986

These acts make it illegal to discriminate against a person because of his or her sex, e.g. advertising a job as 'for women only'. Certain exceptions are allowed.

(iv) Equal Pay Act 1970

Women must not be paid a lower rate than men employed in the same job or work of 'equivalent value' where all employees are of one sex. For example, a canteen supervisor in a shipyard convinced a court that her work was as skilled as that of engineering foremen who received higher wages.

(v) Race Relations Act 1976

It is illegal to discriminate against a person because of their race, e.g. by refusing to employ Asian or Irish workers.

(c) Competition Law

The Government tries to ensure competition between firms by various means, including:

1. Investigating mergers which might restrict competition. This is recommended by the Office of Fair Trading (see above). The investigation is carried out by the Monopolies and Mergers Commisssion, which is appointed by the Secretary of State for Trade and Industry.

2. Preventing 'unfair practices' such as price-fixing between firms, which restrict competition.
3. Regulating privatised firms through regulatory agencies such as Oftel and Ofgas, which supervise the telecommunications and gas industries.

15.5　Local Government

Figure 15.5 Local authority income and spending

Figure 15.6 A council department's services

Local councils in Britain were until recently organised in a 'two-tier' system, with county and district councils (London and Scotland had slightly different structures, but still used a two-tier scheme).

In Greater London and the former *metropolitan counties* – Greater Manchester, Merseyside, Tyne and Wear, West Midlands, South Yorkshire and West Yorkshire – the county councils have been abolished. In these areas the district councils are the main authority, but in some cases there are joint county-wide authorities for services such as police, fire brigade and bus travel.

Local authorities are also responsible for implementing many laws which affect business, such as consumer legislation (see above). Figure 15.6 shows how one council department affects local businesses.

15.6 Coursework Assignment

How can health and safety be improved in an organisation?

Choose an organisation where you can obtain the co-operation of the owner or manager. Decide whether you want to investigate health and safety in general, or a particular aspect such as fire precautions, machinery and equipment or movement around the building.

Most large organisations have a person responsible for health and safety. Sometimes this person will be a professional health and safety officer, e.g. in large firms. In other cases he or she will have another job but be allowed a certain amount of time for safety duties.

Before starting, read up on the aspect of health and safety you are going to study. You don't need to be a technical expert, but you should have a good general knowledge of the main potential hazards.

The basic method of obtaining information is to survey the building. Try to obtain a map or draw your own. Make a few copies.

Using your blank maps, show any potential danger points. These might include swinging doors or places where people and vehicles might meet. Give details of filing cabinets or machinery.

Describe any problems and suggest possible cures such as moving equipment or doors or putting up warning notices in appropriate places. If possible, find out the likely cost of improvements.

15.7 Worked Example

John Parkes owns a small building firm which combines building of new houses with repairs and home improvements. One of his regular customers is a landlord who rents out houses and flats. The company runs several lorries and vans, and the senior managers have company cars.

Look at the changes announced in the 1988 Budget (Figure 15.2).

(a) Choose and explain **two** changes which might benefit John's business. (4)

(b) Choose and explain **two** changes which could be bad for the business. (4)

Answer

(a) Corporation tax reduced, so company will keep more of its profits.
    Lower income tax – people have more to spend upon housing. (2 each)
(b) e.g. Mortgage changes making it more expensive to buy housing.
    Fuel and company car taxes increased – vehicles more expensive to run.
(2 each)

15.8 Self-Test Questions

Question 1

Study the following extract from a local paper.

LOCAL BUSINESS VISITED BY HEALTH AND SAFETY INSPECTOR

Dangerous chemicals found near wall next to school yard. Firm instructed to put them in a fireproof container.

"It's disgusting – such things shouldn't be allowed" – **local resident.**

"We are very concerned for our members' welfare" – **union representative.**

"There is no danger to the public now" – **fire officer.**

"The visit was a complete surprise to us – someone must have rung the HSE. The cost of building a fireproof container could have serious effects on our plans for the future." – **Management.**

(a) How would the following people react to this news:
  (i) a couple trying to sell their nearby house. (4)
  (ii) a local fire protection services firm. (4)
  (iii) the Local Authority. (4)
(b) What does the 'HSE' do? (4)
(c) What kind of action could the unions consider if the firm does not improve its safety standards? (6)
(d) Write down the ways in which the firm could improve its public image – which has been damaged by this incident. (10)
(e) What did the management mean when it spoke about 'The cost of building a fireproof container could have serious effects on our plans for the future'? (10)

(SEG)

ADVERTISEMENT A (22 MARCH 1988)

BUY A SONAR 20" TELEVISION
WITH REMOTE CONTROL
for superb viewing

ONLY £200 CASH

OR
£20 DEPOSIT AND
12 MONTHLY PAYMENTS OF £17
APR 14%
VISION-ON LTD
2 CROOK ST
BELFAST

ADVERTISEMENT B (29 MARCH 1988)

BUY A SONAR 20" TELEVISION
WITH REMOTE CONTROL
THE BEST TV IN BRITAIN

ONLY £200 CASH

REDUCED FROM £250!!!!!
EASY CREDIT TERMS AVAILABLE
NO DEPOSIT —
12 MONTHLY PAYMENTS OF £20
VISION-ON LTD
2 CROOK ST
BELFAST

Question 2

(a) (i) Which two laws are being broken by advertisement B? (2)
    (ii) How has each law been broken? (4)

Mrs Kerr bought one of the above TV sets. When it was delivered she found the remote control would not work. When she contacted the shop she was told to contact the manufacturer.

(b) Which consumer law has the shop broken? (2)
(c) (i) Give the names of **two** agencies which could help Mrs Kerr with this problem. (2)
    (ii) In what way could each help? (4)
(d) Why should complaints about faulty goods be made to the shop rather than to the manufacturer? (2)
(e) What role does the Office of Fair Trading play which may help to avoid these situations? (4)

(NISEC)

16
Aiding and Controlling Business

SEG	LEAG	NISEAC	WJEC	NEAB	MEG	Topic	Date attempted	Date completed	Self Assessment
✓	✓	✓	✓	✓	✓	16.1			
✓	✓	✓	✓	✓	✓	16.2			
✓	✓	✓	✓	✓	✓	16.3			
✓	✓	✓	✓	✓	✓	16.4			
✓	✓	✓	✓	✓	✓	16.5			
✓	✓	✓	✓	✓	✓	16.6			
✓	✓	✓	✓	✓	✓	16.7			
✓	✓	✓	✓	✓	✓	16.8			
✓	✓	✓	✓	✓	✓	16.9			

As well as the Government, businesses can obtain advice and assistance from many private sources. Private organisations also have influence and control over business activity.

16.1 Banking

Banks provide many services for firms. These include the following.

(a) Current Accounts

Current accounts are for making and receiving payments from other accounts.

(b) Deposit Accounts

Deposit accounts are for spare cash which can earn interest.

(c) Standing Orders

Standing orders are regular fixed payments. A business such as a magazine publisher may ask its subscribers to pay by standing order.

(d) Direct Debits

Direct debits allow a firm to claim payment direct from a customer's bank. The amount may vary from time to time. For example, a customer may arrange a direct debit for a telephone company. When the bill becomes due the telephone company will ask the customer's bank for the amount. The direct debit system is most suitable for payments such as those for gas and insurance, where the amount payable cannot be known in advance, or to save the bother of changing standing orders every year.

(e) Advice and Assistance

Advice and assistance from the banks' specialists may cover matters such as taxation, finance and business. A bank may also provide a trade reference for a customer seeking to obtain supplies on credit.

(f) Safeguarding of Valuables

Safeguarding of valuables such as important documents is often done by banks. Businesses such as shops, which are largely paid in cash, can make use of *night safes* which are secure metal boxes set into the wall of the bank. Money can be deposited in a night-safe after banking hours have finished.

(g) International Payments

The risk of non-payment for exports is much higher than for domestic trade. There are two special methods of payment for international transactions.

Bills of Exchange (see Figure 16.1) are drawn up by the exporter and sent to the importer for agreement. Once a bill is signed by the importer it is a legally-binding agreement to pay. A bill of exchange may be guaranteed by a bank.

The *documentary credit* system uses banks in the countries of the exporter and importer to make and receive payments on their behalf. The importer's bank guarantees payment when the goods are received.

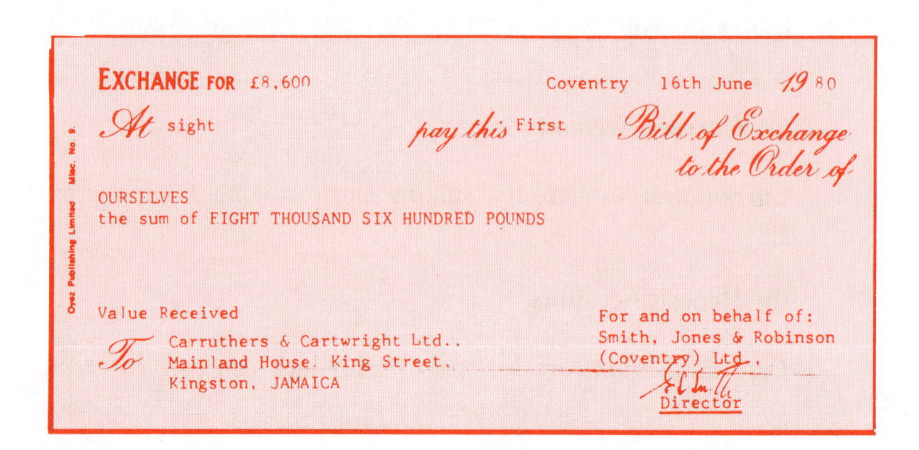

Figure 16.1 Bill of exchange

(h) Loans

Loans of various types are available. These are discussed in Chapter 6.

16.2 Insurance

Without adequate insurance many business activities would be too risky to undertake, because firms could not afford the loss caused by disasters such as fires or theft. Some of the major types of insurance cover and the risks that they cover are as follows.

(a) Employers' Liability

Accidents or illnesses arising out of their employees' work are covered by employers' liability.

(b) Public Liability

Claims such as those from explosions or airline accidents come under this heading.

(c) Product Liability

A firm's activities or products causing injury or illness, such as a drug causing deformities in babies, are covered under this heading.

(d) Buildings

Both the building and contents such as furniture and equipment should be insured.

(e) Money

It is possible to insure against the theft of cash, cheques and other valuables.

(f) Goods in Transit

Theft or damage to goods while being transported can be covered under this heading.

(g) Credit

It is possible to insure against creditors who do not pay their bills.

(h) Fidelity Guarantee

Dishonesty by employees, such as theft or fraud by workers responsible for handling money or goods, can be covered under this heading.

(i) Legal Expenses

It is possible to insure against legal expenses incurred in disputes about issues such as contracts or employment.

(j) Business Interruption

A business may have to stop or reduce trading temporarily because of a fire or other accident. This is also called *consequential loss* insurance.

16.3 Transport

(a) Importance of Transport

Good transport links are vital for businesses, which rely upon them to move goods and provide mobility for workers and customers.
   Choosing a method of transport involves considering several factors.

(i) Type of goods

All goods (including people travelling to work or business) have different characteristics which affect the type of transport chosen. For example goods may need refrigeration or special handling for safety (e.g. chemicals, nuclear waste, food).

(ii) Speed

Faster forms of transport such as air are often more expensive. A business will have to decide whether the cost is justified. Fast transport may be needed for workers, perishable products such as fruit and newspapers or urgent documents or machinery spares.

(iii) Convenience

Most forms of transport apart from road transport involve people or goods being switched from one type of transport to another. They may also work to a fixed timetable. Road travel is often the most convenient and flexible method, but businesses often deliberately locate close to another form of transport, e.g. offices may be near railway stations, warehouses near airports.

(iv) Cost

A business will usually try to keep transport costs as low as possible.

(v) Size and weight

Bulky low-value goods such as coal or bricks will usually be sent by the cheapest form of transport. For a valuable low-bulk item such as diamonds the cost of transport would be a small fraction of the price, and expensive transport such as air-freight might be used.

(b) Methods of Transport

(i) Road

Road transport is by far the most commonly-used form of transport in Britain. There are over 21 million vehicles in Britain. It is usually faster than other forms of transport over distances up to 200 miles. It is flexible, with door-to-door delivery and no need for a fixed timetable. It is the only form of transport which can reach all destinations in the United Kingdom.

Road transport does have some disadvantages, however. It is often slower and more expensive than rail for distances over 200 miles, especially where there are no motorways. There is a limit to the weight of load which can be carried, and road traffic causes congestion and pollution.

(ii) Rail

Rail transport has declined in recent years, mainly because of the increase in the number of road vehicles. However, it is still very important to many businesses and areas, such as south-east England.

Rail transport is usually quicker than road for distances over 200 miles, particularly on electrified mainline services. Bulky goods such as coal can be transported cheaply by rail.

Rail travel is usually slower over short distances, and does not reach many parts of Britain, especially in Scotland. It is less convenient than road transport, because people and goods have to transfer to and from trains. The fixed timetable may also be inconvenient.

(iii) Sea

Most international freight, and over one-third of passengers, are transported by sea. Sea transport is slower than air, its main competitor, but is much cheaper for goods and can carry heavier loads. Some goods, such as oil, are transported in specially-designed ships.

(iv) Inland waterways

Since the early 1800s the canal system has declined steadily because of competition from rail and road transport. It now accounts for only one-thousandth of goods traffic, but is still economic for bulky cargo such as coal.

(v) Air

Air travel has expanded rapidly during the 1980s, especially for passenger traffic. It is the quickest form of transport for international or long cross-country journeys. However, it is also expensive, particularly for bulky goods. It relies heavily upon other forms of transport, and often suffers from delays because of bad weather, technical problems and strikes.

(vi) Pipelines

These are used for goods such as oil and gas. Pipelines are very expensive to build and are inflexible because they are immobile.

(vii) Containerisation

Containers are large metal boxes built to standard sizes to fit different lorries, trains, ships and planes. The container is packed and sealed by the sender. It can then be transferred unopened from one form of transport to another.

Using containers cuts out much of the handling of goods, reducing the danger of theft and breakage. Because containers are made in standard sizes, it is easy to plan storage. The *Transport Internationale Routier* (TIR) system makes it possible to send sealed containers through other countries unopened, cutting out customs delays.

16.4 Aid for Exporters

There are many private-sector organisations which provide services to exporters. Some of these services are similar to those provided by the Government. Most commercial banks have export departments to provide advice and finance. Merchant banks offer similar specialised services, and some discount or accept bills of exchange.

Many industries have trade associations which provide services to their members. Local Chambers of Commerce and the Confederation of British Industry also assist potential exporters.

16.5 Consumer Organisations

(a) Citizens' Advice Bureau (CAB)

The CAB is an independent organisation which receives some grants from the Government, but relies on unpaid volunteers for much of its work. It has offices in most towns which help with many types of consumer problems.

(b) Consumers' Association

The Consumers' Association campaigns for consumers. It is most famous for *Which?* magazine, which tests and surveys goods and services. The contents of a typical issue are shown in Figure 16.2.

(c) Nationalised Industry Consumer Councils

Each of the nationalised industries has a user's council which represents the interests of consumers. For example, the Post Office Users' National Council has investigated the speed of delivery of letters and parcels.

(d) British Standards Institute (BSI)

The British Standards Institute sets standards for a massive range of goods and services. It is best known for its 'Kitemark' and other safety markings, which show that a good conforms to British Standards. Figure 16.3 shows how British Standards apply to the construction industry.

Figure 16.2 A typical issue of *Which?*

(e) National Consumer Council

The National Consumer Council is appointed by the Government to campaign on behalf of consumers. It regularly publishes reports on matters of consumer interest such as housing problems, hospital waiting lists and pension arrangements.

(f) The Advertising Standards Authority (ASA)

The Advertising Standards Authority (ASA) is an independent body financed by the advertising industry. It is responsible for supervising almost all advertising in the United Kingdom (except for television).

The ASA's slogan is that all advertising must be 'legal, decent, honest and truthful'. Its 'British Code of Advertising Practice' sets rules for all advertisers to follow (see Figure 16.4).

The ASA receives thousands of complaints about advertisements every year. If an advertisement breaks its rules, the ASA will ask the advertiser to change or discontinue it.

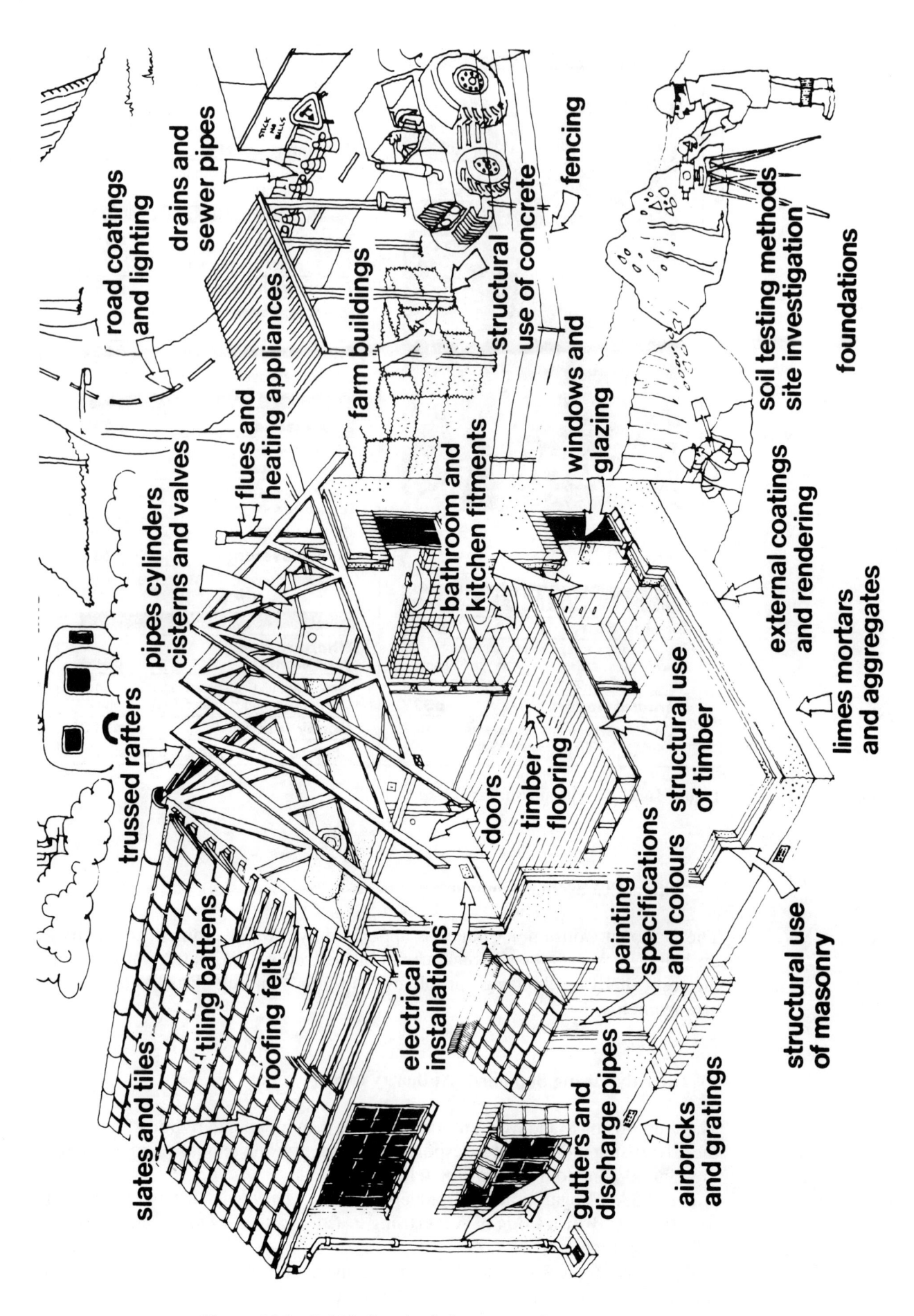

Figure 16.3 British Standards in construction

188

Figure 16.4 Advertising Standards Authority

(g) The Independent Broadcasting Authority (IBA)

The IBA is responsible for controlling television advertising. All TV adverts must be approved before they can be broadcast. About one-third are rejected or changed.

The conditions for television advertising are very similar to those set by the Advertising Standards Authority (see above) but there are some extra rules. Some products, such as cigarettes, cannot be advertised, while others can only be advertised late at night.

16.6 Pressure Groups

Pressure groups are organisations which seek to influence the decisions of business and Government. Many are large formal organisations such as the Consumers' Association or Greenpeace. However, a group of local residents campaigning about noise or nuisance from a factory is also a pressure group.

Pressure groups can have a large influence upon the activities of firms. In recent years, for example, environmental pressure groups have caused companies to change their policies upon matters such as the use of chlorofluorocarbons (CFCs) in aerosols, supplying unleaded petrol and controlling exhaust fumes from cars.

16.7 Coursework Assignment

A study of a local shopping centre

The assignment below is suggested as a range of tasks for a group of students, each of whom might investigate one or two of the tasks listed.

From the resource material available from a study of a local shopping centre, present a report on the different types of business ownership found at the centre and relate the services offered to the use made by the public of the centre.

Suggested approaches to this task are as follows:

1. Draw a map to illustrate the layout of the shopping centre.
2. Identify different types of retail outlet, such as sole trader, multiple/specialist chain store, supermarket, and explain the organisation of each.
3. Explain the services offered by businesses at the centre, such as banks, estate agents, solicitors, travel agents.
4. Decide whether the centre meets the needs of the users and make recommendations if you think improvements are needed.
5. State the basic facts which should be taken into account before siting a shopping centre.
6. Consider the role of local government in the establishment and running of such a shopping centre.
7. Outline the consumer protection offered to the shoppers.
8. State the different ways by which the shoppers could pay for their purchases.
9. Indicate the use made of modern technology by the different businesses at the shopping centre.

(SEG Specimen)

16.8 Worked Example

A brick manufacturer wishes to assess road and rail transport as a means of delivering loads of bricks to customers nationwide. Use the graph and your own knowledge to answer the questions raised by the manufacturer.

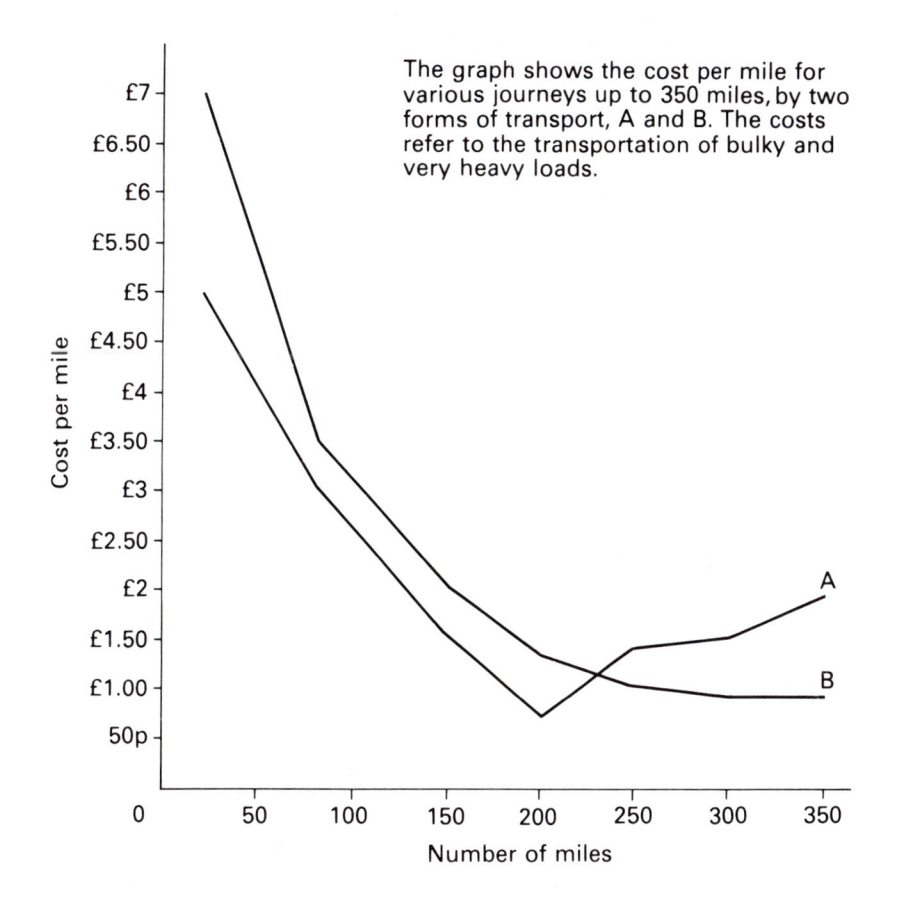

The graph shows the cost per mile for various journeys up to 350 miles, by two forms of transport, A and B. The costs refer to the transportation of bulky and very heavy loads.

(a) (i) Which is the cheaper method of transport for a 100 mile journey, A or B? (1)
    (ii) Which is the cheaper method of transport for journeys over 250 miles, A or B? (1)
    (iii) At what distance does it cost the same by A and B? (1)
(b) What is the difference in *total* cost between A and B for a journey of 200 miles? (2)
(c) Identify the form of transport called A and state your reasons. (3)
(d) Identify the form of transport called B and state your reasons. (3)

Answers

(a) (i) Road (1)
    (ii) Rail (1)
    (iii) 230 miles (1)
(b) Rail costs – £260; road costs – £140; difference = £120 (2)
(c) Road. More expensive over long distances especially for heavy, bulky loads. (3)
(d) Rail. Relatively high fixed costs; cheaper to move long distance loads because costs spread over distance. (2)

(LEAG)

16.9 Self-Test Questions

Question 1

Mr Hunter owns a small electrical goods shop which has a large store at the rear. Business is booming and he decides to expand into larger items such as freezers. Mr Hunter now needs to provide a delivery service for the larger items. He decides upon a suitable van and employs an assistant to drive and do general work around the shop.

(a) (i) Name **two** risks that he has to insure against by law. (2)
  (ii) What other types of insurance cover would you advise Mr Hunter to take out? Give reasons. (6)
(b) What uninsurable risks may Mr Hunter have to bear as a businessman? (4)
(c) Explain why it is important to Mr Hunter to have adequate insurance cover. (4)
(d) How might Mr Hunter benefit from consulting an insurance broker about his requirements? (4)

(NISEC)

Question 2

Read the following newspaper article from the *Welsh Daily Press*, and answer the questions.

> **THREE AFFECTED BY CHEMICAL LEAK AT NATCHEM**
>
> The workers at Natchem were affected by a leak of gas yesterday. The employees, two women and one man, were taken to hospital but were soon allowed home. A spokesman for Natchem explained that a valve had not been properly shut and this had caused the leak. He added that there was no danger to the people living nearby although a cloud of yellow gas was seen above the plant at the time. The Board of Directors are to hold an emergency meeting with the Trade Unions to ensure that the accident could never happen again. All Health and Safety measures are to be checked by the Factories Inspectorate.
> Janet Evans who lives on the local housing estate told the newspaper 'Something must be done. This is the second time this has happened in the last year. We are very worried that our health is at risk, and that the land around us is being polluted'.

(a) The Personnel Manager had the task of contacting the relatives of the three injured employees. What other tasks would he or she perform during a normal working day at the chemical plant? (7)
(b) Give **two** examples of health and safety measures that the Factories Inspectorate will be checking apart from looking for leaks. (2)
(c) The valves used in the plant were the only ones made that have the British Standard kite mark stamped on them. Why did the firm buy this make of valve? (3)
(d) What other steps might Janet Evans take to try to stop such a leak happening again? (6)

(WJEC)

17 Coursework Assignments

SEG	LEAG	NISEAC	WJEC	NEAB	MEG	Topic	Date attempted	Date completed	Self Assessment
✓	✓	✓	✓	✓	✓	17.1			
✓	✓	✓	✓	✓	✓	17.2			
✓	✓	✓	✓	✓	✓	17.3			
✓	✓	✓	✓	✓	✓	17.4			
✓	✓	✓	✓	✓	✓	17.5			
✓	✓	✓	✓	✓	✓	17.6			
✓	✓	✓	✓	✓	✓	17.7			
✓	✓	✓	✓	✓	✓	17.8			

17.1 Why do Coursework?

Examination coursework is part of GCSE Business Studies syllabuses for several reasons:

- It allows you to investigate a topic at length.
- The pressure of the exam room is removed.
- It encourages you to work with others.
- Approached properly, it can be great fun and motivate you to produce good work.
- It develops skills such as interpretation of data which are tested in written examination papers.

17.2 Coursework Requirements

All the GCSE syllabuses describe the way in which examination coursework is to be undertaken and marked. Each syllabus has its own requirements about matters such as subject content, number and length of assignments. These are set out in summary form in Figure 17.1.

	LEAG	MEG	NEAB	NICCEA	SEG	WJEC
% of marks	25	30	30	20	30	30
No. of assignments	2	3	1, 2 or 3	1	3	2, 3 or 4
Length/time taken	Normally not more than 800–1000 words each	Not more than 1500 words/ 10 hours work each	Need to be more than 3000 words in total	Not more than 2500 words	Not specified	Total of approximately 30 hours work
Other conditions/ information	From 6 titles set by Examining Group in year of examination	From different areas of syllabus	Can be presented in written, oral or visual form	Can be presented only in written or printed form	From different areas of syllabus	Maximum of 30 hours work

Figure 17.1 Summary of coursework requirements

17.3 How Coursework is Marked

Like the written examinations, GCSE coursework assignments are marked according to the coursework mark schemes given in the syllabus. To get good marks, your assignment must show that you can use the skills specified in the scheme for your syllabus.

This point can be illustrated by looking at the mark scheme for the MEG Business Studies syllabus (shown in Figure 17.2). This shows how the marks for coursework are awarded.

OBJECTIVE	MARKS
1. An understanding of the aim is displayed together with an understanding of the facts, principles, terms, techniques or ideas central to that part of the syllabus to which it relates and appropriate to the particular assignment.	10
2. Information chosen is appropriate for use in the assignment.	5
3. Information is presented in an accurate, logical and effective manner.	4
4. Data has been analysed involving the interpretation of information in narrative, numerical or graphical form using skills and techniques developed within the course.	5
5. Main findings have been presented, which involve reasoned explanation, developed arguments, valid inferences, solutions and conclusions as appropriate.	6

Figure 17.2 MEG coursework mark scheme (1990)

Each syllabus has a different mark scheme, but the skills that examiners are looking for are similar in all GCSE Business Studies syllabuses. You will need to look at the scheme for your particular syllabus. It may be difficult to follow, so you might have to ask your teacher to explain some points.

It is worth considering the MEG scheme in more detail to see exactly what is expected of you. It looks complicated, but can be explained simply. Some of the objectives overlap, and can be considered together.

> *1. An understanding of the aim is displayed together with an understanding of the facts, principles, terms, techniques or ideas central to that part of the syllabus to which it relates and appropriate to the particular assignment.*
> *(10)*

State the purpose of your assignment, e.g. to find the best location for a shop, to investigate the health and safety procedures in an organisation etc. As explained in Section 17.5 below, it is best to phrase your assignment title as a question or a hypothesis.

These marks are for using and applying the ideas that you have learned during your course. Use business terms such as 'costs', 'productivity', 'break-even' and 'turnover' where they are relevant. As explained in Section 17.6 below, this will be much easier if you consider the appropriate concepts *before* you start collecting information.

2. Information chosen is appropriate for use in the assignment (5)
3. Information is presented in an accurate, logical and effective manner. (4)

Marks are given for including *relevant* information and explaining what it shows and why it is useful in relation to the aim of the assignment. Don't 'pad' your assignment with irrelevant material or jumble your data together in a confusing manner.

4. Data has been analysed involving the interpretation of information in narrative, numerical or graphical form using skills and techniques developed within the course. (5)
5. Main findings have been presented, which involve reasoned explanation, developed arguments, valid inferences, solutions and conclusions as appropriate. (6)

Many students lose marks because they concentrate on collecting and presenting their information, but do not relate it to the aim of the assignment. At least 20 per cent of the marks will be given for stating and explaining your conclusions or recommendations (which should be backed up by the data you have collected).

17.4 Getting Ideas for Coursework

Your coursework assignments may be set by the Examining Group or your teacher. However, if you do have some choice, there are several ways of generating ideas for coursework.

(a) Notes and Books

Go through your notes and any books you have used or can find in the library. Make a list of any topics that you have found interesting, and try to form at least one question or hypothesis for each one.

Don't limit yourself to the work you have done in Business Studies. You may have been interested in topics in another subject which could be investigated from a business point of view. An example which came from a Home Economics course is given in Figure 17.3. If you do choose an idea from another subject, however, make sure it is relevant to Business Studies.

Lucy and Caroline were interested in food and were very concerned about a healthy diet. They were annoyed that 'low-fat' and 'sugar-free' products were more expensive than the 'standard' versions of similar food and drink. They decided to investigate the reasons for this and settled upon the title:
Why does 'healthy' food and drink cost more than the 'standard' product?

Figure 17.3 'Health food' assignment

(b) Interests and Hobbies

Most people have a particular interest in a sport or hobby. In pursuing this interest they will usually buy goods and services from firms or other organisations. You could study a firm or industry which is involved with your interest, as long as you remember that you are undertaking a Business Studies assignment. For example, you may be fascinated by different computer operating systems, but the examiner will only be interested in the details of MS/DOS and CPM if there is some commercial relevance to the difference.

(c) Newspapers and Magazines

You may be able to find ideas from newspapers and magazines. If you find an article that interests you, you could try to find out more about the particular issue. If it is controversial there will be plenty of people and organisations with something to say about it. Local newspapers are usually a good source. Figure 17.4 shows headlines from an evening paper with ideas for investigation.

DRIVE THE CAR OF YOUR DREAMS AND YOU COULD— WIN £500

▲ How do car dealers attract customers?

Changes for drinks factory

◄ How will a soft-drinks factory be affected by a take-over?

How can local businesses encourage trade in the town? ►

Bright image on the agenda

Figure 17.4 Ideas from a newspaper article.

(d) Competitions

Every year many competitions are organised for school and college students which involve commercial topics such as share prices, local businesses and market research. Some of these may be suitable as coursework for GCSE Business Studies. Entering a competition can provide a 'fun' element to preparing for an examination.

Before entering a competition, however, check that

- The competition entry can be used or adapted for your examination assignment.
- The closing date for the competition allows enough time to complete your entry.

(e) Mini-enterprises

Many students are involved in running 'mini-companies', e.g. under the Young Enterprise scheme. This type of activity could be used as the basis for an assignment if it is carefully planned. You could focus upon a particular theme such as:

- How the product was chosen.
- The methods of market research used.
- Costing and pricing.
- The organisation of production.

(f) Work Experience

You may have a part-time job or the chance of a placement on a work experience scheme. You could use this opportunity to investigate an issue at your place of work such as health and safety or the marketing of the firm's products.

(g) Books on Coursework

Several books on coursework have been published. They often contain good ideas for assignments, but make sure these are suitable for your examination.

17.5 Choosing a Title

Your assignment should be regarded as an *investigation* into a business problem or issue. As can be seen from the example given above, a large proportion of the marks awarded are for stating the aim of the assignment, collecting relevant data and drawing conclusions which are directly related to the aim of the information. If your assignment does not have a specific aim, you will lose about one-third of the marks before you even start.

The best way of avoiding this problem is to phrase your assignment aim as either a *question* or a *hypothesis*.

An example of a *question* that might be investigated is

'What is the fastest-growing industry in this area?'

If your title is a question you will need to answer it. This example would involve looking at what is meant by 'fastest-growing' – e.g. does it mean growth of output, employment, profit etc? You would then need to look for information to answer the question.

A *hypothesis* is a statement about an issue which can be tested by collecting and using information. An example of a hypothesis which might be investigated is

'Private contractors are more efficient than local authorities at providing refuse collection services.'

If you decided to test this hypothesis you would need to consider what is meant by 'efficient' – does it mean cheap, good quality of service, use of labour etc? You could obtain information and opinions from a variety of sources such as trade unions, firms, local councillors and the public.

Examples of possible titles are given in each chapter.

17.6 What Information is Needed?

In deciding on the data you wish to collect, the most crucial thing to remember is that it should be *relevant* to your title. The most common problem of examination coursework in Business Studies is that too many assignments are simply 'scrapbooks' of mostly irrelevant information.

For example, it is fairly easy to collect lots of material about a large company such as Tesco or ICI. Many students simply rewrite or 'cut and paste' the glossy brochures sent out by these companies, without explaining why they are including this material or why it is relevant to their assignment.

This type of work gains very low marks. Unless a piece of information is directly relevant to the aim of the assignment, it should not be included. One way of ensuring that data is relevant is to always make a point of explaining why it is included, e.g.

'The graph shows that between 1960 and 1990 blodgett imports rose from 5 per cent of total UK sales to 60 per cent. This is one of the reasons for the fall in employment in the blodgett industry'.

Before deciding to look for or include any piece of information in your assignment, ask yourself questions such as:

- Why is this relevant to my assignment?
- What does it prove?
- Is there any connection between this piece of data and other information I have collected?
- Am I including it just because it looks pretty or helps to make the assignment look bigger?

Irrelevant information is regarded by examiners as 'padding' and does not gain marks. If you answer the questions honestly you will produce a better assignment and save yourself a lot of wasted time. You will have to learn to be ruthless in discarding data which does not further the aim of your assignment, however interesting or pretty it may look.

One way of sorting out what information is needed is to ask questions about the subject matter of the assignment. You can then decide which questions need to be answered, and work out how to go about it. For example, the girls who investigated the pricing of 'health foods' (see Figure 17.3) prepared a table like that shown below:

Why does 'healthy' food and drink cost more than the 'standard' product?

QUESTION	ACTION
What is meant by 'healthy'?	Choose ten pairs of products e.g. low-calorie and ordinary orange juice, white and wholemeal bread. Compare products of similar size, weight, volume etc. e.g. 28oz loaf.
Is 'healthy' food and drink more expensive?	Check prices in local shops.
Does 'healthy' food and drink cost more to produce? If so, why e.g. economies of scale with 'standard' products, cost of ingredients?	Write to food manufacturers.
Do manufacturers have a higher mark-up on 'healthy' products?	Write to food manufacturers.
Do retailers have a higher mark-up on 'healthy' products? Is so why, e.g. consumers prepared to pay more, higher storage costs, shorter shelf life?	Write to retailers. Check wholesale prices. Questionnaire for consumers.

By spending some time thinking about what information was needed *before* starting their assignment, Lucy and Caroline gave themselves a sound structure for collecting the information and writing the assignment. They kept wasted time and irrelevant information to the minimum.

17.7 Sources of Information

There are several different methods of collecting information. You should not attempt to use them all – be selective and choose the most appropriate.

(a) Questionnaires

These should only be used where strictly necessary, as they are time-consuming and the answers given are often inaccurate (for example Government surveys show that people admit to smoking only half the amount of tobacco that they actually smoke).

If questionnaires are used you should:

- Ensure that all the questions provide necessary information.
- Stick to a small number of questions.
- Avoid questions which are too personal, e.g. asking strangers their age or income.
- Be polite.
- Not pester people who are obviously too busy to answer your questions.
- Not try to 'lead' people, e.g. 'the wages for nurses are too low, aren't they?'
- Choose a suitable 'sample', e.g. if enquiring about tastes in food include people of different ages and sexes.
- Be wary of 'postal' surveys or giving people questionnaires to take away for completion. You may get a lot of non-replies.

(b) Interviews

Personal interviews allow more detailed answers than questionnaires. They are particularly useful for:

- Interviewing somebody with specialist knowledge and experience.
- Examining opinions or attitudes in more detail.
- Being flexible about the questions which are asked.
- Providing a more relaxed atmosphere. People are likely to tell you more.

If you interview people you will be taking up their time (and your own), so make sure that the interview is worthwhile. To do this you should:

- Decide upon the type of person or persons that you need to interview.
- If you need to talk to people whom you don't know, write or phone politely. Explain what you are doing, why you wish to interview them and how long the interview is likely to take.
- Plan the interview carefully, writing down the questions you wish to ask (be prepared to change these if necessary).
- Turn up on time, but don't be surprised if your interviewee keeps you waiting.
- Thank your interviewee for their help. Follow this up with a written thank-you later.
- Write up your interview notes as soon as possible.
- Decide which parts of the interview are relevant. If you use a direct quote make sure that it is accurate and put quotation marks at the beginning and end.

(c) Visits to Firms

Visits to firms and other organisations have the same benefits as personal interviews, and similar rules apply. If you are allowed to roam about the building be careful. Don't get in the way of people or machinery, and don't disturb people while they are in the middle of lifting boxes or counting figures.

(d) Letters

It is sometimes possible to obtain information by writing to people or firms. Don't be disappointed, however, if you receive no reply or a letter which simply includes glossy brochures which are irrelevant.

Letters should be short, simple and to the point, typed or neatly written on blank white A4 paper and set out in the correct business manner. You should also ask your teacher or lecturer to check the letter before you send it.

(e) Tests and Experiments

Depending on your assignment, tests or experiments may be useful. For example, if you are studying market research or running a mini-company you might carry out 'blind tastings' to find out if people can distinguish between 'own-brand' and 'brand-name' products.

(f) Observation

Observation means looking and listening very carefully, e.g. watching people at work, a manufacturing process or shoppers in a supermarket. You might also be a 'participant observer', e.g. using a work experience placement to see what it is like to work in a particular firm.

If you intend to use observation as a research method, think about:

- What you are trying to observe.
- Whether people will know that you are watching them (people may be hostile if they think you are 'spying' on them).
- Whether you will take notes as you go along.

Examples of observation being used successfully are given in Figure 17.5.

(g) Newspapers and Magazines

Newspapers and magazines can be very useful. Some, such as *The Times* and the *Economist*, have indexes of articles, which should be available together with back numbers in a good reference library. If you are investigating a particular industry there may be a trade journal which will be helpful. A local newspaper may allow you to consult its cuttings files.

Articles can also be used as 'leads'. The names of people or organisations mentioned should be circled and considered as sources of information. Figure 17.6 gives an example.

(h) Television and Radio

If your assignment concerns an issue which is currently in the news you may be able to use TV or radio programmes to obtain information. This will mean paying attention to programmes such as 'Panorama' and 'Newsnight' rather than watching 'Neighbours' or listening to Radio One. It is advisable to check through the *Radio Times* and *TV Times* for details.

A group of students was trying to find out which parts of a small town were the best locations for shops. They arranged themselves in pairs and counted the number of people passing particular points in the town centre. The most suprising result was that three times as many people passed one end of the main street as the other. This would obviously make a difference to the trade of a shop.

Cleo was investigating the issue of introducing parking charges in a town centre. Local shopkeepers said that this would destroy their trade. She wanted to find out if restricting parking to one or two hours would solve the problem of parking without charges being introduced. She took the registration numbers of cars at 9 a.m. and checked to see how many were still there at 5 p.m. Her results were then plotted on a map as shown below.

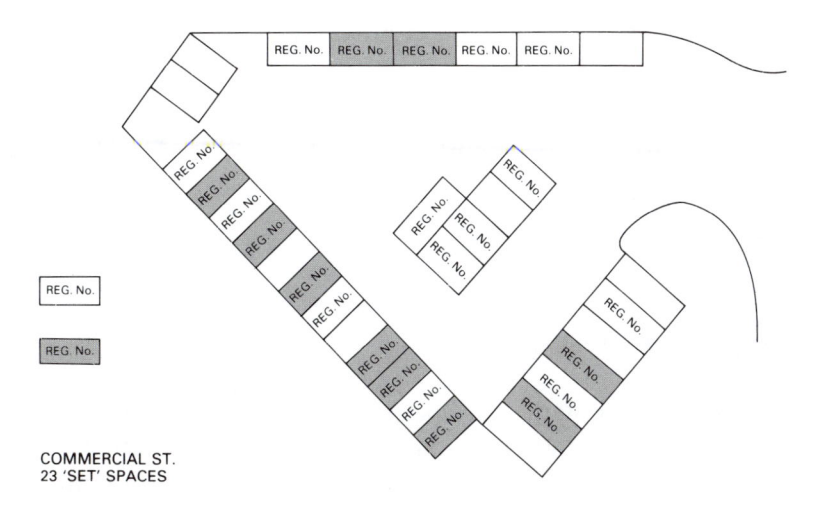

COMMERCIAL ST.
23 'SET' SPACES

Figure 17.5   Examples of observation

Kentish Gazette May 27, 1988

Killer bug fear in quarry plan

by STEVE HEDGES

PATIENTS at Maidstone Hospital could be put at risk from the often fatal Legionnaires disease if proposals to quarry nearby are allowed, say objectors.

The fears were raised when Maidstone council decided to fight the proposals for ragstone working at Hermitage Farm, 800 yards from the hospital.

Cllr Jennifer Fenn (Con), who is also a member of the Maidstone Health Authority, said councillors had to seriously consider the possible danger from the disease that could thrive on quarry dust.

She said: "It's now acknowledged that dust gets into air systems and the bacteria feeds upon it. The disease is particularly fatal to the sick and elderly."

Barming parish councillor Peter Wakefield said the link between dust and the disease had been illustrated by experts investigating the recent outbreak at Broadcasting House, London.

Cllr Wakefield said the dust and noise created by quarrying could not be tolerated either when homes were only 500 metres away.

Mark Ostheimer, who presented a 276-signature petition to the council, said people in Barming Heath were strongly opposed to the scheme.

They believed it would seriously affect the environment, causing problems of safety, noise, dust and associated pollution.

Maidstone planners voted unanimously to object to the scheme submitted by contractor Pat Gallagher. It will now be determined by the county.

Under Mr Gallagher's plan, 250,000 tonnes of ragstone a year would be quarried over a 15-year period.

He has also offered to spend £500,000 on roadworks and a new woodland screen in Hermitage Lane if the plan is approved.

Cllr Paul Oldham (Con) said: "Half a million pounds spent on improving is going to make very little difference to Hermitage Lane and will do absolutely nothing about the problems of the junctions at either end."

Cllr Oldham said the scheme, which would mean an increase in lorry traffic, would be a serious threat to homes and hospital.

He said: "After a long wait Maidstone has a fine general hospital. Have we realy waited that long to have it ruined by this kind of development?"

Although the plan has united hospital chiefs, councillors and villagers in opposition, Mr Gallagher has claimed the scheme would create more benefits than problems.

Landscape architect Tom La Dell, who spoke on behalf of Mr Gallagher, said the proposed £500,000 road works was a very positive offer.

He claimed that if the matter went to appeal it was possible no road improvements would be required.

Figure 17.6   Using newspaper articles as leads

If possible, record a programme so that you can check on details or listen to arguments at your own pace. Your school or college may also have recordings which are relevant to your topic.

(i) Books

Although one of the aims of Business Studies coursework is to get away from textbook theories, books can be useful for providing background information, explaining terms and providing facts and figures.

To find relevant books:

- Look in your own textbooks.
- Ask your teacher.
- Try the school or college library.
- Go to the central reference library for your area.
- Find out the Dewey Decimal number for the subject area. The librarian will look this up for you if you ask nicely. You can then check the shelves and catalogue for suitable books.

(j) Reference Sources

Reference and statistical books are published by the Government and other organisations. The major sources are listed at the end of the book. If you are studying an industry you should be able to find information on matters such as employment, sales, foreign trade and prices.

If you use reference sources be careful to explain why they are important. You may find them difficult to interpret, so be prepared to ask for help. Remember also that the information may be biased or unreliable.

(k) People

People you know can be the most useful resource of all. Be ready to consult your teacher and anybody else. Even your parents may know more than you think, or know where to look for information!

17.8 Writing the Assignment

If you have planned and researched your assignment thoroughly the actual writing should be easy. The best assignments will be a good interesting read. This will happen if you:

- List the contents of your assignment, e.g. introduction, methods of research, section titles, conclusion, acknowledgements.
- Start by explaining the aim of the assignment, i.e. what you wanted to find out.
- Explain how you decided on your research methods.
- Use original material and explain why it is important.
- Label all diagrams and figures and say why they are included.
- Use different ways of showing information, e.g. graphs, piecharts, pictures, maps etc.

- Ruthlessly discard irrelevant data. Your assignment should not be a 'scrapbook'.
- Indicate possible bias or inaccuracy in your information, e.g. by pointing out data which may be based upon opinion rather than fact.
- Present your assignment logically and attractively with clear sections and headings.
- Put quoted material in inverted commas and write down the source (copying material without acknowledgement could be classed as 'cheating').
- Give the names of people who have helped (you will probably be expected to do this on an official form).
- Use business terms and ideas where relevant.
- Give conclusions and recommendations justified by the data you have collected.
- Stick to the format and number of words specified in the syllabus.

Index

acknowledgement 77
ACORN system 98, 100, *101*
accounting 68–75
advertising 94–99
   control of 187–9
aids to trade 14
Advertising Standards Authority (ASA) 187, *189*
advice note 77
air transport 185
ancillary firms 114
application forms 138
aptitude tests 138
arbitration 151
Articles of Association 34–5
assembly line 110–11, 118, *119*
assets 71–72
authority 63–4
average cost 69, 112, 115
Assisted Areas *120*, 170

balance of payments 21–3
balance of trade 22
balance sheet 71–2
banking services 50, 99, 181–2
barter 11
batch production 109
'Big Bang' 52
bill of exchange 182
Board of Directors 33, 60
bonuses 127
borrowing 50–1
branding 93
break-even analysis 69–70
British Overseas Trade Board (BOTB) 171
Business Expansion Scheme (BES) 171
business names 29
British Standards 186, *188*

capital 72
   liquid 75
   owner's 75
   return on 75
   working 75
capital goods 13
cash-flow 49, 70–1
centralisation 64
Certificate of Incorporation 35
Certificate of Trading 35
chain of command 63
change, business and 11–13
Channel Tunnel 11, 15
channel of distribution 99
closed shop 147
collective bargaining 147, 150–1
command economy 5
commercial services 14
commission 126
communication 115, 118, 156–60
Common Market *see* European Community
companies
   types of 29–37
   registration of 34–5
Companies Acts 29
competition
   international 13–14
   legislation 174–5
computers 116–18, 159–60
Confederation of British Industry (CBI) 150, 186
conglomerates 114–15, *116*
Consumer Credit Act 173
Consumer Protection Act 173
consumer durables 13

consumer law 172–4
consumer organisations 186–9
Consumer Association 186, *187*
containerisation 186
contracting out 43
contract of employment 139
control, span of 63–4
Co-operatives 35–7
Co-operative Development Agency (CDA) 35
Co-operative Retail Society (CRS) 36–7
Co-operative Wholesale Society (CWS) 36–7
corporation tax 167
cost of sales 73
costs 68–9
   average 69, 112, 115
   fixed 68–9, 112–13
   total 69
   unit *see* average costs
   variable 69
credit note 80
creditors 72
credits 80
current accounts 181
curriculum vitae 138

database 100, *101*, 108
data processing 118
debentures 51
debits 80
debtors 72
decentralisation 64
deductions, from pay 129–30
deindustrialisation 14
delegation 61–2
delivery note 77
denationalisation 41
demand 3
deposit accounts 181
desk research 100
depreciation 72
deregulation 43
Development Areas *120, 159*
direct debits 181
direct mail 98–9
direct selling 94, 95
direct services 14
diseconomies of scale 115
distribution 99
diversification 114
division of labour 110–12
documentary credit system 182
documents, business 77, *78, 79*, 80
durable goods 13

economies, types of 3–6
economies of concentration 114–15, 121
economies of scale 112–15
electronic mail 160
embargo 20
employers' associations 150 (*see also* CBI)
Employment Protection Act 174
Enterprise Agencies 171
Enterprise Allowance Scheme 171
environment and business 189
Environmental Health Department 173–4
Equal Pay Act 174
European Community (EC) 19, 24–5
exchange controls 20
excise duties 167
expenses 73–4
Export Credit Guarantee Scheme (ECGD) 171

exports 21–4
   assistance for exporters 171, 182
   payments for 182
   difficulties of exporting 23–4
external economies of scale 114–15
external sources of finance 50–1
extractive industries 13

factoring 51
Fair Trading Act 173
facsimile transmission 160
fax machines 160
field research 100, 102
finance for business 49–55
finance houses 50
fixed assets 72
fixed costs 69, 112–13
fixed-term loan 50
flow production 109–10
Food and Drugs Act 173
footloose industries 119
free enterprise 3
free market economy 3–4
fringe benefits 127

goods
   capital 13
   durable 13
   single-use 13
Government
   assistance to business 51, *120*, 121 168–71
   finance 166–7, *168, 175*
   local 175–7
   control over business 172–7
   statistics of 100, *169*
gross pay 129
gross profit 73–4
gross profit margin 76
group selection of employees 139

Health and Safety Act 174
holding company 61
horizontal integration 115–16

incentive pay 127
income tax 129–30, 166, *168*
incorporation 30
industrial distribution 13–14
imports, restriction of *see* protectionism
Independent Broadcasting Authority (IBA) 189
induction of employees 138–9
industrial action 150–1
industrial inertia 121
industrial relations 147–51
industrial structure 13
inland waterways 185
insurance 182–3
integration 115–16, *117*
interdependence 11
Intermediate Areas *170*
internal economies of scale 112–14
internal sources of finance 49
internal organisations of business 60–64
international trade 19–26
   balance of payments accounts 21–3
   European Community (EC) 19, 24–5
   finance 182
   payments 182
   problems of exporters 23–4
   protectionism 20–1
interviews
   job 138
   market research 102
invisible trade 21–2

invoice 77, *79*
issuing house 54

job description 134–5
job production 109
joint-stock companies 29–30, 33–5

Labour Relations Agency 151
labour turnover 112–13
lateral integration 116
leasing 50
liabilities 71–2
limited companies 29–30, 33–35
limited liability 29
limited partner 31
liquid capital 75
Loan Guarantee Scheme 171
loans for business 50–1
local authorities 175–7
loss leaders 94
location of industry 119–21

management, functions of 57, 59
Manpower services Commission (MSC) *see* Training Agency
manuals 159
manufacturing 109–10
margin
   gross profit 76
   net profit 76
mark-up 76
market economy 3–4
market-makers in shares 52, *53*
market research 100, 102
market share 59, 115
market segments 90
marketing 88–102
   campaigns *89*
   mix 88
   place 94, 99
   price 88, 94
   product 88–93
   promotion 94–99
mass production 19, 112–15
meetings 158
memoranda (memo's) 158
Memorandum of Association 34
merchant banks 54, 186
mergers 59, 115–16, 174
merit payments 127
microfilm 159
mixed economy 6
modems 160
monopolies
   control of 174–5
   natural 42
   statutory 42–3
Monopolies and Mergers Commission 174
motivation 125–6
multinational companies 61, 114, *116*

National Consumer Council 187
National Insurance 130, 166
nationalisation 41–3
nationalised industry consumer councils 186
net pay 130
net profit 72–4
net profit margin 76
net worth 75
night safe 182
non-monetary benefits 127

objectives of business 59–60
Office of Fair Trading (OFT) 173–4
Official Statistics 100, *169*
order 77, *78*
ordinary shares 51
organisation 57, 60–1, *62*, 63–4
organisation charts 60
outstanding balance 80
overdraft 50
overtime pay 126
own-brands 99
owner's capital 75

partnerships 31–2
pay 125–30
Pay as you earn (PAYE) 130
payslip 129–30
pendulum arbitration 151
performance targets *59*, 60
personal selling 94, *95*
personnel description 135–6
picketing 151
piece rates 126–7
planned economy 5
planning, for business 57
population 11
preference shares 51
pressure groups 189
Prestel 160
prices, importance of 3–5
pricing methods 88, 94
primary industry 13
private limited company 32–3
privatisation 41, 43–5, 175
product 88–93
   development 90–1
   life cycle 92–3
   mix 90–1
production 109–21
   methods 109–10
productivity 111
profit
   gross 73–4
   importance of 59
   incentive 4
   net 73–4
   retained 49
profit and loss account 73–4
profit-sharing 127, *128*
profitability 68, 76–7
promotion 88, 94–9
protectionism 20–1
pro-forma invoice 80
psychological tests 139
public corporations 42–3
public limited companies 33–4
public relations (PR) 159
purchases 73
place, in marketing 94, 99

quality control 58, 118
questionnaires 100
quota sampling 102
quotas, import 20
quotation 77

Race Relations Act 174
rail transport 185
random sampling 102
rates, local authority 167, *169*
receipt 80
recruitment 125, 134–9
regional policy *120, 170*
Registrar of Companies 34
registration of companies 34–5
remittance advice note 80
research and development 113
responsibilities of business 11–12
responsibility 61, 63
retained profit 49
return on capital 75
revenue
   of firms 69
   of Government 166–7, *168*
road transport 184–5
robots 118, *119*

Sale of Goods Act 172
sales, in accounts 73
sampling 100–2
scarcity 2
sea transport 185
secondary industry 13
selection, of employees 137–9
service industries 14
Sex Discrimination Acts 174
shareholders 49

shares
   buying and selling 52, *53*, 54
   new issues 54
   types of 51
shop steward 147–8
small firms
   assistance for 171
   reasons for survival 115
Small Firms Service 171
social benefits 15
social costs 4, 14
sole proprietor *see* sole trader
sole trader 30–1
span of control 63–4
specialisation 11 *see also* division of labour
sponsorship 98
standing orders 181
statement of account 80
stock 72–4
stock turnover 74
Stock Exchange 29, 33, 51–4
Stock Exchange Automated Quotation System (SEAQ) 51, *53*
strikes 151
structure of industry 13–14
subsidiary firms 61, *62*
subsidies 20
superannuation 130
supply 3
Supply of Goods and Services Act 172
surveys 100–2

take-home pay 130
takeovers 59, 115–16
tariffs 20
tastes, consumer 12, 24
tax code 130
taxes 129–30, 166–7, *168*
technology 112
Telex 160
teletext 160
tertiary industry 14
test marketing 102
Third Market 52
time rates 126
total costs 69
trade associations 100, 186
Trades Description Act 172
trade unions 130, 147–51
Trades Union Congress (TUC) 150
trading account 73–4
Trading Standards Department 173–4
training 114, 125–6, 140–1
Training Agency (formerly Training Commission, Manpower Services Commission) 140–1
Training Commission *see* Training Agency
transport 121, 184–6
Transport Internationale Routier (TIR) 186
turnover, stock 74

Unfair contract Terms Act 172
unions, trade 130, 147–51
unit costs *see* average costs
unlimited liability 29
Unlisted Securities Market (USM) 51
Unsolicited Goods and Services Act 172–3

Value Added Tax (VAT) 166
variable costs 69
vertical integration 116
visible trade 21–2

wages *see* pay
Weights and Measures Act 173–4
Which? *186*, 187
wholesaler 99
word processing 116–17, *118*
working capital 75

Youth Training Scheme (YTS) 141

Macmillan Work Out Series

For GCSE examinations
Accounting
Biology
Business Studies
Chemistry
Computer Studies
English Key Stage 4
French (cassette and pack available)
Geography
German (cassette and pack available)
Modern World History
Human Biology
Core Maths Key Stage 4
Revise Mathematics to further level
Physics
Religious Studies
Science
Social and Economic History
Spanish (cassette and pack available)
Statistics

For A Level examinations
Accounting
Biology
Business Studies
Chemistry
Economics
English
French (cassette and pack available)
Mathematics
Physics
Psychology
Sociology
Statistics